EDUCATIONAL NEUROSCIENCE FOR LITERACY TEACHERS

Bridging the world of reading instruction and applied cognitive neuroscience, this book presents research-backed reading instructional methods and explains how they can be understood through the lens of brain processes.

Dispelling myths about neuroscience, Spence and Mitra explore how brain-based research informs literacy research in a way that is clear and accessible to pre-service teachers. Chapters address theories of reading, social-emotional learning, phonological processes, embodiment, multilingualism, reading comprehension, and more. Featuring examples of instruction and consistent "Did you know?" and "Food for thought" sections, readers will come away with a greater understanding of the reading brain and how neuroscience can inform effective instruction.

Delving into the extent to which neuroscience can underpin reading research, this text is ideal for pre-service teachers, educators, and students in the fields of language arts and literacy, as well as cognitive neuroscience.

Lucy Spence is a Professor of Language and Literacy Education in the Department of Instruction and Teacher Education at the University of South Carolina, USA.

Ayan Mitra is a Postdoctoral Research Associate at the Hoeft Laboratory for Learning Engineering and Neural Systems (BrainLENS Laboratory, University of Connecticut and University of California, San Francisco) with a joint appointment at the Brain Imaging Research Center (BIRC) at the University of Connecticut, USA, Department of Psychological Sciences.

EDUCATIONAL NEUROSCIENCE FOR LITERACY TEACHERS

Research-backed Methods and Practices for Effective Reading Instruction

Lucy Spence and Ayan Mitra

Routledge
Taylor & Francis Group
NEW YORK AND LONDON

Designed cover image: Jesse David Lilly

First published 2023
by Routledge
605 Third Avenue, New York, NY 10158

and by Routledge
4 Park Square, Milton Park, Abingdon, Oxon, OX14 4RN

Routledge is an imprint of the Taylor & Francis Group, an informa business

Library of Congress Cataloguing-in-Publication Data
Names: Spence, Lucy K., author. | Mitra, Ayan, author.
Title: Educational neuroscience for literacy teachers : research-backed methods and practices for effective reading instruction / Lucy Spence and Ayan Mitra.
Description: New York, NY : Routledge, 2023. | Includes bibliographical references. |
Identifiers: LCCN 2022060526 (print) | LCCN 2022060527 (ebook) | ISBN 9781032187785 (hardback) | ISBN 9781032183947 (paperback) | ISBN 9781003256199 (ebook)
Subjects: LCSH: Literacy. | Reading. | Learning--Physiological aspects. | Cognitive neuroscience. | Educational psychology.
Classification: LCC LC149 .S64 2023 (print) | LCC LC149 (ebook) | DDC 370.15--dc23/eng/20230118
LC record available at https://lccn.loc.gov/2022060526
LC ebook record available at https://lccn.loc.gov/2022060527

ISBN: 978-1-032-18778-5 (hbk)
ISBN: 978-1-032-18394-7 (pbk)
ISBN: 978-1-003-25619-9 (ebk)

DOI: 10.4324/9781003256199

Typeset in Sabon
by MPS Limited, Dehradun

CONTENTS

FOREWORD

It is hard to imagine a skill that is more fundamental to participation in the modern world than reading. Reading, the act of decoding and understanding written language, is necessary for gleaning many types of information and for engaging in many types of communication. Reading is also foundational for the broader development of literacy. Functional literacy goes far beyond reading and involves capacities to engage effectively with written language embedded in various contexts and media, and coordinated capacities to produce written language for self-expression. Literacy is a gateway to unlimited information, opportunities, and enjoyment. Deprived of literacy, one is quite simply unable to fully partake of contemporary society.

Yet, according to the NAEP, only about one-third of U.S. fourth and eighth graders scored "proficient" in reading in 2019 (*The Nation's Report Card*, https://www.nationsreportcard.gov/highlights/reading/2019/), and only a minority of U.S. high school students report reading for pleasure. Sadly, poor reading outcomes are more common among students of color and students experiencing poverty, and the inequities exposed by the global COVID-19 pandemic have further exacerbated these pernicious race and class-based disparities (Gotlieb et al., 2022). How can teachers and schools make headway on remediating our students' reading ability and literacy development? How can they help all young people become literate, and take advantage of all that literacy provides?

As Spence and Mitra explain, though phonological decoding and reading comprehension rely on cognition, becoming a reader is not simply a cognitive process. Like all cultural learning of complex developmental skills, learning to read involves and shapes many dimensions of a child's personal and social world. In the brain, learning to read co-opts and repurposes systems evolved for social communication, emotion, language, executive control, meaning, memory, and narrative among others. Decades of neuroimaging research have demonstrated that learning to read literally reorganizes key brain networks in ways that result in measurable changes to the brain's structure and function. The full development of literacy, which takes place across the lifespan, is so fundamental to our intellectual and cultural lives that its impact is impossible to fully measure or comprehensively describe.

Taken as a whole, this book provides an accessible, useable summary of important research findings about how children learn to read, and about how adults can support and teach this process in socially, emotionally, culturally, linguistically, and cognitively appropriate ways. From complex neuroscientific data to practical implications for diverse K-12 classroom contexts, Spence and Mitra take educators on a journey into the science and practice of teaching reading to help young people become literate in the full sense of the term. Enjoy!

Mary Helen Immordino-Yang
Rossier School of Education
University of Southern California

ACKNOWLEDGMENTS

This is not just a book; this is our story. Spence and Mitra met at the College of Education at the University of South Carolina when Ayan moved to the United States to work on his Ph.D. His dream of bridging neuroscience and education led him to Professor Spence, an expert in literacy, language, and instruction. Through six years of dense readings, re-readings, and more reading, we were able to somewhat achieve our vision of having the two disciplines speak to each other. Mitra's experience at the Applied Cognitive Neuropsychology Laboratory under the supervision of Dr. Scott Decker and his wonderful lab mates—Chris, Michael, and Jessica helped him develop the required expertise in neuroimaging and cognitive neuroscience.

Over these years, Spence and Mitra delved into the nexus of translational science, methodology, applied sciences, educational research, and neuroimaging. We cemented our collaboration through publications, presentations in national and international conferences, and research posters. Finally, Karen Adler—a senior editor at Routledge noticed our presentation at the Literacy Research Association. She reached out to us and invited us to work on a book project on *Educational Neuroscience for Literacy Teachers*. We were ecstatic and after an initial proposal submission and rounds of peer review, we were able to land this book contract.

This book would not have been possible without the village of people who supported, critiqued, and stood by us. A page of acknowledgments is never enough to express the gratitude we feel toward every single person who made this dream a reality. We would like to thank our families, John Spence, Jesse Lilly, Bidisha Mitra, and Vidira Mitra. We would like to express our gratitude for the graduate students, families, and children. Without their participation in some of our courses and literacy lab, we would not have been able to conceptualize this project. They gave us valuable feedback about the need for a book like this, their interest in the brain processes, and how that might help us in reaching preservice and in-service teachers, which is pivotal to the fundamental idea of the book. We would also like to thank BrainLENS Laboratory

(UCONN-UCSF) and the Brain Imaging Research Center (BIRC) for giving Dr. Mitra the opportunity to hone his skills in neuroimaging and reading.

Our warmest thanks to the array of brilliant researchers, George Hruby, Catherine Compton-Lilly, Pamela Jewett, Patricia Paugh, Yang Wang, Mary Helen Immordino-Yang, Nikki Arrington, Zhichao Xia, and Rebecca Gotlieb, who read our drafts and gave us essential feedback and encouragement and helped us move forward. We especially thank Mary Helen Immordino-Yang, a champion of educational, affective, and developmental neuroscience for agreeing to provide the foreword for our book. We are heavily influenced by her work, and we feel it was only fitting for someone like her to introduce our book to the world.

INTRODUCTION

This book develops a vision of literacy networks by exploring the brain and literacy together. Literacy is a uniquely human ability that helps to shape the cultural world we live in today. Our ability to read and write builds on our biological capacity for language. The ability to verbally communicate with one another enables us to develop and use a written language system. As we engage with our culture's writing system, our neural pathways for vision and speech are modified and the ability to read and write is developed over time. Parents, caregivers, families, and schoolteachers provide the necessary basis for reading and writing.

Neuroscience is a hot topic in the news cycle, as new findings are constantly emerging. Journalists write about these findings, sometimes in an impartial way, and other times to persuade readers to accept a related opinion. Busy educators may not have the time to read neuroscience research and may be wary of accepting opinion-oriented journalism. This book gives educators a reliable and readable account of neuroscience studies of literacy and research-backed literacy instructional practices.

The authors, Ayan Mitra and Lucy K. Spence, teamed up to share their specific expertise on literacy. At the time of this writing, Ayan was a post-doctoral research associate at the Hoeft Laboratory for Learning Engineering and Neural Systems in the Department of Psychological Sciences at the University of Connecticut. His work involved assisting with a broad range of neuroimaging studies including studies on reading. Lucy is a professor in the Language & Literacy program in the Department of Instruction and Teacher Education at the University of South Carolina, where she has taught undergraduate and graduate courses in literacy for 15 years. Her research has added to the body of literacy scholarship within language acquisition, reading instruction, and writing assessment. Lucy was also a reading specialist and an ESL teacher for 17 years in Arizona. Ayan and Lucy's interests converged when Ayan studied reading and

DOI: 10.4324/9781003256199-1

the brain with Lucy and a psychology professor at the University of South Carolina.

As Ayan and Lucy delved into neuroscience research on literacy, they became concerned that preservice teachers and other educators were not receiving sound information on the neuroscience of literacy and advice on how to use such information (Cassidy, et al., 2022). They began to present some of this information in the courses they taught and found that students were eager for more information on literacy and the brain. They began presenting this information at educational conferences and found out that teacher educators were also eager to have neuroscience research condensed and explained. Understanding the brain is important to literacy teachers and other educators, yet many educators are not exposed to this information. This book fills that need.

This book is unique in presenting a side-by-side look at both neuroscience research and literacy research. Neuroimaging studies build on and are connected to the field of psychology which has traditionally used observations, experiments, and surveys to understand human thoughts, feelings, and behaviors. Neuroimaging studies use technological tools such as MRI, EEG, and TMS to produce images of the structure and activity of the brain. Neuroscience, psychology, and education research come together to inform educational neuroscience as shown in Figure I.1.

Few educators delve into the journals that report neuroscience findings. In writing this book, we studied journals such as *Brain and Language, Cognition, Neuroimage, Journal of Neurolinguistics, Neuropsychologia, Human Brain Mapping,* and many others. We examined education journals such as *Reading Research Quarterly, Literacy, Scientific Studies of Reading, Reading and Writing Quarterly, Early Childhood Education Journal,* and *Developmental Psychology* to determine effective instructional methods. As a result, we connected

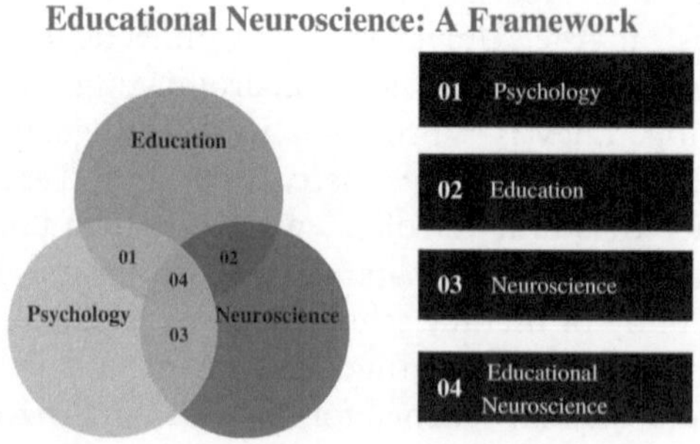

Figure I.1 Fields of Study that Inform Educational Neuroscience.

methods of literacy instruction to brain functions described by neuroscience research.

Educational studies of literacy have been in progress for over 100 years, and some have foreshadowed current findings in neuroscience. We draw from studies of literacy published since 2011, performed with a variety of methods that involved collecting information in both real-world and lab settings. Participants in the literacy studies ranged from prekindergarten to 12th grade. Each chapter includes examples of literacy instruction gleaned from these studies. Each example includes preparation, goals, and procedures for the lessons.

This book will discuss what has been learned to date through neuroimaging research in areas pertinent to literacy. These findings offer potential connections between neuroscience and research-based instructional practices. Still, the neuroscience of literacy is only partial and ever-emerging. Direct correlations between neuroscience research and literacy instruction are not possible at this time because neuroscience findings in many areas have yet to be replicated adequately.

You may have questions about what brain research says about specific types of literacy instruction. Many of these questions have not been answered yet due to the constraints of neuroimaging equipment, highly controlled stimuli, the type of tasks, and methods of analysis. However, brain research methods are rapidly advancing, and new insights are continually emerging.

Organization of This Book

Chapter 1, "Neuroscience and Literacy," presents our stance on literacy learning and some basic understandings of brain development. In Chapter 2, "Literacy Theories," we build on this understanding through theories found within the fields of literacy education, educational psychology, and educational neuroscience. In chapters 3 through 9, we delve further into neuroscience studies to explore six important aspects of literacy: embodiment, social and emotional learning, multimodality, making meaning, phonology, and languaging.

In Chapter 3, "Embodied Brain," we explore embodiment—how our body interacts with the environment through our brain, nervous system, and endocrine system. We present examples of instruction that encourage students to use materials, their bodies, and the environment for learning.

In Chapter 4, "Social and Emotional Brain," we explore social interaction and emotion in learning. We describe how our interactions with other people build our brain's network connections. We show how emotion influences learning. Examples of instruction illustrate how dialog and collaboration enhance learning. One example guides students to use their emotions to understand literary works.

In Chapter 5, "Multimodal Brain," we explore how different modes of expression such as writing, image making, and speaking are combined. This chapter includes discussions of writing instruction and learning through technology. Examples of instruction guide students to manage information found on the internet and other complex texts.

In Chapter 6, "Making Meaning," we explore reading comprehension. This chapter describes the executive functions of the brain and the importance of memory, metacognition, and prior knowledge in learning. We provide examples for developing meaning through applying cognitive strategies and building vocabulary.

In Chapter 7, "Phonology," we present information on decoding, phonics, phonemic awareness, beginning reading, and dyslexia. Examples of instruction include guided reading, explicit phonics instruction, and interactive writing.

In Chapter 8, "Languaging," we discuss how multilingual speakers use their languages in school settings. We describe how the brain processes multiple languages. The chapter includes examples of instruction for students who are learning English as an additional language.

Finally, Chapter 9, "Literacy Networks," provides a summary of the six areas of neuroscience and literacy research included in the book and their implications for teachers. We close with our argument for a nuanced view of literacy development that builds a bridge between neuroscience findings and educational research on literacy.

Throughout the chapters, we argue for a view of literacy that reflects the "situated, embodied, and embrained human mind" (Immordino-Yang et al., 2018, p. 195). This means that our brains need our living bodies, and our bodies depend on our environment to exist. Brain, body, and environment interact together during literate activity. Thus, we explore human thinking and action in response to interactions and learning from the physical and cultural world. This book explores how our senses perceive the world as we integrate new information into what we already know and believe (van Moort, et al., 2020). We show how our brain reacts to our body and biochemical influences as our brain continues to grow and change throughout the lifespan due to biological, chemical, and social events. The biopsychosocial brain (Engel, 1977) thus develops and engages with the cultural construct of literacy in what we like to call literacy networks.

Bibliography

Cassidy, J., Grote-Garcia, S., & Ortlieb, E. (2022). What's hot in 2021: Beyond the science of reading. *Literacy Research & Instruction*, *61*(1), 1–17. 10.1080/19388071.2021.2011236

Engel, G. L. (1977). The need for a new medical model: A challenge for biomedicine. *Science, New Series, 196*, 129–136.

Immordino-Yang, M. H. (2016). *Emotions, Learning, and The Brain: Exploring The Educational Implications of Affective Neuroscience*. W.W. Norton & Company.

Immordino-Yang, M. H., & Gotlieb, R. (2017). Embodied brains, social minds, cultural meaning: Integrating neuroscientific and educational research on social-affective development. *American Educational Research Journal, 54*(1S), 344S–367S. DOI: 10.3102/0002831216669780

Immordino-Yang, M. H., Darling-Hammond, L., Krone, C., & Aspen Institute, National Commission on Social, Emotional, and Academic Development (NCSEAD). (2018). The brain basis for integrated social, emotional, and academic development: How emotions and social relationships drive learning. Aspen Institute.

van Moort, M. L., Jolles, D. D., Koornneef, A., & van den Broek, P. (2020). What you read versus what you know: Neural correlates of accessing context information and background knowledge in constructing a mental representation during reading. *Journal of Experimental Psychology: General, 149*(11), 2084–2101.

1
NEUROSCIENCE AND LITERACY

Teachers can benefit from an understanding of neurobiological and sociocultural factors related to learning. One preservice teacher shared her thoughts below:

> I was fascinated by Dr. Mitra's lecture on the reading brain. Throughout my studies, I have never experienced a lecture on the specifics of the brain and how the different parts are used while reading. The visual that Dr. Mitra provided was especially helpful with understanding the different parts of the brain (Figure 1.1). As more research is conducted over time, I am interested in seeing different ways to approach education, teaching, and learning to help benefit future students.

The preservice teacher we quote here, echoed by others in our classes encouraged us to write this book. We aim to provide literacy teachers with current information on how the brain functions in literacy learning together with literacy instructional methods. K-12 literacy teachers are incredibly important to their students' brain and literacy developments. From the time children enter preschool until they write that final senior thesis, teachers nurture reading, writing, and many other aspects of literacy.

Literacy teachers also work with families and parents to affirm and encourage literacy in the home. They reach out to the community to engage students through field trips, guest speakers, and cultural events. Through these engagements, teachers not only nurture learners' brains but develop students' literacy through their interconnected social, emotional, and cognitive worlds.

As we engaged in research for this book, we gradually began to see the importance of networks in both neuroscience and literacy. Neuroscience has moved toward a view that considers cognitive function to involve large-scale distributed networks (Menon & Uddin, 2010). Brain networks develop in conversation with the body, environment, and social interactions. Literacy involves networks of meaning-making activities. Thus, when we talk about the brain and literacy, we are describing literacy networks that involve books, our brains, and so much more.

DOI: 10.4324/9781003256199-2

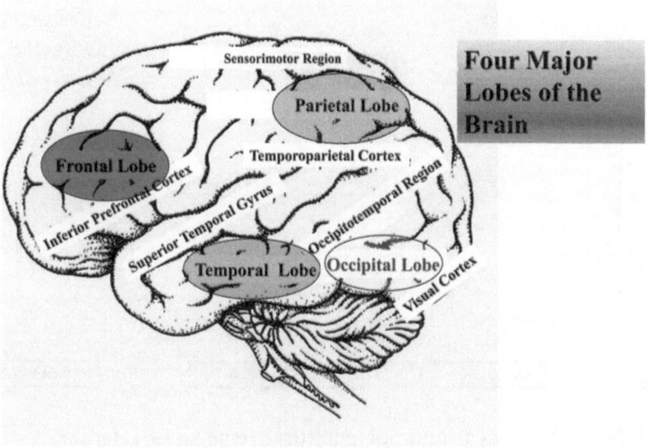

Figure 1.1 Four Major Lobes of the Brain.

Note: The brain is divided into left and right hemispheres. This figure is the left cerebrum (Bui & Das, 2021).

Our Stance on Literacy Learning

We position literacy within theories and research that integrates mind, body, and society. In this view, thinking and cognition are developed and influenced by society and culture (Gee, 1996). Literacy involves complex social practices of reading, writing, talking about texts, and using texts for a variety of social and personal purposes (Street, 1984).

Within the following chapters, we examine the growing body of neuroscience that supports this conceptual approach. Immordino-Yang and Gotlieb (2017) are neuroscientists who are interested in K-12 students. Their work describes how neurobiological and sociocultural developments are codependent. **Neurobiological** refers to the brain and nervous system of the human body. **Sociocultural** refers to how humans interact within their society and culture.

Child and adolescent brain developments are influenced by interactions with others and experiences in the world. Personal interactions, emotions, and physical experiences are intertwined with cognitive functions (Immordino-Yang, Darling-Hammond, & Krone, 2019). As literacy teachers, we must consider the whole person including past experiences, home life, societal influences, health, and emotion because all these aspects of life affect how our students learn.

In an example from a first-grade classroom, students integrated social interaction with their cognitive development. During a read aloud of the book, *How Does it Move?* by Gallimard Jeunesse, the teacher paused occasionally for the children to talk together about a physical motion

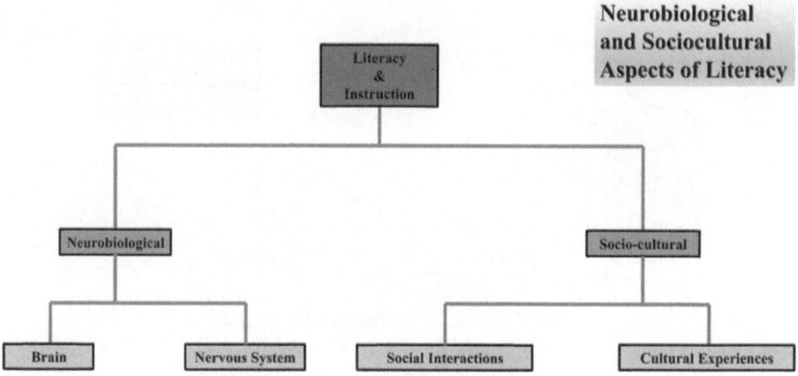

Figure 1.2 Neurobiological and Sociocultural Aspects of Literacy.

introduced in the book. The children had different background experiences and language abilities to express their ideas and they shared these with each other. These children came to school well-fed and rested. The children's physical and emotional well-being was supported in a classroom environment that was nurturing, clean, and safe. Figure 1.2 shows the interaction of neurobiological and sociocultural aspects of literacy.

Literacy and the Biological Sciences

Our bodies are made up of interconnected systems that together engage in complex literate activities including reading, writing, and representing ideas. Letters on a page are only one aspect of literacy. For example, looking at a website it is clear that we make meaning through words, photographs, drawings, font, color, hyperlinks, speech, music, sounds, and possibly other modalities. This approach to communication is called **multimodal literacy**. Multimodal literacy involves the integration of multiple modes of communication for composing and reading texts.

Just as we are beginning to understand literate activity as constellations of meaning-making activities, we are understanding the constellations of connectivity in body and brain processes and networks. We know that our brain receives information from the world through our senses: sight, hearing, touch, smell, and taste. Our brain also receives information from our heart, gut, and other parts of our internal body.

The heart and gastrointestinal tract generate their own electrical activity and send information to the brain. We experience this when we are hungry. We plan, search, navigate, and use our learning and memory to find food. Many other life-sustaining behaviors connected to high-level sensory and cognitive functions are internally driven (Azzalini et al., 2019).

Our body also produces hormones and neurotransmitters that function as messengers of the body and control our functions and our psychology. Hormones and neurotransmitters are important for learning because they contribute to how the brain is organized and the development of neural circuitry (Gore et al., 2019).

As a person reads, the body is actively sending information to the brain. For example, children's letter recognition is frequently assessed in kindergarten. This may be pleasurable to some children as they compete with themselves to recognize more of the alphabet. Other children may feel stress or anxiety during the assessment. Children also react to literacy materials. If a child has fallen behind in kindergarten and first grade, they may react negatively when given the same type of remedial texts that have frustrated them in the past. Children may experience fatigue or feel sick. A surge in hormones may trigger a need to flee to safety. On the other hand, hormones can produce pleasure when a student is given an eagerly anticipated book from a favorite author.

Neuroscience Research on Reading

Neuroscience does not offer a simple solution to literacy problems. However, experimental findings of recent research can inform reading educators and lead to a greater understanding of reading and writing. Neuroscience research on reading began with finding which areas of the brain are activated during tasks such as reading individual words. Then the research progressed to finding brain networks involved in more complex processes such as sentence comprehension (Schuister et al., 2021).

Neuroscience can help us understand beginning reading instruction as well as the comprehension processes of more advanced readers. It offers insights into the social and emotional aspects of learning. Neuroscience is also beginning to address language processes such as bilingualism, which can give teachers insights into their students who speak more than one language. Neuroscience study of literacy remains underway and new findings are constantly emerging.

Why We Can Read and Write

Let's start our voyage into the neuroscience of literacy by looking at select pieces of educational neuroscience that explore the human capacity for reading and writing. Only humans have the ability to construct a language as well as a written system that is composed of a small set of symbol shapes. Over time, cultural groups of humans developed written marks to symbolize individual sounds, syllables, or meanings to represent their oral language. Different cultures around the world developed written languages over millennia based on people's needs and functions. Scientists wonder what gave humans this ability for language and writing that stands out as unique among all the living creatures in our world.

Some scientists theorize that the brain has evolved to recognize people's faces. Neural connections for face recognition allowed humans to work together to survive in a hostile environment. They needed to distinguish between friend and foe. Similar neural connections are repurposed to recognize print. It seems there is an overlap between word and face perception (Boring et al., 2021). Both face perception and reading involve extended and dynamic brain pathways. These pathways are activated across both hemispheres of the brain in distinct networks that support social interaction and language.

Scientists continue to learn about our capacity for reading through advanced neuroscience imaging machinery, computing innovations, and analytical methods. These advances are adding to what we know about how our brains process the printed word. This is a complicated undertaking that scientists must break down into individual components. Piece by piece, the highly detailed results of many experiments have established fundamental principles of neurocognitive functions underlying perception and action (Matusz et al., 2019).

Neuroscience research in literacy is typically conducted in highly controlled settings with precise experimental designs and a minimal number of factors to isolate specific tasks. More recently, new methods attempt to understand brain activity in more real-world settings.

Brain Anatomy

For neuroscientists, anatomy was the starting point for understanding how the brain processes written text. All four major lobes—the frontal, temporal, parietal, and occipital lobes—of the brain have been associated with language and reading processes. Networks of white matter connect across the lobes. The **white matter** tracts transmit signals to and from various gray matter regions of the brain (Borden et al., 2015). Some attributes of each lobe are listed below to give you an idea of their functions.

- The **frontal** lobe is associated with executive functions, such as decision making, working memory, motivation, problem-solving, planning, monitoring, attention, and inhibitory control
- The **parietal** lobe is associated with integrating sensory input and processing language
- The **temporal** lobe is associated with understanding language, retaining visual memories, and processing and remembering emotions
- The **occipital** lobe is associated with processing stimuli from the external world and assigning meaning to and remembering visual perceptions

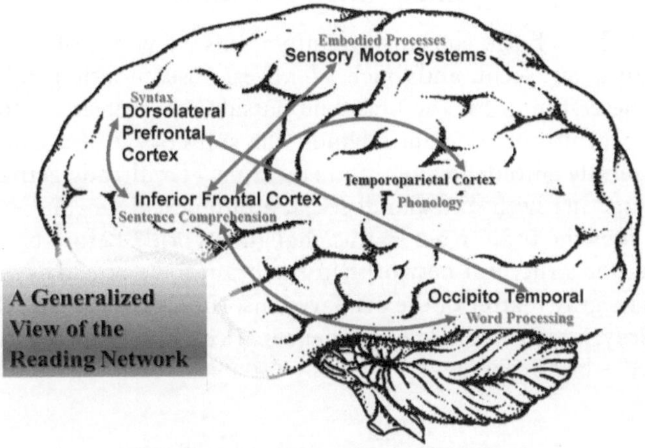

Figure 1.3 A Generalized View of the Reading Network.

Note: Major brain regions that are implicated in reading (D'Mello & Gabrieli, 2018).

Neuroscience looks closely at individual areas and functions within the major lobes and how they are connected. A **reading network** connects specialized brain areas during reading. The network engages the inferior frontal, superior temporal, temporal–parietal, and temporal–occipital areas (Pugh et al., 2001). The reading network is a model of how brain areas develop connectivity as the ability to read is acquired. Figure 1.3 shows how areas across the brain are involved in reading. The figure does not illustrate the neural assemblies that extend across the brain and come together in the areas shown.

Reading Network Development

The neural connections for language begin developing before birth. Specialization for reading develops throughout childhood and is refined in adolescence. As the brain develops, cells (neurons) move from one place to another. Life experiences and a person's behaviors lead to stronger or weaker connections between the neurons. This remarkable ability to adapt and change is called **neuroplasticity**. Upon exposure to written language, the brain responds by adapting and changing. Reading development involves the emergence of specialized neural connections and connectivity across brain regions (Perdue et al., 2022).

Infant Brain Networks

When a baby is born, she emerges into a sensory world of sound, light, temperature, air, scent, and touch. Her eyes, nose, mouth, ears, and skin absorb these stimuli for the first time outside the protective womb. She feels the warmth of someone's hands, the soft cotton of a blanket, and she is carefully enfolded in her mother's arms. Her already active brain is now interacting with our shared social and physical world.

How does the brain react to this changing world? Before birth, major white matter structural networks in the brain have already been established. The gray matter of the primary sensorimotor regions is already in place. **Gray matter** is made up of neuronal cell bodies in the outermost layer of the brain (Figure 1.4).

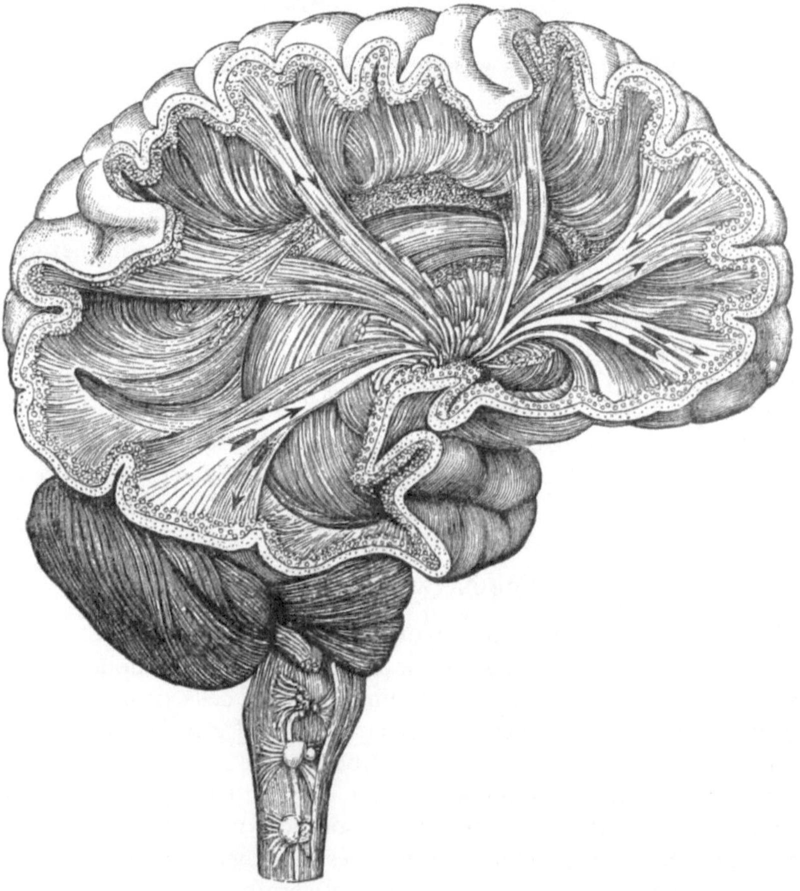

Figure 1.4 Some of the White Matter Fibers in the Brain.

Before birth, there are already somewhat mature network configurations of auditory, visual, and sensorimotor functional networks. These networks support the processing of smell, touch, vision, hearing, balance, spatial awareness, visual tracking, coordination, and movement. After birth, an infant's early experiences and gene expression refine the primary brain networks, making them more efficient.

Infants gradually improve other functional networks for thinking and sensing. The infant's social relationships and engagements with ideas and situations continue to influence patterns of brain structure and function as the child grows (Ilyka, Johnson, & Fox, 2021). The continued development of sensorimotor functional networks is critical during early childhood.

It is clear that prenatal and infant care are important to brain and sensory development. Babies need to be surrounded by caring family members. They need to be held and fed. Families should talk and sing to their babies. They need good healthcare and a healthy environment so they can grow and thrive.

Child Brain Networks

> Reed is almost four years old as he travels by car through the Great Smokey Mountains. His family is taking a road trip and he is strapped into a child's car seat next to his two siblings. His older brother has been reading some of the road signs along the way as the children eagerly anticipate arriving at the cabin. Suddenly Reed points to a road sign and blurts out, "Oconaluftee!" How was this three-year-old able to read that sign?

Based on his knowledge of the alphabet and his parents' discussion of their destination, Reed decoded the road sign. **Decoding** is the process of translating print into speech. Children usually begin to read between the ages of 4 and 8. During this time, their visual pathways and phonological coding systems develop in what is known as the visual word form area (Dehaene et al., 2015) (Figure 1.5). During early childhood, children's brains change dramatically as sensory stimulation from the environment leads to sensorimotor network development. Once a child begins to read, this visual word form area responds to written words and enables rapid recognition of strings of letters and their associated sequences of sounds. As children are learning the symbol-sound relationship, they are developing a complex and dynamic functional circuit for processing written language.

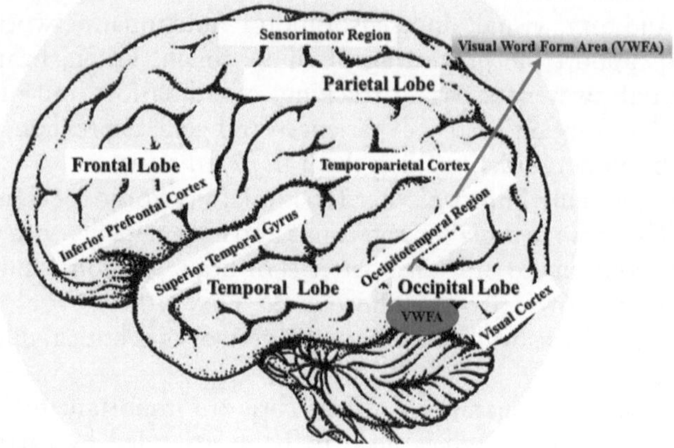

Figure 1.5 Visual Word Form Area.

> When Reed was learning to speak, around 1–2 years old, he was acquiring new words a bit slower than typical and had some difficulty articulating some sounds. His mother consulted a speech therapist who began working with Reed and his older brother, who also needed speech therapy. The children played games and puzzles involving words and letters. Reed quickly learned the English alphabet. Eventually, he was able to read words in the environment around him. Not all children make the sound-to-letter connection in exactly this way, but the experiences with a speech therapist helped Reed in his early path to reading.

Most children begin to associate letters with sounds and associate some printed words with meanings before formal schooling. You may have seen a young child's picture of a house and family members with "mom" and "dad" labeled. Drawing and making marks on paper help children build foundational literacy skills (Rowe, Shimizu, & Davis, 2022). Early experiences with printed symbols develop children's brain systems for print, speech, and the connections between speech and print. Parents and caregivers can encourage this development by providing children with materials for writing and drawing, reading aloud to them, encouraging pretend reading, and opportunities for imaginative play (Rand & Morrow, 2021).

Imaginative play is important for brain development. The brain's frontal region is thought to contribute to conceptual change, attention, working memory, and planning. You may have seen children completely focused on playing house, planning the roles and actions of each character in the household. This play scenario illustrates the brain activity of the frontal region and the connections between regions of the brain that go beyond the visual word form area and are very important to reading development.

As they begin to read, children develop networks across regions of the brain including the frontal lobe. The frontal lobe is involved because reading requires focusing and shifting attention. As children read, they represent and maintain information in working memory. **Working memory** can be defined as the ability to temporarily maintain, update and manipulate information to guide goal-directed behavior.

Areas within the frontal, temporal, parietal, and occipital lobes work together as readers map sounds onto text, as they read whole words, and as they associate written language with meaning. When phonological processing is needed, such as when encountering an unknown word in an unfamiliar context, phonological processes are used (Wang et al., 2020). When the word is familiar, it is processed immediately without the need for attending to each letter sound. Children gradually build neural systems to integrate print processing with speech and to control the reading process through working memory, attention, planning, and social interactions.

Child Development

Early childhood literacy educators understand the importance of developing children's speech-to-print connections at home and in early school experiences. In addition to reading stories, and exploring writing and drawing materials, teachers may prompt the child to tell a story, writing down the child's speech, then giving the pencil to the child to add known letters and words. Understanding how the alphabet represents sound is crucial to developing the reading network.

As children progress, literacy educators continue to promote ever-expanding print experiences. In school, children are exposed to different genres and reading materials such as narrative stories, informational and procedural texts, poetry, songs, play scripts, and websites. They learn how to navigate, enjoy, and understand different types of reading material. Motivation for reading can be encouraged through the independent choice of reading material and informal conversations about what children are reading. These literacy experiences are important for brain development. The brain changes throughout childhood, adolescence, and beyond. These changes are mainly through generating, pruning, and reorganizing neural connections that reflect a person's experiences, allowing a person to adapt to their world (Immordino-Yang et al., 2019).

The ability to rapidly recognize words or word parts is developed in childhood. By the time children reach adolescence, they are generally fluent readers. The perception of visual words emerges from a slow effortful process to a rapid automatic process that occurs within the span of several hundred milliseconds in a skilled reader (Schlaggar & McCandliss, 2007). It is important for children to develop reading fluency because reading materials become increasingly dense and complex as children progress through school. Reading **fluency** combines accuracy and speed in word recognition allowing for attention to be focused on meaning (Zimmerman et al., 2019).

Adolescent Brain Networks

> When Hector was 15, he suddenly became interested in piano. He asked his parents for a keyboard and began watching internet videos of piano instruction. He spent much of his free time learning from the videos and was soon playing with skill. However, the videos did not teach him to read music or understand music theory, so he began formal lessons. At his first lesson, he breezed through *Adult Piano Book One* in a few hours.

Hector's interest and rapid learning can be seen in many teenagers. His neural circuits were built and strengthened during his childhood. Then in adolescence, his brain began to change. During adolescence, the brain's networks become more efficient for processing certain tasks, including reading. Adolescent brains are in a very plastic phase of development. One aspect of adolescent brain development involves compressing and reducing the size of some neural connections, allowing for more efficient processing of information (Dennis et al., 2013; Zielinski et al., 2010). These changes occur in response to experiences. When adolescents have experience and practice in academic subjects, their brains activate and change in response. For educators, this means that adolescence is a key phase for expanding students' academic capacities.

Social Restructuring

Adolescents are required to learn complex and abstract academic content in middle and high school. At the same time, they are undergoing drastic changes in social behavior. They spend more time with peers than with adults and family. Romantic and sexual interests emerge. These social experiences receive intense neural processing because of hormonal restructuring, maturation, and learning (Nelson et al., 2005). During this phase of social re-orientation, it is important for adolescents to integrate themselves into new social support groups such as teams, clubs, or classes. These support networks act as a buffer to social or academic stress.

Literacy teachers can provide experiences that support the restructuring of adolescent brains. Choice of independent reading materials and time to read and talk about books give students opportunities to interact socially with their peers. This also builds motivation for reading both in and out of school. Teachers can immerse students in academic content and social issues by facilitating their research into interesting topics they have chosen, and structuring debates or discussions (Spence et al., 2022).

Infancy, childhood, and adolescence are important times for brain development. The home environment and school play important roles in the brain and literacy. That is why educators are eager to learn more about how the brain functions and how literacy learning can be enhanced. Let's look at how neuroscientists study the brain.

How to Study the Brain

Have you ever been to a hospital or clinic with imaging equipment? Similar equipment is also used in neuroscience studies of language, reading, writing, and other literacy processes. Figure 1.6 is a photo of a magnetic resonance imaging (MRI) machine in a neuroscience lab. Experiments that scan and analyze brain data are helping us understand how literacy is achieved in humans, but the brain is complicated. The brain contains approximately 1 trillion cells, 100 billion neurons, and is made up of gray and white matter.

The complex nature of the brain means that researchers have designed and carried out many studies over time to begin to understand what happens in the brain during reading. Neuroimaging research builds on a history of work that includes psychological experiments, studies of brain damage, and brain dissection. This has resulted in a detailed and labeled anatomical map of the brain. These areas have been associated with human behaviors.

Your brain is part of your central nervous system. The central nervous system sends and receives electrical signals from nerve cells to their target cells all over the body. This system regulates our hormones and our response to stress. It keeps our heart pumping and our lungs breathing. It controls muscle movement, memory, learning, feelings, sleep, healing, digestion, and senses. The central nervous system involves the brain and body and is connected through **neurotransmitters**, which are the body's chemical messengers. Neurotransmitters such as amino acids, serotonin, and dopamine transmit messages between cells. These can excite, inhibit or modulate the nervous system's electrical signals.

The neuroendocrine system is the interface between the nervous and endocrine systems. The **endocrine system**, also known as the hormone system, regulates the body. Hormones are made by glands throughout the body and are recognized by receptors in various organs and tissues.

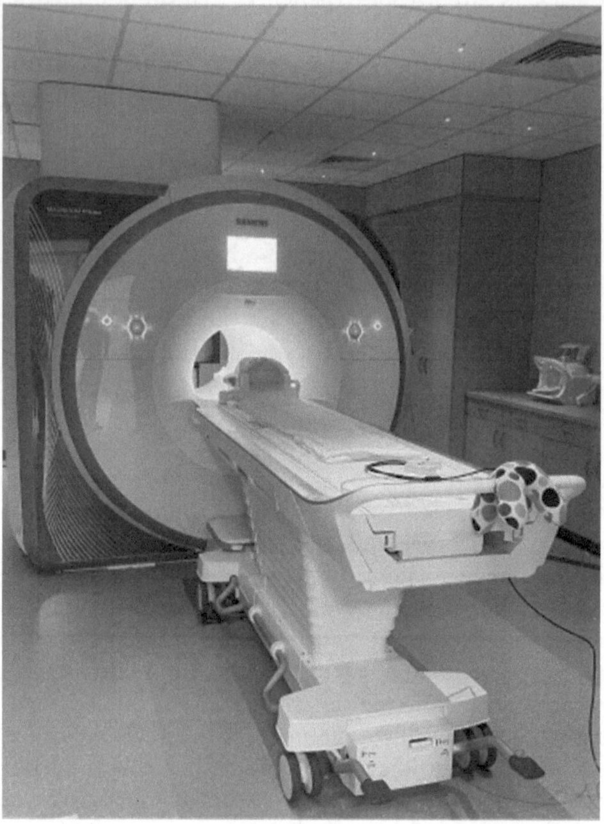

Figure 1.6 Magnetic Resonance Imaging (MRI) Machine.

Hormones also function as messengers of the body and control our functions and our psychology. They help our body stay in balance.

Hormones help the body deal with stress, control our sleep cycles, bring on puberty, control sexual development and reproduction, regulate appetite and blood sugar, and contribute to pleasure and motivation among many other functions.

Our brain also receives information from our heart, gut, and other parts of our internal body. Internal signals from the heart and gastrointestinal tract are involved in brain dynamics and with the brain, form a single complex system. The heart and gastrointestinal tract generate their own electrical activity and send information to the brain that helps us to self-regulate our emotions, stress, and resilience. These and continued scientific discoveries about the brain and body can contribute to providing an optimum environment for children and adolescents.

Research continues to focus on brain networks and the body's systems. Current research is also exploring how social, emotional, and cognitive processes are interconnected. Immordino-Yang (2019) describes this interconnectivity as the "situated, embodied, and embrained human mind" (195).

Understanding the active, social, and emotional aspects of brain function is crucial for literacy. The brain in action in the real world has been described as the **biopsychosocial** brain (Engel, 1977). Bio refers to the biology of the human body including genetics and functional processes. Psycho is a shortened form of psychological and refers to an individual's cognitive development. Social refers to interactions with others within a social context.

Biopsychosocial studies are increasingly important but are not always suited for the lab, where subjects are isolated and stationary during neuroimaging (Kasai, 2015). To move out of the laboratory and into the real world, portable scanning devices have been developed. New techniques such as hyperscanning can record data from two or more brains at the same time. With new imaging techniques, scientists can study what happens in the brains of two or more people while they are interacting. Some scientists are taking portable scanning devices into classrooms to study groups of students.

How to Use Neuroscience Findings

Over time neuroimaging has produced an increasingly nuanced understanding of literate activity and we will continue to learn from future studies. Meanwhile, novel information about the brain and reading processes has attracted the attention of literacy educators (Hruby & Goswami, 2019). Enthusiasm for the rapid increase in neuroscience information has sometimes led to misapplications of basic lab research in classrooms. For example, some educators have ignored aspects of reading instruction that go beyond decoding and the initial stage of beginning reading (Shanahan, 2020).

Basic lab research helps us understand reading more fully but does not directly translate into how we teach reading in the classroom. Neuroscience does not offer a simple solution to literacy problems. However, the experimental findings can be enlightening for literacy educators, leading to a greater understanding of the processing involved in beginning reading instruction, the comprehension processes of more advanced readers, and other literate practices.

Rather than making the mistake of trying to translate neuroscience studies directly to classroom instruction, in this book we use effective studies of instructional practices. Many of these studies have been conducted over time and positive results have been implemented in literacy classrooms. We attempt to build a bridge between educational research and studies of brain functions.

Neuroscience and Educational Policy

Everyone cares about literacy. Students, parents, teachers, administrators, school boards, community groups, religious groups, journalists, commentators, state legislators, governors, political groups, and elected representatives are all concerned. Some of these people know a little and some take the time to learn a lot about education and literacy. Some know a little about neuroscience, but very few take the time to read neuroscience studies. Many of these people rely only on media reports of neuroscience.

One real problem in literacy education comes from special interest groups who use neuroscience to build a flimsy structure to support their stance on how children should be taught. These special interest groups can influence media reports, elected representatives, and legislators. Legislation requiring certain types of instruction has proliferated across the United States because of the efforts of these special interest groups. Laws have been enacted enforcing phonics instruction and dismissing balanced literacy instruction. Laws have enforced English-only instruction and severely limited bilingual instruction in some states. State legislators have also tried to ban teaching the history of racial discrimination and addressing social-emotional aspects of learning in schools.

Special interest groups that support curriculum enforcement by legislation would benefit from understanding neuroscience findings on the interconnected nature of learning. We make some of these connections below.

Phonics and Balanced Literacy

A careful review of research on beginning reading shows the importance of learning letter-sound correspondence and connecting this knowledge in order to read and write. This is the **alphabetic principle** and is one of several aspects of learning to read (Rayner et al., 2001). However, reading theorists differ when it comes to focusing predominantly on phonics. **Phonics** is a method of teaching reading through the alphabetic principle. This relies on the idea that reading for meaning does not occur until after a child understands how each letter represents a sound.

Other theories suggest that reading depends on a combination of factors including the child's prior experiences with print, language, social interactions, emotional factors, and cognitive processes such as attention and memory (Hindman et al., 2020). **Balanced literacy** includes explicit literacy instruction including the alphabetic principle. It balances this with guiding children to explore language structures. Balanced literacy focuses on reading and writing as meaning-making processes. Neuroscience studies have noted connections between reading and meaning making. For example, cross-modal brain activity includes regions that promote understanding of observed human behavior connected with areas associated with reading (Gullick & Booth, 2014).

English-only and Bilingual Instruction

Bilingual education programs promote speaking, reading, and writing in two languages (Garcia, 2020). Bilingual programs have been politicized in the United States and over two decades ago, legislation abolished bilingual programs in several states. However, research has shown that English-only instruction has effects only up to second grade, while bilingual programs have better results as students proceed to middle school. Studies show that using students' languages in bilingual education benefited students academically (Valentino & Reardon, 2015).

Neuroscientists have described the benefits of bilingualism. For example, bilinguals have been found to have improved executive control functions and increased efficiency in task performance over time when compared to monolingual speakers (Di Pisa et al., 2021). As people have learned of these benefits, bilingual programs have spread across the United States. English-speaking children and their families want to participate in bilingual programs and the number of students speaking languages other than English has grown.

Teaching about Racial Discrimination

Another policy issue that affects educators involves teaching about racial discrimination. Those who are concerned about this issue could benefit from neuroscience research. Several states have passed legislation to ban teaching about systemic racial discrimination in the history of the United States. The politicization of this topic came about from a fear that white people living today would be blamed for what has happened in the past. This fear led to books being removed from school libraries and teachers being fired (Teitelbaum, 2022).

Teaching the history of racial discrimination is important to literacy educators because literacy is integral to maintaining a strong democracy. Attempts by special interest groups to legislate instruction are counter to democratic ideals such as developing informed citizens that have access to independent sources of information. Students can benefit from understanding how discrimination affects our society and individuals. Neuroscience has revealed some of these effects.

Studies of discrimination have found that multiple negative interactions over time are associated with long-lasting changes in resting state brain networks (Han et al., 2021). **Resting-state networks** are thought to support internal mental activity and connect internal and external attention to monitoring one's surroundings. Stress also affects the brain. Prolonged stress exposure has been shown to affect how the brain responds to stress including decreased attention control (Soares et al., 2013).

Social-emotional Learning

In some US states, policymakers have criticized the teaching of social-emotional skills. **Social-emotional learning** focuses on skills such as collaboration, self-efficacy, self-regulation, goal setting, and communication (Fisher et al., 2019). The attempts to ban social-emotional learning arose from a fear that schools would take from parents the role of teaching moral values. Literacy instruction that includes social-emotional learning helps students to consider others' perspectives, express empathy, and care about the world around them. Such education is necessary because sociocultural development is co-dependent with neurobiological development. The brain and social life influence one another as the child develops (Immordino-Yang & Gotlieb, 2017). Everyone should care about literacy instruction, but over-reaching policies and laws are burdensome for teachers who are responsible for children's education. Although policies and laws affect daily instruction, it is teachers who impact student outcomes (Rowan et al., 2002).

Teachers are responsible for student learning, and they can benefit from neuroscience studies related to teaching practices. Brault Foisy et al. (2020) pointed to five aspects of teaching that relate to the developing brain: orienting students' attention, strategy instruction, engaging students cognitively, setting the learning context, and interacting with students. We give examples of these aspects of teaching that were used in a third-grade teacher's writing workshop (Manak, 2011). These teaching practices lead pupils to process and retain information, which may strengthen existing brain networks or develop connections with new brain areas (Table 1.1).

The example of interactive read-aloud demonstrates how the teacher included strategies for both reading and writing in her demonstration. The children were seated on a rug, close to the teacher, so the pages could be shown to the students as the students and teacher talked about what they noticed in the book. The teacher set the tone for the lesson, which was respectful of others, yet low risk so that students felt comfortable thinking and sharing. Dimensions of literacy such as setting the context, orienting student attention, strategy instruction, engaging cognition, and interacting are integral to teaching students to make sense of texts.

Table 1.1 Teaching Practices and Interactive Read-Aloud Examples

Setting the learning context	The third-grade teacher situated the interactive read-aloud within the previous lessons and the overall writing workshop unit.
Orienting student attention	The teacher pointed out aspects of the author's craft while reading a picture book aloud to students.
Strategy instruction	The teacher modeled how to read headings, diagrams, and captions within nonfiction books.
Engaging students cognitively	The teacher stopped after every couple of pages to ask what students were noticing.
Interacting with students	As students responded to the book or noticed aspects of the author's craft, the teacher acknowledged and extended their responses.

Literacy Networks

Literacy is a multidimensional concept with visual, phonological, motor, and cultural dimensions (Dehaene et al., 2015). Neuroscience helps us understand the multiple dimensions involved in literate practices including embodied processing, semantic processing, social semantic processing, emotional valence, phonological processing, and languaging. These dimensions of literacy involve the brain, body, and the social environment.

Literacy instruction impacts the developing brain during the critical periods of early childhood, childhood, and adolescence. We focus on six dimensions of literacy that are important to us as literacy educators (Figure 1.7). The chapters within this book discuss each of these six dimensions and provide examples of literacy instructional methods that illustrate them.

Embodied processes	Connecting the meaning of language with action-related semantic information.
Semantic processing	Accessing the meaning of language through memory, prior knowledge, and prior experience.
Social and Emotional	Accumulation of social meanings from language. Emotional content as an aspect of language.
Multimodal	The way different modalities such as voice, text, and images come together to communicate ideas.
Phonology	Connecting the visual look of a letter to the sound. And connecting a sound to a letter that is used to represent the sound.
Languaging	Using any of the linguistic resources available to communicate with others and function in a social context.

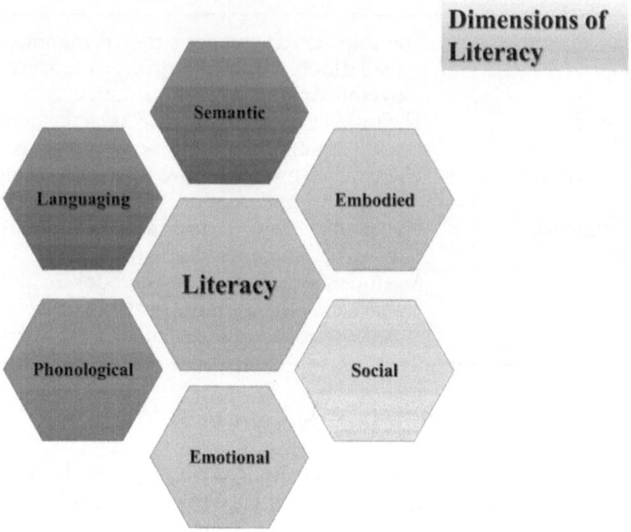

Figure 1.7 Dimensions of Literacy.

These aspects of literacy reflect our vision of literacy networks. This vision combines an understanding of the brain, body, emotion, social interaction, and environment, along with oral and written language. Our goal is to present teachers with both neuroscience findings and research-backed literacy instructional methods that can inform teachers' everyday practice.

Did You Know?

With increasingly rich and complex brain data, scientists have changed how they view the relationship between the brain and behavior. At first, the focus was on regions of the brain. Then scientists began charting connections and pathways between brain regions. Now scientists are describing the networks and distributed components across the brain that enable human behavior (Vanderah, 2020).

Food for Thought

A variety of techniques are used to obtain and study images of the brain. These are referred to as neuroimaging. Neuro refers to the brain and imaging refers to pictures of structure or activity the neuroimaging techniques produce. Some of the major methods used to study reading are EEG, fMRI, TMS, DTI, MRS, PET, and others. After the images are produced, researchers use statistical modeling to analyze the data.

EEG	Electroencephalography
TMS	Transcranial magnetic stimulation
DTI	Diffusion Tensor Imaging
fMRI	Functional magnetic resonance imaging
PET	Positron emission tomography
MRS	Magnetic resonance spectroscopy

Bibliography

Azzalini, D., Rebollo, I., & Tallon-Baudry, C. (2019). Visceral signals shape brain dynamics and cognition. *Trends in Cognitive Sciences*, *23*(6), 488–509. 10.1016/j.tics.2019.03.007

Borden, N. M., Forseen, S. E. M., & Stefan, C. M. (2015). *Imaging Anatomy of The Human Brain: A Comprehensive Atlas Including Adjacent Structures*. Demos Medical.

Boring, M. J., Silson, E. H., Ward, M. J., Richardson, R. M., Fiez, J. A., Baker, C. I., & Ghuman, A. S. (2021). Multiple adjoining word- and face-selective regions in ventral temporal cortex exhibit distinct dynamics. *Journal of Neuroscience*, *41*(29), 6314–6327.

Brault Foisy, L.-M., Matejko, A. A., Ansari, D., & Masson, S. (2020). Teachers as orchestrators of neuronal plasticity: Effects of teaching practices on the brain. *Mind, Brain, and Education*, *14*(4), 415–428.

Bui, T. M. & Das, J. (2021, July 31). *Neuroanatomy, Cerebral Hemisphere*. In: StatPearls [Internet]. StatPearls Publishing. https://www.ncbi.nlm.nih.gov/books/NBK549789/

Clay, M. M. (2005). *An Observation Survey of Early Literacy Achievement (2nd ed.)*. Heinemann.

Dehaene, S., Cohen, L., Morais, J., & Kolinsky, R. (2015). Illiterate to literate: Behavioural and cerebral changes induced by reading acquisition. *Nature Reviews Neuroscience*, *16*(4), 234–244. 10.1038/nrn3924

Dennis, E. L., Jahanshad, N., McMahon, K. L., de Zubicaray, G. I., Martin, N. G., Hickie, I. B., Toga, A. W., Wright, M. J., & Thompson, P. M. (2013).

Development of brain structural connectivity between ages 12 and 30: A 4-Tesla diffusion imaging study in 439 adolescents and adults. *NeuroImage, 64*, 671–684.

Di Pisa, G., Pereira Soares, S. M., & Rothman, J. (2021). Brain, mind and linguistic processing insights into the dynamic nature of bilingualism and its outcome effects. *Journal of Neurolinguistics*, 58. 10.1016/j.jneuroling.2020.100965

D'Mello, A. M., & Gabrieli, J. (2018). Cognitive neuroscience of dyslexia. *Language, Speech, and Hearing Services in Schools, 49*(4), 798–809. 10.1044/2018_LSHSS-DYSLC-18-0020

Engel, G. L. (1977). The need for a new medical model: A challenge for biomedicine. *Science, 196*, 129–136.

Fisher, D., Frey, N., Marsh, J. P., & Gonzalez, D. (2019). The links between social and emotional learning and literacy. *Journal of Adolescent & Adult Literacy, 63*(1), 115–117.

Foster, P. P., Baldwin, C. L., Thompson, J. C., Espeseth, T., Jiang, X., & Greenwood, P. M. (2019). Editorial: Cognitive and brain aging: Interventions to promote well-being in old age. *Frontiers in Aging Neuroscience, 11*, 268. 10.3389/fnagi.2019.00268

Garcia, A. (2020). A new era for bilingual education in California. *Phi Delta Kappan, 101*(5), 30–35.

Gee, J. P. (1996). *Social Linguistics and Literacies: Ideology in Discourses (2nd ed.)*. Routledge.

Goodman, K., Fries, P. H., & Strauss, S. L. (2016). *Reading—The Grand Illusion: How and Why People Make Sense of Print*. Routledge/Taylor & Francis Group.

Goodman, K. S. (1967). Reading: A psycholinguistic guessing game. *The Journal of the Reading Specialist, 6*(4), 126–135. 10.1080/19388076709556976

Gore, A. C., Krishnan, K., & Reilly, M. P. (2019). Endocrine-disrupting chemicals: Effects on neuroendocrine systems and the neurobiology of social behavior. *Hormones & Behavior, 111*, 7–22.

Gullick, M. M., & Booth, J. R. (2014). Individual differences in crossmodal brain activity predict arcuate fasciculus connectivity in developing readers. *Journal of Cognitive Neuroscience, 26*(7), 1331–1346.

Han, S. D., Lamar, M., Fleischman, D., Kim, N., Bennett, D. A., Lewis, T. T., Arfanakis, K., & Barnes, L. L. (2021). Self-reported experiences of discrimination in older Black adults are associated with insula functional connectivity. *Brain Imaging and Behavior, 15*(4), 1718–1727. 10.1007/s11682-020-00365-9

Hindman, A. H., Morrison, F. J., Connor, C. M., & Connor, J. A. (2020). Bringing the science of reading to preservice elementary teachers: Tools that bridge research and practice. *Reading Research Quarterly, 55*(Suppl 1), S197–S206.

Hruby, G. G., & Goswami, U. (2019). Educational neuroscience for reading educators. In D. E. Alvermann, N. J. Unrau, M. Sailors, & R. B. Ruddell (Eds.), *Theoretical Models and Processes of Literacy*. Routledge.

Ilyka, D., Johnson, M. H., & Lloyd-Fox, S. (2021). Infant social interactions and brain development: A systematic review. *Neuroscience and Biobehavioral Reviews, 130*, 448–469.

Immordino-Yang, M. H. (2016). *Emotions, Learning, and the Brain: Exploring the Educational Implications of Affective Neuroscience*. W.W. Norton & Company.

Immordino-Yang, M. H., Darling-Hammond, L., & Krone, C. R. (2019). Nurturing nature: How brain development is inherently social and emotional, and what this means for education. *Educational Psychologist*, *54*(3), 185–204.

Immordino-Yang, M. H., & Gotlieb, R. (2017). Embodied brains, social minds, cultural meaning: Integrating neuroscientific and educational research on social-affective development. *American Educational Research Journal*, *54*(1S), 344S–367S. 10.3102/0002831216669780

Kasai, K., Fukuda, M., Yahata, N., Morita, K., & Fujii, N. (2015). The future of real-world neuroscience: Imaging techniques to assess active brains in social environments. *Neuroscience Research*, *90*, 65–71.

Manak, J. (2011). The Social construction of intertextuality and literary understanding: The Impact of interactive read-alouds on the writing of third graders during writing workshop. *Reading Research Quarterly*, *46*(4), 309–311.

Matusz, P. J., Dikker, S., Huth, A. G., & Perrodin, C. (2019). Are we ready for real-world neuroscience? *Journal of Cognitive Neuroscience*, *31*(3), 327–338.

Menon, V., & Uddin, L. Q. (2010). Saliency, switching, attention and control: A network model of insula function. *Brain Structure and Function*, 214(5/6), 655–667. 10.1007/s00429-010-0262-0

Mercadante, A. A., & Tadi, P. (2021, July 31). *Neuroanatomy, Gray Matter*. In: StatPearls [Internet]. StatPearls Publishing. https://www.ncbi.nlm.nih.gov/books/NBK553239/

National Center for Educational Statistics (2022, September 1). *9-Year-olds' reading and mathematics scores drop since start of pandemic*. [Press release] https://www.nationsreportcard.gov/media_video_archive.aspx

Nelson, E. E., Leibenluft, E., McClure, E., & Pine, D. S. (2005). The social re-orientation of adolescence: A neuroscience perspective on the process and its relation to psychopathology. *Psychological Medicine*, *35*(2), 163–174.

Perdue, M. V., Mahaffy, K., Vlahcevic, K., Wolfman, E., Erbeli, F., Richlan, F., & Landi, N. (2022). Reading intervention and neuroplasticity: A systematic review and meta-analysis of brain changes associated with reading intervention. *Neuroscience & Biobehavioral Reviews*, *132*, 465–494.

Pugh, K. R., Mencl, W. E., Jenner, A. R., Lee, J. R., Katz, L., Frost, S. J., Shaywitz, S. E., & Shaywitz, B. A. (2001). Neuroimaging studies of reading development and reading disability. *Learning Disabilities Research & Practice*, *16*(4), 240. 10.1111/0938-8982.00024

Rand, M. K., & Morrow, L. M. (2021). The contribution of play experiences in early literacy: Expanding the science of reading. *Reading Research Quarterly*, *56*(1), S239–S248.

Rayner, K., Foorman, B. R., Perfetti, C. A., Pesetsky, D., & Seidenberg, M. S. (2001). How psychological science informs the teaching of reading. *Psychological Science in the Public Interest: A Journal of the American Psychological Society*, 2(2), 31–74. 10.1111/1529-1006.00

Rowan, B., Correnti, R., & Miller, R. J. (2002). What large-scale research tells us about teacher effects on student achievement: Insights from the prospects study of elementary schools. *Teachers College Record, 104*(8), 1525–1567.

Rowe, D. W., Shimizu, A. Y., & Davis, Z. G. (2022). Essential practices for engaging young children as writers: Lessons from expert early writing teachers. *Reading Teacher, 75*(4), 485–494.

Schlaggar, B. L., & McCandliss, B. D. (2007). Development of neural systems for reading. *Annual Review of Neuroscience, 30*(1), 475–503.

Schuster, S., Himmelstoss, N. A., Hutzler, F., Richlan, F., Kronbichler, M., & Hawelka, S. (2021). Cloze enough? Hemodynamic effects of predictive processing during natural reading. *NeuroImage, 228*, 1–11.

Shanahan, T. (2020). What constitutes a science of reading instruction? *Reading Research Quarterly, 55*, S235–S247.

Soares, J. M., Sampaio, A., Ferreira, L. M., Santos, N. C., Marques, P., Marques, F., Palha, J. A., Cerqueira, J. J., & Sousa, N. (2013). Stress impact on resting state brain networks. *PLoS ONE, 8*(6), 1–9. 10.1371/journal.pone.0066500

Spence, L. K., Costa, P. J. B. M., & Cullars, A. (2022). "They're killing our imaginations": Dialogue and reflexive writing development in historically marginalized students. *Reading Research Quarterly, 57*(3), 847–862. 10.1002/rrq.449

Street, B. (1984). *Literacy in Theory and Practice.* Cambridge University Press.

Teitelbaum, K. (2022). Curriculum, conflict, and critical race theory. *Phi Delta Kappan, 103*(5), 47–53.

Valentino, R. A., & Reardon, S. F. (2015). Effectiveness of four instructional programs designed to serve English learners. *Educational Evaluation & Policy Analysis, 37*(4), 612–637.

Vanderah, T. W. (2020). *Nolte's the Human Brain in Photographs and Diagrams (5th ed.).* Elsevier.

Wang, K., Banich, M. T., Reineberg, A. E., Leopold, D. R., Willcutt, E. G., Cutting, L. E., Del Tufo, S. N., Thompson, L. A., Opfer, J., Kanayet, F. J., Lu, Z., & Petrill, S. A. (2020). Left posterior prefrontal regions support domain-general executive processes needed for both reading and math. *Journal of Neuropsychology, 14*(3), 467–495.

Zielinski, B. A., Gennatas, E. D., Zhou, J., & Seeley, W. W. (2010). Network-level structural covariance in the developing brain. *PNAS Proceedings of the National Academy of Sciences of the United States of America, 107*(42), 18191–18196.

Zimmerman, B. S., Rasinski, T. V., Was, C. A., Rawson, K. A., Dunlosky, J., Kruse, S. D., & Nikbakht, E. (2019). Enhancing outcomes for struggling readers: Empirical analysis of the Fluency Development Lesson. *Reading Psychology, 40*(1), 70–94.

2

LITERACY THEORIES

> A newborn baby, wrapped in a soft blanket is held for the first time by her mother. The baby opens her eyes and looks up at a loving face. She feels warm arms and soft fabric. She hears excited voices and feels the comfortable temperature of the room. This baby is sensing the world around her and her brain is very active. She is already learning. Even before birth, she heard the sound of language as her auditory system developed. Her language networks will quickly grow stronger and more complete. Although this baby's brain is not wired for reading, it has the ability to develop literacy. In her brain, the language networks will be crucial for learning the literacy practices of her society and culture.

Literacy theories have been generated through observations and cognitive experiments over the past 100 years. The fields of education, linguistics, psychology, and biology have contributed to this work. Theories have addressed reading and writing development, as well as how people engage in literacy including their contexts, relationships, identities, and cultures. The field of neuroscience has also developed theories of reading and writing and has more recently begun to address social interaction and emotional aspects of literacy.

It may seem like theories from education and neuroscience would clash, but by engaging with these different perspectives, educators can enhance their overall understanding of literacy. In turn, scientists can learn from the research and practical experiences of literacy educators and the theories that guide their practice. The purpose of this chapter is to look at a few theories that undergird the ideas in the ensuing chapters.

Education Theories

Rather than list all the learning theories that could possibly impact instruction, we touch on concepts that are foundational to the ideas

DOI: 10.4324/9781003256199-3

presented in this book. Social constructivist learning theories include the zone of proximal development (ZPD), scaffolding, and culturally relevant pedagogy. We also use metacognitive theory to explain the instructional implications of brain research.

Social Constructivist Theories

Social interaction is a key idea in social constructivist theory. As learners interact, they construct new knowledge. Constructing knowledge means that learners make their own knowledge through experiences. The ways people interact to construct knowledge can be explained by the ZPD and scaffolding.

Zone of Proximal Development

> Kalen and Brayton sat together on the classroom rug, sharing a copy of *The Pirate Kids: The Very Quiet Parrot* by Johanna Gohmann. Their teacher Ms. Madden offered them this book, knowing they would be able to read most of the words and follow the plot. However, some words were slightly more challenging, and the boys would have to infer some of the more subtle plot details. Brayton had a better sight vocabulary, and Kaylen had great comprehension. They were well suited as reading partners because they could help each other read fluently and with understanding.

This scene highlights two children in a classroom that is structured for students to interact together while enjoying books. The teacher used social constructivist theory by encouraging the children to enjoy a book they can successfully read with help from another child. The children built their understanding as they read and talked about the book. **Partner reading** involves two students reading the same book, who stop to talk at designated points in the book or reading selection. Before reading, the teacher or students use sticky notes to tag stopping places in the book. The teacher structured this reading engagement so that students would construct their knowledge through social interactions.

Social learning theories help us understand that learning is influenced by interactions between people. Lev Vygotsky (1978) studied children's learning and developed the concept of a ZPD. This zone is just beyond the child's current abilities and is the place where the child is able to perform with help. Using Vygotsky's ideas, teachers set up instruction so that learners interact toward achieving a reachable goal.

In the partner reading example, Ms. Madden had previously assessed the students reading process and determined the strengths and needs of each student in the class. The students were paired with partners who could potentially help them progress in their ZPD. When one student needed help, the partner jumped in to provide help with a word or explanation.

Scaffolding

A related concept is Jerome Bruner's concept of **scaffolding** (Bruner, 1990; Wood, Bruner, Ross, 1976). To scaffold learning, teachers simplify or demonstrate to guide learners in successfully using the skills they are in the process of acquiring. Scaffolding is used as a metaphor. A physical scaffold is used for working at heights. It is removed when a part of the project is complete. Similarly, instructional scaffolds are removed when the learner can complete a task independently. Ms. Haney scaffolded Oscar as he read, *I Can Make This Promise* by Christine Day.

> Ms. Haney sat beside Oscar, a fifth-grader, listening to him read. She noticed that Oscar sometimes did not use punctuation. He read, " … a huge banner that shouts fire." Ms. Haney asked him to read it again, pausing at the punctuation to see if it changed the meaning. He read again. " … a huge banner that shouts, 'fireworks.' That makes more sense," Oscar said.

Ms. Haney scaffolded Oscar's reading by prompting him to use punctuation instead of stopping at the end of a line of text. She used this prompt one more time as a reminder, but he soon remembered on his own. Ms. Haney continued to monitor his reading but no longer needed to prompt him to use punctuation.

Teaching at the ZPD and scaffolding are key concepts in constructivist learning theory. Constructing knowledge in these ways helps build concepts necessary for understanding literature. Some examples of structures for knowledge construction are whole class or small group discussion of literature, using graphic organizers to visually represent elements of literature, and even acting out scenes from a story. Chapters 6 and 7 will reference the ZPD to discuss how readers use phonology and other cues to construct meaning as they read.

Vygotsky's theory of the ZPD was a result of his work on sociocultural learning that explained how people's interactions and the culture they live in shape their mental development. In US schools, students come from various cultural backgrounds. Culturally relevant pedagogy addresses the cultural aspect of learning.

Culturally Relevant Pedagogy

> An eighth-grade class had completed a study of *Mississippi Solo: A River Quest* by Eddy L. Harris. They enjoyed this memoir of a young Black man as he journeyed by canoe down the Mississippi River. After reading the story, they began brainstorming ideas for their own memoirs. Mr. Colter asked, "What was an impactful moment in your life?" The class thought quietly for a minute, then Mr. Colter said, "Maybe an accident where you needed stitches, or setting a broken bone." The students soon came up with ideas: a family's car accident, helping a grandfather with piglets, and visiting a grandmother.

This scene depicts one teacher's culturally relevant pedagogy. In a rural, largely African American classroom, Mr. Colter introduced a contemporary memoir written by an African American man. He connected themes in the book to the students' own lives and they wrote about personal experiences.

Culturally relevant pedagogy involves these tenets: Connecting curriculum to students' lives and culture, fostering students' intellectual and moral development; developing cultural competence, and developing critical consciousness (Ladson-Billings, 1994). Teachers approach instruction with the expectation that students will succeed academically. They instill cultural competence for understanding and valuing students' cultures and the cultures of others. They promote critical consciousness for identifying, analyzing, and solving real-world problems, including societal inequalities. In Chapters 5 and 6, we present information on how cultural competence is achieved in the developing brain.

Theories of instruction that are related to culturally relevant pedagogy include culturally relevant teaching and culturally sustaining pedagogy (Paris, 2012). All these theories focus on instruction that builds on students' cultures. Students engage with academic content that is connected to their identities and lived experiences. Students maintain the cultural and linguistic competence of their communities while gaining access to dominant cultural competence. Teachers support students' cultural experiences including dialects, languages, and perspectives. Teachers plan instruction with books and study topics that highlight or connect to students' cultural experiences.

Another related idea is **funds of knowledge** (Moll, 1992), which brings students' home and family knowledge into the classroom. Resources that are integral to family functioning are seen as resources for learning in school.

Figure 2.1 Intersection of Learning Theories.

Connecting Learning Theories for Literacy Instruction

Many literacy educators connect the concepts of constructing knowledge, scaffolding at the ZPD, and culturally relevant pedagogy (Figure 2.1). These compatible theories are easily translated into classroom practice. Many of the examples of instruction in Chapters 4–9 rely on combinations of these theories.

Constructivist and sociocultural theories help teachers plan instruction. This involves getting to know the students, their families, and their communities. Teachers get to know students and their families through individual conferences, questionnaires, formative assessments, participating in community events, and home visits.

Metacognition

Teachers can learn about their students by using **formative assessments.** These are methods of collecting information while learning is in progress. The teacher uses this information to meet the student's immediate learning needs.

In the following example, Mr. Canty used a reading interview to learn about Javier's reading process.

> At the beginning of the school year, Mr. Canty interviewed his fifth-grade students to encourage them to think about their reading process. Mr. Canty was particularly concerned about Javier because he was reading below grade level.

Mr. Canty: When you are reading and come to something you don't know, what do you do?
Javier: I kind of sound it out at first. If it sounds a little weird, then I ask someone what the word is.
Mr. Canty: Do you ever do anything else?
Javier: No

Following the interview, Mr. Canty planned to teach Javier additional strategies for solving unknown words during reading. They continued to meet weekly throughout the school year to discuss Javier's reading process. Javier learned to discuss and think about his reading process, and he learned a variety of strategies to read and comprehend different kinds of texts.

Over the last 40 years, psychologists have developed theories of metacognition. **Metacognition** involves being aware of one's thought process. It is a person's ability to monitor and regulate their thoughts. There are two aspects of metacognition, metacognitive monitoring, which is being aware of one's thoughts and behavior, and metacognitive control, which involves modifying one's thoughts or behavior. The flow of information between what one is experiencing, and metacognition during the experience allows a person to both initiate thoughts and observe those thoughts (Hacker, 2018).

Metacognition is clearly related to reading and writing development. Readers must continuously control their reading skills and monitor comprehension (Goodman et al., 2005). Writers must think about how to transfer ideas into words while monitoring to make sure the text is cohesive. Brain networks are involved in selecting the most relevant stimuli from among other competing stimuli. For example, when reading an unknown word, the reader must choose the best fit from several possible words (Zacharopoulos et al., 2022). In the next section, we connect the literacy and psychological theories discussed above with the biological theories that support them.

Biological Theories

Amber was an active baby who preferred to be pushed in a stroller outside rather than take a nap indoors. As a child, she enjoyed riding on the merry-go-round and being pushed high in the swing. As a teen, Amber traveled to Asia and all over the United States. Then as an adult, she scrupulously saved her money for more international travel.

Amber's adventures illustrate how a baby can be born with genes that predispose them to certain personality traits. Amber was a bit of a risk-taker and sought out new experiences. Abmer's experiences also influenced her development. Both nature and nurture are influential. Babies are born with genes that will help them thrive through all the stages of life, but experiences affect how those genes are expressed.

Biological theories such as evolution and genetics have informed theories of learning. Evolutionary developmental psychology proposes that some aspects of infancy and childhood have developed through natural selection for adaptation to the child's environment (Bjorklund, 2018). These ontogenetic adaptations help the child deal with the current context (Hall & Oppenheim, 1987). **Ontogenetic adaptation** suggests that changes in children's development are due to evolutionary factors that help the child survive and thrive during a specific time during development. Ontogenetic means the development of an individual over the lifespan and adaptation is the process of a species becoming fitted to its environment.

Unless they have a rare genetic disorder, children are all born with the necessary genes for brain development and learning (Immordino-Yang et al., 2018). Although we inherit our genes from our parents, our genes also change in response to environmental cues. These forces in our environment are called epigenetics. **Epigenetic** means "above the genome" and refers to environmental forces that turn genes on and off, copying and arranging them without changing the underlying genetic code of the DNA.

Due to the influence of epigenetics, optimal environments are needed to support growth, development, thinking, and learning. Optimal environments include clean drinking water, a nutritious diet, clean air, a stable home, a nurturing family, and intellectually stimulating experiences. These elements optimize positive early neurodevelopmental preparation for learning and socioemotional development (Boyce & Kobor, 2015).

Combining the biological theories of ontogenetic adaptation and epigenetics, we can see that the human species adapted to its environment over time so it could survive and thrive. Individuals go through developmental stages that enable them to survive under the care of their parents and within the environment. These adaptations show up in an individual's genes. As a child gestates and grows, he is influenced by his environment and some genes are modified by this influence (Figure 2.2). Because of the influence of the environment, it is important for a mother to have prenatal care, and for a child to be treated well in the home, live in a healthy environment, engage in optimal educational opportunities, and have supportive relationships (Immordino-Yang, 2016).

Models of Neurological Processing

> Two children, five-year-old Tyrone and his older brother Caleb were seated on the floor reading the picture book, *Brown Bear, Brown Bear, What do you See?* By Bill Martin Jr.

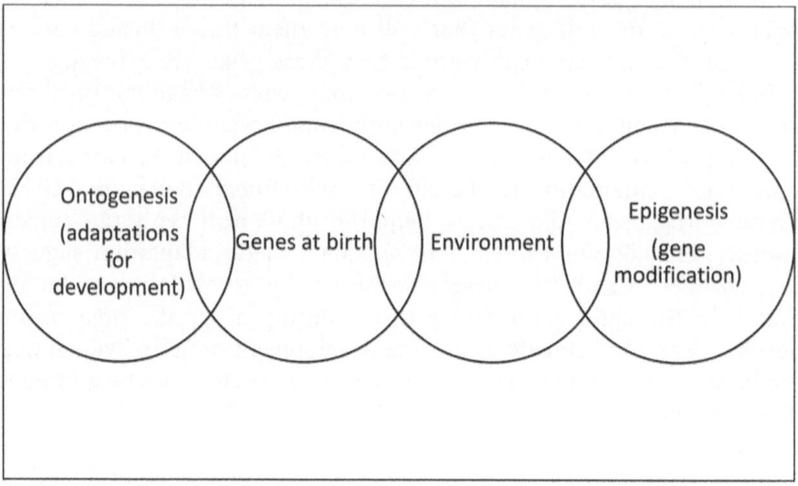

Figure 2.2 Influence of Adaptations, Genetics, and the Environment.

> Caleb pointed to a word and asked his little brother, "What is this word?"
>
> Tyrone pointed to the word, Brown and said, "buh."
>
> "Brown," Caleb told him. Then he read, "Brown Bear, Brown Bear, what do you see? I see a red bird looking at me."

Both boys were relying on reading networks within their brains, but Caleb took a more direct route for immediate word recognition. Tyrone engaged an indirect route by sounding the individual letter B. After listening to Caleb read the repetitive text, Tyrone began to recognize the phrases, "Brown Bear, Brown Bear, what do you see?" and "I see a___ looking at me." He began to recognize the word forms "Brown" and "Bear." As Tyrone gained experience with words, he would eventually rely more on the direct route of accessing whole words stored in memory.

The Dual-Route Model

The **dual-route model** describes the two routes of brain activation during reading, the ventral (direct route), and the dorsal (indirect route). Figure 2.3 shows the location of the dorsal and ventral routes. The direct route involves recognizing whole words and retrieving the word's sound and meaning from memory. These associations build as the reader comes in contact with the word many times. This route is used for reading words that more commonly occur as well as irregular words such as

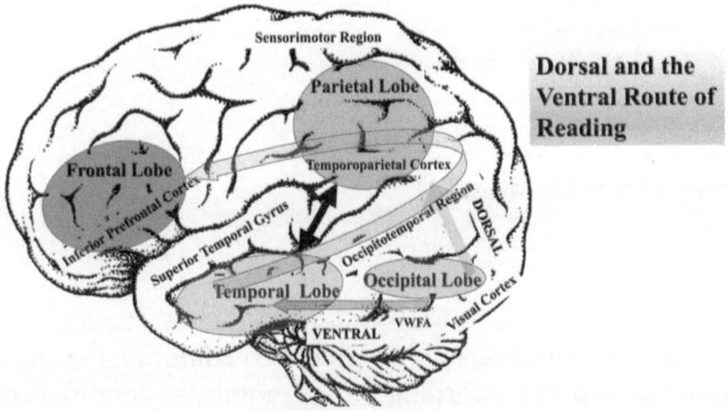

Figure 2.3 Dorsal and Ventral Routes in Reading.

Note: Neural network mediating word reading (Fletcher & Grigorenko, 2017).

"once" that do not have a clear letter–sound correspondence (Cummine et al., 2015). The dual-route model will be referenced again in Chapter 8, which discusses "Languaging."

The indirect route maps the visual representation of print onto the sound structures of language. This route is associated with slow decoding, which involves a rule-based analysis of the printed word. This requires learning the **alphabetic principle**, the understanding that letters represent speech sounds. This is critical for learning and using the relationships between the spelling of the word and the sound of the word (Pugh et al., 2001).

Both the direct and indirect routes are involved in reading. However, readers activate these areas in different ways. Highly skilled readers mostly activate a path of letter combinations and meaning without the need for phonemic processing (Jobard et al., 2011). Lower skilled readers are more likely to activate phonemic processing with letter combinations and meaning. This suggests there are differences in how processing routes are used by individuals.

Ventral and dorsal processing is aided by white matter pathways and connections between areas of the brain. These pathways allow efficient communication between brain areas (Gupta & Srivastava, 2020). The white matter pathways develop into a connected reading network as a person learns the alphabetic principle.

Recent Brain Models for Reading

Benjamin and Gabb (2012) summarized the state of brain research on reading, "Historically, reading fluency has been modeled as the product of discrete skills such as single word decoding. More recent

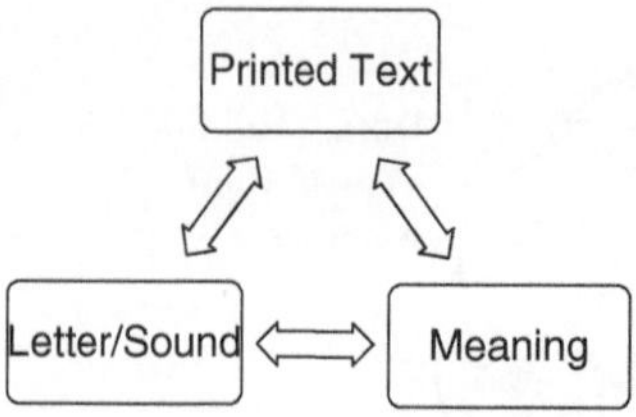

Figure 2.4 Interactive Model of Reading.

conceptualizations emphasize that fluent reading is the product of competency in, and the coordination of, multiple cognitive sub-skills (a multi-componential view)" (p. 2572).

Models of reading are not settled facts. Researchers contest the dual-route model and suggest the need for other models. For example, **interactive models** explore networks across brain regions and suggest that phonological and semantic processing are engaged interactively and in parallel (Harm & Seidenberg, 2004; Stites & Laszlo, 2017). Some students draw more on phonology and some draw more on semantics (Fischer-Baum, 2017). Rather than following a set pathway in one direction, interactions occur between sensory regions and higher order processing regions through forward and backward feedback loops (Price & Devlin, 2011). This means that when a reader sees printed text, multiple areas of the brain are activated at the same time. Figure 2.4 includes arrows going both ways to show the back-and-forth interaction between brain areas that process sounds and letters and brain areas that process word meanings.

Reading teachers mostly help students as they read real words within stories and other texts. Sometimes lists of words or even nonwords are used for testing purposes. Processing nonwords (e.g., snave) is more strongly associated with phonological and orthographic processing, which involves sound and spelling patterns (McNorgan et al., 2015). The processing of real words is more strongly associated with semantic functions, such as memory. Semantic processing, meaning, memory, and comprehension will be discussed further in Chapter 6.

Models of reading continue to be developed based on cognitive psychology, continued experimental research, and computer modeling. The models are developed over time and are always subject to improvement as additional information is discovered. Educational neuroscientists suggest that to continue building strong models, large-scale population studies and longitudinal studies with reproducible methods are needed (Meisler & Gabrieli, 2022). Studies involving different types of people such as females, males, adults, children, adolescents, bilinguals, strong readers, and poor readers are necessary to gain a full understanding of the brain's reading process among different types of readers. Both neuroscience and literacy research increasingly points to the multidimensionality of literacy development and use among learners (Compton-Lilly et al., 2020). These multiple dimensions include social and cultural factors as well as different learning trajectories of individual students.

Using Theories and Frameworks in Teaching

As literacy educators, we can draw upon theories and models of reading as we work with students. Spence's experience as a classroom teacher highlights the practical use of theories of learning.

> When I think about starting a new school year, I have a lot of hope in my heart. I have ideas, plans, and a theory. If students are engaged in their learning, not just by reading and writing about things, but by doing things—they will learn. I probably believe so strongly in this theory because it is how I learn—by doing. I construct my own knowledge by jumping in feet first and figuring it out as I go along, using my prior experiences as a guide. Educational theorists have helped me understand why learning by doing is so powerful.
>
> Students learn from other people as they construct new knowledge. Teachers scaffold students to achieve new skills and understandings. Students learn from each other as they work out problems cooperatively. They learn through using language as a means of thinking.
>
> Classrooms should be places where children talk, write, draw, and build. In active classrooms, students listen attentively to what others have to say because it helps them work toward a goal. Whenever children interact with one another, they are learning. Interaction can support children in bridging the gap between what they know and what they can learn about a topic. My work as an elementary and middle school teacher was grounded in social constructivist learning theories. I saw these concepts in the children I taught. For some years, it was easy to be a constructivist teacher. I had a curriculum, a job, and administrators that encouraged me to teach following social constructivist theory. Other years, I was at odds with the curriculum I was given. The curriculum materials and standardized tests were restrictive. There were too many standards to cover, and my students' test scores would be scrutinized and compared to other teachers. My fear paralyzed me. When I tried

to teach by the book, I was unhappy. I had a theory of teaching and learning. How could I make it work—even when I was pressured by misguided constraints?

Over time I figured out that even when I did not have a supportive curriculum or administrators, my theory of teaching and learning would support me. I decided that covering too much material in one school year was counter-productive because real learning did not occur when students were rushed from one topic to another. My students could memorize things for the next test but did not apply or transfer that knowledge. So, I began to teach the important concepts in depth rather than trying to cover everything that was handed to me. I began to connect concepts across subjects, topics, and the school year.

For several years, I taught Spanish-speakingstudents who were transitioning into an all-English curriculum. Literature was often difficult because of the extensive vocabulary. Regardless of the difficulty, we studied *James and the Giant Peach* by Roald Dahl, a British author. I read a chapter of the book aloud each day, then gave them the version written as a playscript. Our goal was to present the play to several classes, using the stage in the cafeteria. Each student had a part in making the play a success, even though they had widely varying English proficiency. Every student was interested and motivated throughout. The classes that watched the play were so engrossed that everyone forgot about the intermission.

Authentic audiences create purpose and motivation for learning. The audience can be other students in the classroom, the classroom next door, family members, or community groups. Classmates are an excellent audience and provide motivation and purpose, especially when students take the lead in directing activities. Throughout these purposeful learning engagements, students should be talking together about what they are doing because as Vygotsky showed us, language is necessary for the development of ideas and for learning new concepts.

Through an in-depth study of the novel and performing the play, my students understood and enacted many of the state standards for language arts and improved their ability and confidence with the English language. I read the novel aloud chapter by chapter after lunch each day. Then the students read the play script and we stopped to discuss it along the way. To help the children understand the plot, I wrote out the major plot points on strips of tagboard and gave one randomly to each child. Their task was to line up around the periphery of the classroom in order of the plot sequence. They eagerly walked around the classroom, reading, and talking, lining up, then repositioning, and finally proudly reading off each section in order.

James and the Giant Peach in play form happened to be available at my school. However, my largely Hispanic students would have benefited from a more culturally relevant experience. Books with Hispanic characters such as *The Dreamer* by Pam Muñoz Ryan and Peter Sís can be adapted for performing as a more culturally relevant experience for Hispanic students. I understand that not every book can be performed as a play, but purposeful learning can happen when students have goals for the work they do. Doing is an essential part of learning. Doing a play, doing a project, building a model, drawing a diagram, performing a poem, giving a speech, and creating visual art; are just some ways to learn by doing. Adding to my theory of learning, I later learned that biological theories of development show us the importance of rich experiences because children's brains and bodies are influenced by their environmental conditions.

Neuroscience research has strengthened my understanding of the embodied nature of literacy. This means that how a person experiences literacy is impacted by experiences, social interactions, emotional responses, and cognitive functions. My theory and approach to instruction involve finding out about my students' backgrounds and interests. I talk to parents to learn about my students' lives at home and I consider their physical and emotional needs. I use formative assessments to determine my students' current skills and plan instruction to move them forward by providing a curriculum that is rich, student-centered, and interesting.

Instructional Frameworks

In addition to sociocultural, psychological, and biological theories of learning, a variety of instructional frameworks can guide our teaching. The writing process, reader response, dialogic teaching, inquiry learning, critical literacy, and social justice frameworks are some ideas that guide teachers' practice. These frameworks will appear in the instructional examples we provide in later chapters, connected to brain research. We briefly discuss each framework below.

Writing Process

Within this structure, students engage in writing about topics of their choice with an audience in mind. They discuss their writing as they make writing decisions including revisions. The focus is on the process of writing rather than the final product. One important aspect of the writing process is to write before writing (Murray, 1978). This has been called prewriting, brainstorming, planning, or rehearsal. Students must have a chance to form their thoughts, rather than immediately churning out a predictable essay.

Drafting gives the writer a chance to write quickly without letting the inner critic censor their ideas. Revision allows the writer to change and form their text. Time to re-read and revise a piece of writing acknowledges that writers struggle with the imbalance between what they intend to say and how to express it (Graves, 1982).

Editing and publishing are the final phases of the writing process as the text becomes more like a finished product for sharing with others. Editing prepares the text for an audience. Publishing presents the text to an audience. Stapling pages into a booklet, preparing a digital text, reading the text aloud, or posting it on a bulletin board, are just a few ways to publish student work.

As students write in a workshop setting, they are using sensory-motor and social information to modulate the activation of the semantic network (Lin et al., 2018). This draws on the student's accumulated, connected meanings.

Reader Response

This is a theory of reading, in which the reader actively constructs the meaning of a text. Readers transact with texts to create meaning while reading. Differences in culture or experiences may influence the meanings that readers construct. Teachers acknowledge that there is not one defining interpretation of a text. Literature circles and response journals are two ways that students can freely respond and transact with what they are reading. Reader response theory connects with our understanding of semantic processing, as semantic connections are made with prior experience and building meaning during reading.

Dialogic Teaching

Students and teachers engage in extended dialog to construct knowledge and understanding. This shifts the power dynamic away from the teacher as students think more deeply and question ideas. Teachers move away from asking questions with the expectation of a specific answer. Instead, they try to create a dialog among the students as they explore ideas together. Structures such as a circle of voices give each student an opportunity to talk. Students can engage by discussing issues, debating perspectives, and generating questions. Teachers demonstrate how to use oral language effectively. Dialogic interactions can help to sculpt and mature neuronal networks as they become more efficient and connected.

Inquiry Learning

Throughout an inquiry unit of study, students generate questions, investigate multiple resources, and revise their understandings. Inquiry learning begins with questions. Questioning is continued and encouraged throughout the unit of study. As students generate questions, they contribute to the content under investigation. Teachers guide students toward critical thinking and assist students in finding strong resources to explore the inquiry topic. Inquiry learning can provide students with tasks in which they take more initiative yet receive plenty of teacher support. This combination is implicated in brain areas that are associated with learning, planning, reward, and motivation (Nakai et al., 2017).

Critical Literacy

Within this structure, students and teachers approach the world's socially constructed socio-political systems through examination and questioning. Texts are not seen as neutral, and the way people read texts is not neutral.

Students read about societal issues, especially issues that concern them or their community. They choose and read texts critically. Reading several different texts on a topic provides a variety of perspectives. Students consider why the author wrote the text and the choices the author made including what was included and what was omitted. Through critically reading, writing, and discussing societal issues, students may devise action plans for improving their community or the larger society.

Students may study patterns of injustice, social stratification, and systemic social issues. They engage in self-reflection. Teachers provide texts that address these issues and encourage discussions and personal experiences. Students take action to address social inequalities in their lives and communities.

Instruction that includes critical literacy and social justice provides students with expanded perspectives on social life, which is critical to education. Neuroscience has shown that the configuration of the human brain changes shortly after a learning experience, and this is related to memory performance. Expanding student perspectives is one more way to impact brain development.

Making it Work in the Classroom

Making it work in your classroom requires knowing the theories and frameworks that guide your teaching and trusting what you know. Every instructional decision you make can be guided by theory including what to focus on, what materials to use, and how to structure student engagement. When your teaching is guided by a strong theory, your students will be interested, and their goals will be purposeful. Students will observe, imagine, discuss, and interact to accomplish their goals.

Together, educational, psychological, and biological theories provide a wide view of learning. Yet from their different starting points, they are converging on principles of literacy learning. Children's brains, minds, and bodies develop in response to their environment and experiences. It is up to teachers to provide many of those experiences.

Bibliography

Benjamin, C. F. A., & Gaab, N. (2012). What's the story? The tale of reading fluency told at speed. *Human Brain Mapping*, 33(11), 2572–2585. 10.1002/hbm.21384

Bjorklund, D. F. (2018). A metatheory for cognitive development (or "Piaget is dead" revisited). *Child Development*, *89*(6), 2288–2302.

Boyce, T. W., & Kobor, M. S. (2015). Development and the epigenome: The 'Synapse' of gene-environment interplay. *Developmental Science*, *18*(1), 1–23.

Bruner, J. (1990). *Acts of Meaning: Four Lectures on Mind and Culture.* Harvard University Press.

Coltheart, M., Rastle, K., Perry, C., Langdon, R., & Ziegler, J. (2001). DRC: A dual route cascaded model of visual word recognition and reading aloud. *Psychological Review*, *108*(1), 204–256.

Compton-Lilly, C. F., Mitra, A., Guay, M., & Spence, L. K. (2020). A confluence of complexity: intersections among reading theory, neuroscience, and observations of young readers. *Reading Research Quarterly*, 55, S185–S195. 10.1002/rrq.348

Cummine, J., Dai, W., Borowsky, R., Gould, L., Rollans, C., & Boliek, C. (2015). Investigating the ventral-lexical, dorsal-sublexical model of basic reading processes using diffusion tensor imaging. *Brain Structure & Function*, *220*(1), 445–455. 10.1007/s00429-013-0666-8

Fletcher, J. M., & Grigorenko, E. L. (2017). Neuropsychology of learning disabilities: The past and the future. *Journal of the International Neuropsychological Society: JINS*, *23*(9–10), 930–940. 10.1017/S1355617717001084

Goodman, Y., Watson, D., & Burke, C. L. (2005). *Reading Miscue Inventory: From Evaluation to Instruction (2nd ed.).* Richard C. Owen Publishers, Inc. ISBN: 978-1572747371.

Graves, D. H. (1982). How do writers develop? *Language Arts*, *59*(2), 173–179.

Gupta, A., & Srivastava, M. P. (2020). Newer paradigms in language neurobiology. *Annals of Indian Academy of Neurology*, *23*, S73–S81.

Hacker, D. J. (2018). A metacognitive model of writing: An update from a developmental perspective. *Educational Psychologist*, *53*(4), 220–237.

Hall, W. G., & Oppenheim, R. W. (1987). Developmental psychobiology: Prenatal, perinatal, and early postnatal aspects of behavioral development. *Annual Review of Psychology*, *38*(1), 91. 10.1146/annurev.ps.38.020187.000515

Harm, M. W., & Seidenberg, M. S. (2004). Computing the meanings of words in reading: Cooperative division of labor between visual and phonological processes. *Psychological Review*, *111*, 662–720. 10.1037/0033-295X.111.3.662

Immordino-Yang, M. H. (2016). *Emotions, Learning, and the Brain: Exploring the Educational Implications of Affective Neuroscience*. W.W. Norton & Company.

Immordino-Yang, M. H., Darling-Hammond, L., Krone, C., & Aspen Institute, National Commission on Social, Emotional, & Academic Development (NCSEAD). (2018). The Brain Basis for Integrated Social, Emotional, and Academic Development: How Emotions and Social Relationships Drive Learning. Aspen Institute.

Jobard, G., Vigneau, M., Simon, G., & Tzourio-Mazoyer, N. (2011). The weight of skill: Interindividual variability of reading related brain activation patterns in fluent readers. *Journal of Neurolinguistics*, *24*(1), 113–132.

Ladson-Billings, G. (1994). *The Dreamkeepers*. Jossey-Bass Publishing Company.

Lin, N., Wang, X., Xu, Y., Wang, X., Hua, H., Zhao, Y., & Li, X. (2018). Fine subdivisions of the semantic network supporting social and sensory–motor semantic processing. *Cerebral Cortex*, 28, 2699–2710. 10.1093/cercor/bhx148

McNorgan, C., Chabal, S., O'Young, D., Lukic, S., & Booth, J. R. (2015). Task dependent lexicality effects support interactive models of reading: A meta-analytic neuroimaging review. *Neuropsychologia*, *67*, 148–158.

Meisler, S. L., & Gabriel, J. D. E. (2022). A large-scale investigation of white matter microstructural associations with reading ability. *NeuroImage*, *249*, 118909.

Moll, L. (1992). Bilingual classroom studies and community analysis: Some recent trends. *Educational Researcher*, *12*(2), 20–24.

Murray, D. M. (1978). Write before writing. *College Composition & Communication*, *29*, 375–381. 10.2307/357024

Nakai, T., Nakatani, H., Hosoda, C., Nonaka, Y., & Okanoya, K.o (2017). Sense of accomplishment is modulated by a proper level of instruction and represented in the brain reward system. *PLOS One*, *12*, e0168661. 10.1371/journal.pone.0168661

Paris, D. (2012). Culturally sustaining pedagogy: A needed change in stance, terminology, and practice. *Educational Researcher*, *41*(3), 93–97. 10.3102/0013189X12441244

Price, C. J., & Devlin, J. T. (2011). The interactive account of ventral occipitotemporal contributions to reading. *Trends in Cognitive Sciences*, *15*(6), 246–253. 10.1016/j.tics.2011.04.001

Pugh, K. R., Mencl, W. E., Jenner, A. R., Lee, J. R., Katz, L., Frost, S. J., Shaywitz, S. E., & Shaywitz, B. A. (2001). Neuroimaging studies of reading development and reading disability. *Learning Disabilities Research & Practice*, *16*(4), 240–249.

Stites, M. C., & Laszlo, S. (2017). Time will tell: A longitudinal investigation of brain-behavior relationships during reading development. *Psychophysiology*, *54*(6), 798–809.

Vygotsky, L. S. (1978). *Mind in Society: The Development of Higher Psychological Processes*. Harvard University Press.

Wood, D., Bruner, J. S., & Ross, G. (1976). The Role of tutoring in problem solving. *Journal of Child Psychology & Psychiatry & Allied Disciplines*, *17*(2), 89–100.

Zacharopoulos, G., Hertz, U., Kanai, R., & Bahrami, B. (2022). The effect of feedback valence and source on perception and metacognition: An fMRI investigation. *Cognitive Neuroscience*, *13*(1), 38–46. 10.1080/17588928.2020.1828323

3

EMBODIED BRAIN

> Ms. D, a fifth-grade teacher was enjoying spring break at the beach. She was standing in the surf watching the waves come in. She felt the water as it rushed toward her, covering her calves, and giving her a little push. The sun was beginning to set, turning the tide and sky a pale peach. She smiled and felt her tension go out with the receding water. Her shoulders relaxed and she breathed the salty air deeply.

Our bodies and the environment around us impact how we think and what we feel. Being a teacher or student can be very stressful. Competition, tests, paperwork, and time constraints are just some factors that can overwhelm us and our students. The school and classroom environment certainly plays a role in teaching, learning, and literacy.

Where do you like to read? At a desk, on your bed, or couch? On the porch or patio? What do you like to read? Do you ever talk about what you are reading? How do you write? Notepaper, journal, voice dictation?

Literacy involves material objects and our bodies within spaces. It involves doing something with our body and mind. It involves our feelings and interactions. Embodiment is how these things come together within and around us. The term **embodiment** is used to describe how our minds and bodies interact with the environment.

Embodied literacy considers the total literacy environment including the materials, people involved, the space they are in, their feelings, memories, and interactions as they engage with literacy (Boldt & Leander, 2020). Reading and writing involve our senses. We are all familiar with the senses of sight, hearing, taste, smell, and touch. The biological sciences have clarified how our senses are important to our perception of ourselves and the world around us (Young, 2021).

DOI: 10.4324/9781003256199-4

In this chapter, we discuss embodiment in relation to brain systems, the peripheral nervous system, the endocrine system, the visceral system, and the environment.

In this chapter, we explore how our brain is influenced by our bodies, the environment, and social interaction as illustrated in the artist's impression in Figure 3.1.

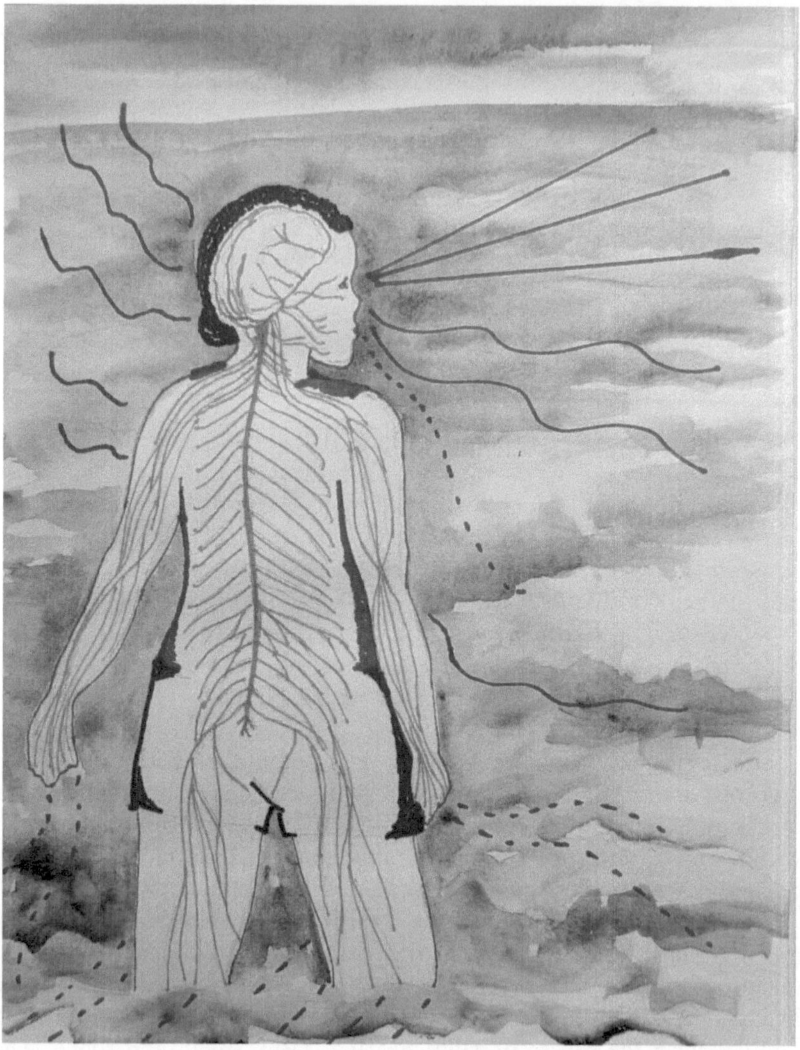

Figure 3.1 Artists' Impression of the Central and Peripheral Nervous Systems Interacting within the Environment.

Embodied and Embrained in the Environment

Embodiment involves the brain as a part of the central nervous system, which extends down the spinal column and connects with nerves in the skin, muscles, and joints. This allows our brain to collect and organize information from the rest of our body and our environment. As we interact in our environment, our senses send information about the environment and our activity to the brain (Tessari et al., 2010).

Our **peripheral nervous system** transmits information to the central nervous system. For example, the sense of touch sends signals about balance and coordination, pressure, vibration, pain, and temperature to the brain. This constant flow of information allows us to move through the world and react to objects and the environment. Our brains interact with our whole body as we sense the environment around us, including other people. As we sense the world around us, we form mental representations of objects and our environment. This works through our **somatosensory system,** networks of neurons that help us perceive our body, objects, textures, movement, and social cues (Azañón & Haggard, 2009).

Your brain also processes information that gives you a sense of self. Your body's vestibular system provides your brain with information about motion, head position, spatial awareness, and awareness that your body belongs to you (Harris, 2020). The brain must be aware of what is going on in your body. This includes interoception and proprioception. **Interoception** is the awareness of your internal functions. Signals such as hunger, thirst, the heartbeat, and breathing tell you how your body is functioning. **Proprioception** is the awareness of one's body and its location in space (Orlov et al., 2010).

In the classroom, you may have students who experience stress in their lives outside of school. When they come to school, they may be in an agitated state, breathing shallowly, or heart racing. Teachers sometimes find themselves in these states as well when dealing with unruly students or school politics. Both students and teachers can benefit from awareness of their body functions and learn to self-regulate in emotional situations. Students may vary in awareness of their body in space. Some students are graceful and coordinated and some may tend to bump into people or things, or accidentally drop objects. It helps teachers to understand that some students are less aware of their body and the objects around them.

The concept of embodiment refers to interactive functions and systems within the body and one's sense of self within the environment. These concepts help us see how the mind extends beyond the brain.

We can see literacy as an embodied process that includes how we sense and feel as we read and write.

> Ms. Holly is a teacher of four-year-old children. As the children drift into her classroom from the bus or parent drop-off, Ms. Holly greets them enthusiastically. They find their photograph on the daily attendance table and make their marks or signature next to their photo. Then they choose an interesting picture book and a comfortable spot to enjoy the pictures, words, and stories in the books. Some children find a friend to share their book with. Ms. Hope sits next to some children to talk about their books. Some children use the felt board or puppets to act out the stories.

Teachers can promote embodied literacy through play and movement throughout childhood and adolescence. Play and movement are essential for early literacy development and physical activity has been associated with beneficial changes in brain and body function. Children must be encouraged to move their bodies at home and at school because sustained physical activity affects cognition and academic performance (Meijer, 2020).

Children's interactions in flexible environments allow for free movement and exploration of language, books, and objects (Daniels, 2021). Learning centers are one way to provide opportunities for freedom of movement. In learning centers, children choose to engage in activities such as dramatizing, illustrating, and exploring topics of interest. Teachers can set up small areas in the classroom for these activities. Concrete objects, books, writing materials, digital composing materials, and craft materials can be set up in learning centers based on children's interests or instructional content. The following is an example of a read and respond center (Flint, 2020).

Read and Respond Center

Preparation

Choose a storybook for the center (for example, *Abuela* by Arthur Dorros). Make three index cards with pictures of characters in the storybook. Attach the cardstock to popsicle sticks for the children to hold as they play.

Goals

Use play as a story response.

Talk about and depict children's engagement with the story.

Procedure

Read the storybook aloud to the whole class and then place it in the learning center.

Explain to the whole class that in this learning center they will read a storybook. They can use the character cards to talk about the book or play the parts of the characters. They can also play and talk about the book in other ways.

Small groups of children use the learning center while other children use additional learning centers around the classroom.

The Read and Respond center provides a space where children can freely use materials and their bodies for meaningful learning. They may tell and retell extended stories, make story predictions, clarify story events, extend vocabulary, analyze story structure, and help each other learn. When children respond playfully to stories, they use their life experiences, knowledge, and feelings to connect with the story and with each other.

As an aspect of embodiment, movement is a part of the learning experience. Movement or action can be classified according to a person's intentions or goals. A person can perform a physical action, imitate an action, internally represent an action, watch someone perform an action, learn how to perform an action, or prepare for action (Papitto et al., 2020). In the Read and Respond Center, children performed physical action by manipulating the character cards. They may also watch or imitate other children. Through these actions, children learn to interact in literate ways. They perform plot, dialogue, and sequence as they play.

We have discussed the many senses that can possibly be engaged during literate activity. Obviously, sight is involved when reading, but surprisingly, even motor activity can be engaged while reading (Deen & McCarthy, 2010). The brain's **sensory-motor** areas are associated with physical motion and activate when we move our arms, hands, fingers, legs, and other body parts. When we read sentences and words that indicate action, the sensory-motor regions in our brains activate. For example, in a study where participants read, "The instructor is grasping the steering wheel very tightly," brain areas for movement were activated (Desai et al., 2013, p. 863). When we read about action, our brains activate the same areas as when we actually perform the action.

Action is important to learning. We imitate others to learn how to play a sport, dance, paint a picture, and many other pursuits. How do humans learn through imitation? Scientists are studying a type of brain cell called mirror neurons that respond when an individual executes a specific motor act and when they observe the same or a similar act by another individual (Kilner & Lemon, 2013). Although there is still much to be learned about the role of mirror neurons in learning, it is a promising line of research that helps us to understand how our brains interact with other people's movements as we learn (Heyes & Catmur, 2022).

Our bodies are resources that help us make mental representations. For example, we can use our fingers to count things, holding up one finger at a time. We can also count with our fingers by slightly moving each finger in a barely noticeable way. We are still making a mental representation. We can also do this completely internally as we co-opt the physical action to assist in thinking (Wilson, 2002). During reading, we draw upon our prior experiences to make mental representations of the text (van Moort et al., 2020).

Literacy Environment

The physical space where students read and write affects their bodies and their reading process. In a traditional classroom, students sit at a desk with a book, computer, or paper in front of them. Some students might be focused on reading or writing, while others may be distracted. The desk may not fit the person's body or there may be a bothersome noise or movement in the space. The student may be sleepy or focused on personal problems. Observing your students can give you clues for designing the classroom environment. Cluttered walls and surfaces may be distracting, while empty spaces allow the mind to focus on the learning task.

To help students engage, teachers can set up classroom spaces that promote reading. Some teachers allow students to choose their space for independent reading. Soft furniture, tables, soft lighting, partitions, and other creative solutions can be designed based on student needs. Early childhood teachers might provide very low tables so children can use the table while sitting on the floor. Middle and high school teachers might offer bean bag seating for those students who prefer to lounge as they read.

The classroom can be arranged to encourage stimulating conversation, reflection, and higher-level thinking. These experiences are important for the child and adolescent's developing brains. Rather than sitting all day at a desk, students might lounge on soft seating to read with a partner. Students may move to a small table for a literature discussion or guided reading group. Different spaces in the classroom can be used for specific literary purposes such as small group book discussions. Teachers can demonstrate how to talk about books and encourage literary dialogue between students.

Literacy Materials and Structures

Materials and structures are part of an embodied literacy experience and are therefore important for brain development. To energize and motivate students to read, interesting books and time for reading must be provided. In a traditional classroom, the same book or anthology is read at the same pace by all. When this is the only exposure to literature, students often lose interest. On the other hand, a reading workshop structure allows students to choose their own books or choose a shared title to read and discuss with a small group.

People are motivated by different types of reading material. Teachers can expose students to a range of books or texts through short talks that pitch the text as possible independent reading material. A range of texts includes literature, popular fiction, informational books, magazines, newspaper articles, digital texts, graphic novels, poetry, biographies, and more. Students may be interested in mystery, humor, how-to, historical fiction, horror, fantasy, or specific nonfiction areas such as health, cars, or sports.

The following teaching plan includes whole group, small group, and independent reading. The learning goals are accomplished through reading and discussing a series of books written by one author (Manak, 2011). Structuring literacy instruction in this way promotes language development through conversation. It promotes motivation through choice and a variety of materials. A variety of reading structures allows for movement, thinking, and reflecting. In this example, discussing connections between books encouraged higher-level thinking.

Intertextual Connections

Preparation

Create a collection of different book series (for example, Crayons Series, Nate the Great, Percy Jackson & the Olympians, The Hunger Games). Choose from the reading experiences below to structure the literacy workshop and provide enough copies of each title for each experience.

Goals

Make intertextual connections between books.

Enjoy literature.

Understand, discuss, and think analytically about literature.

Use reading strategies for word reading and comprehension.

Reading Experiences

Written activities can be used before, during, or after some of the following reading experiences. Students may choose their written activity. For examples, Venn Diagrams comparing books in a series, or characters in books; Sketch that symbolizes an important aspect of a book; Creative dialogue between two or more of the book characters; Plot diagram showing rising and falling action. Each activity should be demonstrated by the teacher before expecting students to work independently.

Interactive Read-Aloud

Connect students' knowledge of previous books in the collection before the read-aloud. Stop at various points in the book to engage students (for example, demonstrate how to solve difficult words, notice the author's stylistic choices, notice literary elements). After the read-aloud, ask students what connections they made between the read-aloud and other books in the collection.

Partner reading

Two students read one book together. Partners sit anywhere around the room where they feel comfortable. In lower grades, partners read alternate pages and then re-read the book, reading the pages the partner had previously read. In upper grades, students read silently periodically stopping to talk about the book at previously determined stopping points.

Independent reading

The entire class reads silently and independently from one of the books in the series. After completing a book, students prepare a book talk to "sell" the book to classmates.

Literature circles

Groups of five or six students read different books from the series. Literature circles are student-directed with a rotating leader. The literature-circle group members read and discuss the book and may respond to the text in a written activity.

Guided reading

- The teacher works with a group of students to assess their reading progress and teach reading strategies based on the group's needs. The teacher elicits predictions about the upcoming text and previews tricky vocabulary

- Students read silently as the teacher listens to one student read aloud, or the students may all attend to the student who is reading aloud. The teacher teaches reading strategies at the point of need during the session or may have prepared the strategy lesson based on the prior session
- Examples of strategies for comprehension are: Stop to think about the meaning; Stop to question; Stop to predict. Strategies for solving unknown words are: Read on then go back; Use initial letters; Use word parts
- Finally, the teacher leads the group in a meaningful discussion of what has been read that day. For example, analyze character actions; infer meanings that are not directly stated; debate pros and cons

In the lesson example, the students studied a series of fictional books. Series books have a predictable structure because the author organizes the books similarly across titles. This predictability helps readers because they can focus more of their attention on the message of the text. As a bonus, when students enjoy one book, they are motivated to read the next title in the series.

Making intertextual connections between books in a series allows for exploring characters' actions. For example, second graders used a Venn Diagram to compare two books in the *Crayons* series by Drew Daywalt (Figure 3.2). Students might also dig deeper into the characters' motivations, recurring motifs, or the author's writing style. Using a variety of structures to explore series books gives students opportunities to voice opinions, make connections, and use academic language. Talking about books can help in strengthening white matter connections between areas in children's developing brains.

Embodied and Embrained in Social Worlds

Embodiment involves social interactions with others. Learning by watching others is an important part of literacy education. During observational learning, action sequences are modeled by patterns of brain activity, similar to physical practice (Apšvalka et al., 2018). Students can learn by watching teacher demonstrations or observing their peers as they work together. Building on this idea of demonstratingand observing, the following example shows how Ms. Larkin, a high school teacher, set up inquiry groups who studied contemporary topics of their choosing (Spence et al., 2022).

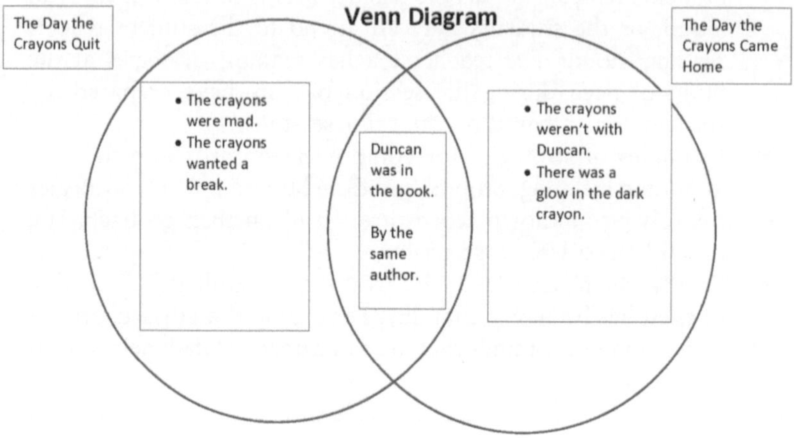

Figure 3.2 Venn Diagram Comparing Two Books in the Crayons Series by Drew Daywalt.

Controversial Topics

Preparation

Students should have a notebook that the teacher will periodically collect to check student progress.

Prepare a whole-class article on a current controversial topic that is of interest to teens. This article will be projected for the whole class to see.

Prepare six copies each of six articles on current controversial topics that are of interest to teens.

Have 1–2 sticky notes for each student and a piece of chart paper. Attach chart paper to the wall by the door and write Exit Slips at the top (for day two).

Make sure students have resources for researching a topic such as digital devices, newspapers, websites, etc.

Goals

Develop communication skills and agency.

Listen and understand different perspectives.

Prepare a speech describing a problem and at least two different perspectives.

Procedure

Day One: Project a whole-class article and read aloud as students follow along. Remind students to listen to others' perspectives and take notes on what their peers say. Elicit a discussion of the article, prompt students to share multiple perspectives.

Make six copies of six different articles on controversial topics that matter to teens. Explain that students can choose an article to read and discuss. After the students have read their article, direct them to group with others who have the same article and listen to each person's perspective on the topic, while also sharing their perspective. Students take notes on what others say.

Day Two: Explain that you want students to discuss the whole-class article in small groups, then later they will brainstorm other controversial topics to explore.

Re-read the whole-class article and allow students to choose groups for discussion. Remind them to listen to others' perspectives and take notes.

Explain that the students will think of a topic that they feel strongly about, research the topic, and write a two-minute speech on the topic. They will give the speech, followed by comments and questions.

Have students begin brainstorming other controversial topics with their groups. The teacher may need to prompt the discussions. Circulate among the groups and give encouragement as needed.

Near the end of the period, have students write their topic on a sticky note and leave it on the Exit Slip chart by the door as they leave the classroom.

After class, cluster the sticky notes into categories of topics.

Day Three: Project a list of the topic categories from the sticky notes. Prompt a discussion and add to the list as necessary. Have students form groups to discuss these topics. Ask each student to choose one topic they feel strongly about and which they would like to research further.

Day Four onward: This could take a few days. Provide instruction on how to research their topic and provide resources as needed. Help students locate accurate information. Discuss how to be critical consumers of information.

Students begin taking notes as they find information relevant to their topic.

After students have found sufficient information, they will prepare a speech following these guidelines: (1) Tell us your topic, (2) Explain your argument and a counterargument(s), (3) Respond to the counterargument(s), and (4) Restate your argument in relation to your topic.

Plan for students to give their speeches. Remind them that they must: (1) Respect each presenter, (2) Validate the presenter's perspective, and (3) Be prepared to ask questions or comment after the speeches.

Plan to extend this unit of study by exploring issues in the students' community. They can use their research skills to address an issue that impacts their community.

In the example lesson above, high school students developed their communication skills and agency by choosing a topic, choosing their group members, preparing, and delivering a speech. They read articles with a variety of different perspectives and learned to listen respectfully as their peers discussed controversial issues. They learned to research and find valid information on a current topic. The teacher modeled these skills, but students also had a chance to learn from each other in their small group discussions. You can believe the controversial topics spurred many lively conversations in the groups!

As these teens developed these cognitively complex skills, they were forming mental representations of themselves as speakers who could explain a topic that mattered to them. Their cultural and social worlds were part of their embodied literacy experience. They observed their peers discussing, researching, writing, and speaking at varying levels of sophistication. It would be safe to say that as they came to terms with multiple perspectives, they supported one another's learning.

Embodied and Embrained Biology

Another aspect of embodiment comes from hormonal systems in the body. We know that adolescence involves important hormonal changes. But hormones also drive early development and contribute to learning throughout the age span. The hormone system is also known as the **endocrine system**. This system regulates the body as glands throughout the body make hormones, which are sent out through the body and are recognized by receptors in various organs and tissues. Hormones function as messengers of the body and control our functions and our psychology. They help our body stay in balance.

Hormones help the body deal with stress, control our sleep cycles, bring on puberty, control sexual development and reproduction, regulate appetite and blood sugar, and contribute to pleasure and motivation among many other functions. Hormones are important for learning because they contribute to how the brain is organized and the development of neural circuitry (Gore et al., 2019).

Our hormones can be affected by the environment. Environmental toxins can disrupt the endocrine system and a person's response to stress. Scientists are studying how stress may alter brain development during sensitive periods such as early childhood and adolescence (Lupien et al., 2009).

In addition to the nervous and endocrine system, our brain receives information from our heart, gut, and other parts of our internal body. Internal signals from the heart and gastrointestinal tract are involved in brain dynamics and with the brain, form a single complex system. The heart and gastrointestinal tract generate their own electrical activity and send information to the brain that helps us self-regulate our emotions, stress, and resilience.

These and continued scientific discoveries about the brain and body can contribute to providing an optimum environment for children and adolescents. Students who experience stressful environments at home can benefit from supportive classroom environments, enriched educational experiences, and social support from members of the community. Such interventions during the early years could have a tremendous effect in preventing the impact of chronic stress or early abuse on the developing brain (Lupien et al., 2009). Early childhood educators play an important role in supporting brain development. Attending to our students' biology, social worlds, and environments can support student learning.

Growing Body and Developing Brain

During infancy until age two or three, there is a massive growth in the number of brain synapses. These are the places where neurons connect to other neurons. This growth is vital to memory formation and learning. During childhood, unnecessary synapses begin to die off. This is called **synaptic pruning**. The remaining synapses are strengthened through the stimulation of experience.

In adolescence, profound changes occur. Short-range connections are pruned, and long-range connections are strengthened while the basic structures of the brain remain stable (Deoni et al., 2015; Dennis et al., 2013). Childhood and adolescence are very plastic periods in brain development, and experiences during this time are significant.

The instructional decisions teachers make are very important to brain development. because teachers provide students with experiences that can benefit the changes occuring in the brain. Experience influences genetics and epigenetics to develop the brain. **Genetics** are inherited from our parents. **Epigenetic** refers to changes in how our genes work based on our behaviors and experiences. Rich, stimulating experiences are needed to make the most of genetic and epigenetic influences (Lupien et al., 2009).

Opportunities to Develop Language

The language networks are already in place at birth and continue to develop in childhood. This is why engaging children in conversation is so beneficial to language and cognitive development. Social interactions are necessary for brain development from birth through adolescence. Social relationships within and outside the family provide opportunities for increased language development in adolescents who are beginning to understand and express more abstract concepts.

Many children and adolescents speak multiple languages at home. Speaking with family and friends in home languages is crucial. The shared language between family members allows for rich conversations and meaningful interactions. The language network is active for all languages and develops through conversations and interactions within personal relationships. Rich and abundant conversations within families are necessary to build relationships and for children and adolescents to feel emotionally secure.

Children also benefit from high-quality language and literacy experiences. Home literacy practices influence the growth of language skills for young dual-language learners (Goodrich et al., 2021). In school, teachers can encourage the rich and diverse languages and literacies brought by students and their families (Compton-Lilly et al., 2012).

To support developmental changes in the brain, children and adolescents must have adequate sleep, rest, and nutrition (Immordino-Yang et al., 2019). The organizing and reconfiguring brain requires a well-fed and well-rested body. The physical environment also impacts the developing brain. Children and adolescents need clean water to drink, clean air to breathe, and an environment free of toxins. They need outdoor exercises such as walking, hiking, or bicycling in forests, mountains, or parks. Some schools provide these outings for students, however, not all schools have available resources such as buses, drivers, and entrance fees. Not all schools allow time away from test preparation, testing, and core curriculum to allow for field trips. All children should have opportunities for safe, uncontaminated, outdoor experiences.

An embodied perspective on literacy clarifies the need for equitable resources for our children and adolescents. They need nutrition, exercise, a clean environment, and educational and civic opportunities for the health and growth of their bodies and brains. If you visit schools in wealthy neighborhoods, you will see an abundance of necessary resources. If you visit schools in poor neighborhoods, you will likely see uneven resources. Some schools resemble Silicon Valley's high-tech office spaces. Other schools deal with broken furniture and decades-old paperback books.

The inequity in resources goes far beyond this simplistic description and many of these are reported in the news cycle. Contaminated water supplies, lack of grocery stores, parents that work two or three jobs to make ends meet, older siblings that care for younger children, gun violence, petty crime, alcohol, and drug use are some debilitating factors that can affect the growth and development of children and adolescents. Regardless of income, our students may face some of these structural and familial issues.

Structural factors beyond school districts also impact students. Race, gender, or socioeconomic status may exclude people from certain opportunities and put them at higher risk for negative emotional and health outcomes. When people are discriminated against because of their status, they experience stress that is associated with poor physical and mental health.

Addressing Inequities

As educators, we must partner with families and communities to ensure that children and adolescents benefit from adequate nutrition, rest, exercise, language use, and safety. Full-service community schools are filling these needs in some areas. Such schools use collaborative leadership in which families have active roles. Partnerships between schools and other institutions provide for health concerns, counseling, food, clothing, and supervised after-school activities, according to the needs of families. These schools work to strengthen families' educational engagement and create welcoming environments (Sanders et al., 2021).

Teachers can contribute to their school's efforts toward equitable opportunities by getting to know students and their families.

> Mr. Colter consistently contacted his students' families. He called them on the telephone after school and used the school's web communication platform. He also met them at school and community events.
>
> One year, Mr. Colter found out that one of his students was diabetic then discovered that many students had family members who were diabetic. He used this knowledge to develop a unit of study on healthy eating. His students researched the types of foods available in convenience and grocery stores in their

neighborhoods, uncovering the ways that unhealthy foods were being marketed and promoted. Then the students took action to protest the vending machine offerings at their school.

Mr. Colter used culturally relevant teaching strategies by using literacy to address a solution to real problems in families and the community. Culturally relevant teaching includes having high expectations, flexible pedagogy, drawing knowledge from students, being part of the community, and giving back to the community (Gay, 2002; Ladson-Billings, 1995). These methods have been enhanced over time and are also known as culturally relevant pedagogy and culturally sustaining pedagogy.

Having high expectations for students means that all students learn when their needs and strengths are recognized and used in the instructional setting. In this student-centered approach, the curriculum must be flexible and tailored to fit the context and meet the needs of individuals. To create a flexible, high-impact curriculum, educators begin by finding out about students and their families including languages spoken, families' social activities, and family and community assets.

Culturally relevant curricula can be promoted by school administrators in the full-service school model. Or teachers can implement it in their own classrooms. There are many ways literacy teachers implement culturally relevant teaching including the following (Spence et al., 2022):

- Use books and other texts written by authors from students' ethnicity
- Use books and other texts with characters from students' ethnicity
- Include books and other texts with both female and male authors
- Include texts with current topics
- Include texts with topics relevant to students' age group
- Encourage writing about student concerns and interests
- Address real issues in students' communities
- Invite guest speakers from the community
- Invite students' family members to share expertise and stories
- Address a variety of narrative structures used in different cultures
- Integrate movement and music with instruction

The ideas above help teachers to build on students' cognitive and emotional goals, knowledge, and context as motor planning in the brain is generated (Immordino-Yang, 2016). As students go about reading, writing, speaking, and listening, the perception and motor areas of the brain converge and support the development of goal-directed skills.

Every student has strengths they bring with them to school and culturally relevant teaching makes use of these strengths to plan instruction. The process of finding student knowledge and using it in instruction is known as **funds of knowledge** (Moll, 1992). One method for obtaining and using funds of knowledge follows (Larrotta & Serrano, 2011).

Funds of Knowledge

Preparation

Document students' interests through observations and interviews.

Select culturally relevant stories that can be models for the literary elements of focus (for example, beginning, middle, end)

Cameras (for example, disposable cameras, cell phones, tablets).

Goal

Create a storybook based on students' lives.

Use literary elements in writing.

Procedure

Explain the purpose of storybook writing using the students' lives as material.

Read culturally relevant stories focusing on literary elements. Encourage students to make personal connections to the stories.

Brainstorm ideas for the stories they will write.

Students take photos to illustrate their storybooks.

Students write drafts and receive feedback on literary elements from peers and teachers. Encourage student self-discovery for revisions and editing.

Compile the final version with the photos into a storybook.

When teachers build instruction based on students' funds of knowledge, they uplift students' cultural backgrounds and strengthen the connection to academics ('t Gilde & Volman, 2021). Connecting academic topics with students' lives also provides intrinsic motivation. **Intrinsic motivation** is motivation to do something because it is satisfying. It is not driven by external rewards.

Reading about people like themselves can change reluctant readers into avid readers because seeing their lives and cultures as important leads to higher engagement. Writing about what matters to students can turn hatred of writing into a restorative and invigorating experience. Free journal writing allows students to reflect on the everyday activities and problems in their lives. Writing stories or essays on topics that impact themselves or their community gives students a real-world reason for writing.

Culturally responsive teaching and funds of knowledge can be used to make students' lives and cultures visible in the literacy curriculum. These methods help us connect with students in our increasingly diverse schools and changing society. Traditional school curriculum often leaves students apathetic toward academic subjects because it does not resonate with their lives. Through culturally sustaining teaching (Paris, 2012) and funds of knowledge, students are invited into a greater understanding of themselves and others as they develop a greater understanding of the world around them.

The benefit of planning instruction based on student knowledge and cultures can be explained by memory and prediction. The brain has a process of forming memories. It also prunes (removes) prediction errors and forms conceptual relationships among events (Kim et al., 2020). When we revisit a familiar situation, our brain anticipates what might come next. When students write about their lives or familiar topics, they can predict based on their prior experience. If we are teaching that stories have a beginning, middle, and end, our students can better understand this concept when thinking about the stories within their own lives.

Embodied literacy considers the total literacy environment, whether it is at home, in school, or in the great outdoors. Child and adolescent bodies must be able to move around. They need to talk, debate and explain in any language. Emotions, memories, experiences, and interactions all work together to develop the brain and literacy.

Did You know?

Neuroscientific research has shown how we recognize the difference between a false and a felt smile. The individual subconsciously simulates the same muscle movements by genuinely or nongenuinely smiling while trying to identify a fake/felt smile in others. Therefore, we can safely assume that experiencing, thinking, and recognizing emotions require an individual to embody the felt/faked emotion (of the other person) in their own body language, posture, movements, and gesture. The Simulation of Smiles (SIMS) model explores how the different components of emotion and their neural mechanisms support embodied simulation. The model identifies the reward systems of the brain, amygdala, somatosensory cortices, and motor centers as the regions of interest in this area of research. However, it still remains unclear what elicits this kind of embodied simulation as opposed to concept/perception-based meaning making (Niedenthal et al., 2010).

Food for thought

A visualization strategy helps students make a mental representation during reading. For example, the teacher might read an action scene aloud, demonstrating how to visualize the scene. Some students even benefit from sketching a representation of what they are reading. These types of tasks help students make mental representations as they read, leading to better understanding.

Bibliography

Apšvalka, D., Cross, E. S., & Ramsey, R. (2018). Observing action sequences elicits sequence-specific neural representations in frontoparietal brain regions. *Journal of Neuroscience*, *38*(47) 10114–10128. DOI: 10.1523/JNEUROSCI.1597-18.2018

Azañón, E., & Haggard, P. (2009). Somatosensory processing and body representation. *Cortex: A Journal Devoted to the Study of the Nervous System and Behavior*, *45*(9), 1078–1084.

Boldt, G., & Leander, K. M. (2020). Affect theory in reading research: Imagining the radical difference. *Reading Psychology*, *41*(6), 515–532.

Compton-Lilly, C., Rogers, R., & Lewis, T. Y. (2012). Analyzing epistemological considerations related to diversity: An integrative critical literature review of family literacy scholarship. *Reading Research Quarterly*, *47*(1), 33–60.

Daniels, K. (2021). Movement, meaning and affect and young children's early literacy practices. *International Journal of Early Years Education*, *29*(1), 41–55.

Deen, B., & McCarthy, G. (2010). Reading about the actions of others: Biological motion imagery and action congruency influence brain activity. *Neuropsychologia*, *48*(6), 1607–1615.

Dennis, E. L., Jahanshad, N., McMahon, K. L., de Zubicaray, G. I., Martin, N. G., Hickie, I. B., Toga, A. W., Wright, M. J., & Thompson, P. M. (2013). Development of brain structural connectivity between ages 12 and 30: A 4-Tesla diffusion imaging study in 439 adolescents and adults. *NeuroImage*, *64*, 671–684.

Deoni, S. C. L., Dean, D. C., III, Remer, J., Dirks, H., & O'Muircheartaigh, J. (2015). Cortical maturation and myelination in healthy toddlers and young children. *NeuroImage*, *115*, 147–161.

Desai, R. H., Conant, L. L., Binder, J. R., Park, H., & Seidenberg, M. S. (2013). A piece of the action: Modulation of sensory-motor regions by action idioms and metaphors. *NeuroImage*, *83*, 862–869.

Flint, T. K. (2020). Responsive play: Creating transformative classroom spaces through play as a reader response. *Journal of Early Childhood Literacy*, *20*(2), 385–410.

Gay, G. (2002). Preparing for culturally responsive teaching. *Journal of Teacher Education*, *53*(2), 106–116.

Goodrich, J. M., Lonigan, C. J., Phillips, B. M., Farver, J. M., & Wilson, K. D. (2021). Influences of the home language and literacy environment on Spanish and English vocabulary growth among dual language learners. *Early Childhood Research Quarterly*, *57*, 27–39. 10.1016/j.ecresq.2021.05.002

Gore, A. C., Krishnan, K., & Reilly, M. P. (2019). Endocrine-disrupting chemicals: Effects on neuroendocrine systems and the neurobiology of social behavior. *Hormones and Behavior*, *111*, 7–22. 10.1016/j.yhbeh.2018.11.006

Harris, L. R. (2020). Does the vestibular system exert specific or general influences on cognitive processes? *Cognitive Neuropsychology*, *37*(7–8), 430–432.

Heyes, C., & Catmur, C. (2022). What happened to mirror neurons? *Perspectives on Psychological Science: A Journal of the Association for Psychological Science*, *17*(1), 153–168. 10.1177/1745691621990638

Immordino-Yang, M. H. (2016). Emotions, learning, and the brain: Exploring the educational implications of affective neuroscience. W.W. Norton & Company.

Immordino-Yang, M. H., Darling-Hammond, L., & Krone, C. R. (2019). Nurturing nature: How brain development is inherently social and emotional, and what this means for education. *Educational Psychologist*, *54*(3), 185–204.

Kilner, J. M., & Lemon, R. N. (2013). What we know currently about mirror neurons. *Current Biology: CB*, *23*(23), R1057–R1062. 10.1016/j.cub.2013.10.051

Kim, H., Schlichting, M. L., Preston, A. R., & Lewis-Peacock, J. A. (2020). Predictability changes what we remember in familiar temporal contexts. *Journal of Cognitive Neuroscience*, *32*(1), 124–140.

Ladson-Billings, G. (1995). But that's just good teaching! The case for culturally relevant pedagogy. *Theory Into Practice*, *34*(3), 159–165.

Larrotta, C., & Serrano, A. (2011). Adult learners' funds of knowledge: The case of an English class for parents. *Journal of Adolescent & Adult Literacy*, *55*(4), 316–325.

Lupien, S. J., McEwen, B. S., Gunnar, M. R., & Heim, C. (2009). Effects of stress throughout the lifespan on the brain, behaviour and cognition. *Nature Reviews Neuroscience*, *10*(6), 434–445. 10.1038/nrn2639

Manak, J. (2011). The social construction of intertextuality and literary understanding: The impact of interactive read-alouds on the writing of third graders during writing workshop. *Reading Research Quarterly*, *46*(4), 309–311.

Meijer, A., Königs, M., Vermeulen, G. T., Visscher, C., Bosker, R. J., Hartman, E., & Oosterlaan, J. (2020). The effects of physical activity on brain structure and neurophysiological functioning in children: A systematic review and meta-analysis. *Developmental Cognitive Neuroscience*, *45*, 100828. 10.1016/j.dcn.2020.100828

Moll, L. (1992). Bilingual classroom studies and community analysis: Some recent trends. *Educational Researcher*, *12*(2), 20–24.

Niedenthal, P. M., Mermillod, M., Maringer, M., & Hess, U. (2010). The Simulation of smiles (SIMS) model: Embodied simulation and the meaning of facial expression. *The Behavioral and Brain Sciences*, *33*(6), 417–480. 10.1017/S0140525X10000865

Orlov, T., Makin, T. R., & Zohary, E. (2010). Topographic representation of the human body in the occipitotemporal cortex. *Neuron*, *68*, 586–600.

Papitto, G., Friederici, A. D., & Zaccarella, E. (2020). The topographical organization of motor processing: An ALE meta-analysis on six action domains and the relevance of Broca's region. *NeuroImage*, 206, 1–15.

Paris, D. (2012). Culturally sustaining pedagogy: A needed change in stance, terminology, and practice. *Educational Researcher*, *41*(3), 93–97.

Sanders, M., Galindo, C., & Allen, K. M. (2021). Professional capital and responses to student diversity: A qualitative exploration of the role of teachers in full-service community schools. *Urban Education*, *56*(10), 1782–1814. 10.1177/0042085918770719

Spence, L. K., Bastos, P. & Cullars, A. (2022). "They're killing our imaginations": Dialogue and reflexive writing development in historically marginalized students. *Reading Research Quarterly*. doi:10.1002/rrq.449

't Gilde, J., & Volman, M. (2021). Finding and using students' funds of knowledge and identity in superdiverse primary schools: A collaborative action research project. *Cambridge Journal of Education*, *51*(6), 673–692.

Tessari, A., Tsakiris, M., Borghi, A. M., & Serino, A. (2010). The sense of body: A multidisciplinary approach to body representation. *Neuropsychologia*, *48*(3), 643–644.

van Moort, M. L., Jolles, D. D., Koornneef, A., & van den Broek, P. (2020). What you read versus what you know: Neural correlates of accessing context information and background knowledge in constructing a mental representation during reading. *Journal of Experimental Psychology. General*, *149*(11), 2084–2101.

Wilson, M. (2002). Six views of embodied cognition. *Psychonomic Bulletin & Review*, *9*(4), 625–636.

Young, E. (2021). How to train your senses. *The Psychologist, May Digest*, 16–19.

4

SOCIAL AND EMOTIONAL BRAIN

> One-year-old Caleb is sitting on his father's lap. Father is reading *The Very Hungry Caterpillar* by Eric Carle. Pointing to the small white dot in the picture, his father reads, "In the light of the moon a little egg lay on a leaf." Caleb puts his tiny finger on the white dot, then watches as his father slowly turns the page.

In storybook reading, Caleb and his father interact socially. Caleb's father acculturates Caleb into an important aspect of social life—reading. Caleb learns that pictures, numbers, and letters correspond to the words his father speaks. Caleb learns about print direction and page-turning. He learns to value and care for books. These experiences help develop the brain's language networks. Storybook reading is also infused with emotion. Caleb feels secure sitting beside his father, listening to his father's deep voice. He connects to the caterpillar's hunger and stomachache and is delighted when it turns into a butterfly at the end of the story.

Social and emotional learning describes how our physical, mental, and emotional interactions with others promote learning. Our brain's language networks are developed through social interaction because of our need to function together as a society. Social learning involves ways of being in our particular social context.

Learning through social interaction begins in infancy, with shared attention between an infant and another person. Brain studies have shown that shared attention begins as early as three months (Gavrilov et al., 2012). Infants and their caretakers engage in **Joint attention**, which includes following another's direction of attention and directing attention to share a common experience. Shared and joint attention facilitates infants in developing social awareness.

This inborn ability for shared attention is what makes social learning so powerful. Children naturally mimic their parents, teachers, and

DOI: 10.4324/9781003256199-5

each other in the process of learning. Home storybook reading initiates joint attention and introduces children to literacy. Children make connections between illustrations, print, and spoken words during storybook reading.

Next, we explore how shared literacy, collaborative groups, and interactive dialogue contribute to students' reading and writing development. We provide examples of these social learning experiences and the brain research that supports this type of instruction. Then we describe how our emotions contribute to learning, the emotional impact of reading, and brain areas involved in our emotional responses.

Shared Reading and Writing

When an infant is born, she enters a social world that is full of emotions and experiences. She can imitate the facial expressions of adults right away, noticing similarities between herself and others. Infants continue to proficiently imitate others as they grow and develop. Around two months old, they will babble, smile, and interact. They already have a social network that includes their parents and siblings and soon recognize the faces of those closest to them. These interactions sculpt and mature brain networks as they become more complex and connected (Lagercrantz, 2016).

In early childhood classrooms, children engage in joint attention through shared reading and interactive writing. In **shared reading**, students and the teacher read a common text such as an oversized, "big" book, a book projected on a screen, or individual copies of the same book or short text. The teacher's voice supports the children as they read along. The teacher and students stop at strategic points to work together on decoding, vocabulary, and comprehension. These experiences engage children's joint attention with the teacher, which can contribute to the development of visual and phonetic pathways in the brain.

Interactive writing is collaborative writing with embedded instruction. The teacher acts as a guide and model, helping students to generate ideas for writing. The teacher demonstrates by thinking aloud about what to write then guides students through the mechanics of writing. This can be done on a large format paper with the whole class, a digitally projected text, or at a table with an individual student. For young children, this includes deciding which letters represent the sounds in a word, spacing between words, and making punctuation decisions. For older students, the teacher guides decisions involving organization, detail, literary elements, or other aspects of composition. The following scene illustrates a small group of students who began writing about sea animals.

> A small group of third graders and a teacher gather around an oversized paper on an easel. They discuss ideas they learned while reading informative books about sea animals. Adam suggests the first sentence and then writes, "All animals need oxygen to breath and live."
>
> "Do you think we need to add a silent "e" to "breathe"? Ms. Ames asks. Adam adds "e" to the paper.
>
> Sheila suggests the next sentence, "Sea creatures come up to the surface to breathe air." Ms. Ames hands the marker to Sheila, who writes her sentence. As the group continues to share the task of writing, Ms. Ames prompts their ideas and focuses their attention on spelling and punctuation when needed.

In this example, the children's attention was directed to the group writing process because they each were responsible for generating sentences and writing them on the shared paper. Ms. Ames encouraged them to compose sentences that would inform a reader about sea animals, thus scaffolding their composing skills. The children also learned from each other as they listened to their peer's sentences and watched them write. Interactive writing provided an opportunity for joint attention during the writing process and scaffolded students' writing skills (Spence, 2023).

Social Learning in Group Work

The human brain is highly evolved to react and adjust to social interactions. These mental adjustments are necessary for humans to survive and thrive. We interact socially through interactions and conversations. Using written language, we send out our written words to others and take in what others have written.

Literacy is not limited to the mind of one individual but occurs within a social context. A study of literacy includes the notion that the mind extends beyond the physical body (Wertsch, 1991). Learning is inherently social as we use our experiences and linguistic knowledge to construct new understandings. In school, group learning engagements and discussions allow for the collective construction of knowledge. Students benefit by talking about their ideas and reflecting on their experiences in individual lessons and throughout the school day.

Social interaction involves working with people who may be culturally different from us. Schools in the United States are increasingly diverse, including students from different cultural backgrounds. When we consider the **sociocultural context** of students, we think about how their relationships and mental processes are shaped by their surroundings and factors such as gender, family structures, regional practices, religion, and nationality.

Neuroscientists have begun to include more diversity in research studies. This is important for understanding how sociocultural contexts influence learning. Scientists have begun to look at the strengths of individuals rather than just deficits. For example, studies that focus on physical or emotional trauma are looking at deficits. Studies that focus on resilience are looking at strengths that help individuals overcome trauma. Because the United States is such a diverse country it is important to understand diverse people from a strength-based perspective.

Research findings from a strengths-based perspective can lead to a greater understanding of factors that help young people be resilient when faced with challenges (Arredondo, 2021). Social interactions that involve students' cultures allow students to share their knowledge. The following scene illustrates adults and students sharing their knowledge as they learn from each other (Spence, 2009).

> Four students gathered in the school library to begin work on their website project. They debated between two topics: Mexico and games, eventually agreeing on Mexico. Jacky suggested the title "Mexican Heritage" and the group agreed. Next, they brainstormed six webpage ideas: Language, *Folklórico*, Jokes and Stories, Aztecs, Travel to Mexico, and Food. The students continued to meet after school in the library for six weeks. Elena, a local website designer volunteered her time to provide technical advice to the team of students. Once the website was published, the students shared the link and explained the project to family and friends at an after-school pizza party.

In the website project, the students discussed, wrote, typed, drew pictures, performed *Folklorico* dance, and video recorded for their project. They used their shared cultural background to create a website that informed their audience about aspects of their Mexican heritage. Background knowledge, interpersonal relationships, and a purpose for writing extended each individual mind to their team and to their audience.

Interactive Dialogue

Interactive dialogue can help students internalize new concepts. When students listen to others, they negotiate different positions, ideologies, and social languages. These exchanges often involve struggle, as people reframe established conceptions. Students benefit from opportunities to engage with new ideas and the time to work out concepts through dialogue. The following classroom scene shows how a seventh-grade teacher incorporated dialogue and social learning for writing instruction (Spence et al., 2022).

> Small groups of students were clustered around their notebook computers as they collaboratively wrote fiction stories. One girl typed on a shared document while another searched the internet for names they could assign to their characters. The two girls bounced around ideas for the setting and plot. At her desk, their teacher opened the girls' shared document to check on their progress. Then she walked over to the girls to provide feedback on their writing, "When I read your story, I need to know why he started the fire. It's important to the plot."

The students learned from each other and expanded their understanding of the elements of fiction. Within the creative process, they used their collective background knowledge including personal experiences and ideas from other texts such as movies, television, books, and other media. Ms. Patton acted as a guide, steering the students forward as they negotiated ideas and organized their writing. The seventh-grade students were within the preadolescent to adolescent stage of life. Social interaction is especially important at this age and into young adulthood. It is a critical period of white matter development in the brain.

White matter is made up of neuronal tracts that transmit signals to and from various gray matter regions of the brain (Figure 4.1). In childhood, gray matter volume increases until about 11 years old.

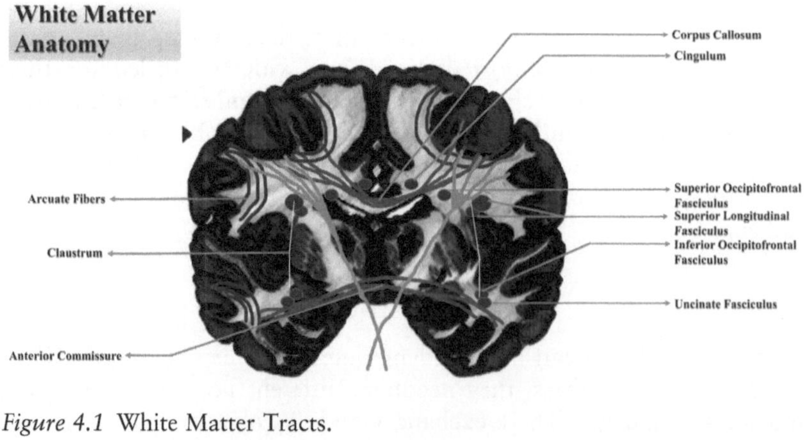

Figure 4.1 White Matter Tracts.

Note: A coronal section of the brain showing the connection between the different commissural fibers of the white matter.

It then begins to decrease while white matter volume increases. This process refines connective pathways making the brain more efficient. The networks that remain active are dependent on the persons' thoughts, environment, and relationship to their immediate surroundings (Adolphs, 2009).

Social relationships become more important as adolescents focus on others outside the family. The school setting provides opportunities for adolescents to interact with peers and teachers. These interactions help them develop their sense of personal identity in relation to others. A crucial aspect of human development is distinguishing oneself from others and understanding how one's thoughts are different from the thoughts of others. Equally important is the ability to make mental representations of the emotions and intentions of others (Herold et al., 2016). During adolescence and throughout the life span we continue to strengthen our sense of self and others.

Children and adolescents learn empathy and build relationships as they interact. Social interactions such as group projects and discussions allow students to listen and respond to the ideas of others. Throughout the school day and in individual lessons, students benefit by talking about their ideas and reflecting on their experiences. In collaborative learning experiences, students interact with others to solve problems. The following example lays out a plan for collaborative inquiry (Guthrie & Klauda, 2014). **Inquiry learning** incorporates active participation of students by involving them in posing questions and making real-world connections through exploration and high-level questioning. In the following example, the teacher introduces a general topic of study to demonstrate inquiry steps. Students then generate subtopics to explore in collaborative groups.

Collaborative Inquiry

Preparation

Gather texts within a topic of study. Make sure the texts are readable for your students. There should be a variety of texts to provide choice and student selection of books. Short sections of texts and videos may be included in the collection. There should be texts on the general topic of study as well as subtopics.

Develop appropriate resources for students to find additional texts.

Prepare examples of cumulative projects such as posters, digital slides, short student-created videos, scrapbooks, etc.

Goals

Actively interact with texts on a topic of study.

Seek conceptual understanding of the topic.

Use cognitive tools to organize text-based knowledge.

Socially share the knowledge construction process.

Day One

Procedure: Introduce the general topic and ask students what they already know about it. Ask students what they are interested in finding out about the topic and possible subtopics. Record students' ideas.

Using the students' ideas for subtopics, form small groups around the subtopics. To form the groups, you can post the subtopics on the walls around the room and have students move to their subtopic of interest.

Invite students to set goals for studying the topic. Make sure the goals can be realistically reached and have the students record their goals.

Work with each group as they choose materials to explore their subtopic. These can be videos, books, digital resources, and selections from texts.

Assign a text on the general topic for reading homework. Tell students they will discuss the reading homework in their subtopic groups.

Day Two

Remind the students they will discuss the reading homework in their subtopic groups and one volunteer will report some of their ideas to the whole class. Circulate through the groups to note ideas from their discussion.

Call on volunteers to share their discussion ideas. Provide feedback and ask probing questions to push their thinking further. Recognize students for the knowledge they gained from reading.

Assign students to a partner to begin reading their choice of text on their subtopic. Allow time in class for this reading.

End class by writing in response to the goals they set for exploring their subtopic. What have they accomplished toward their goal and what do they need to do next? This could also be homework if they do not finish it in class. Tell students they will discuss these responses to their goals in tomorrow's class.

Day Three

Begin by having students silently reread their goals and yesterday's response to their goals. Ask for a few volunteers to share something that helped them reach their goal of learning about their subtopic.

Tell students that one way to learn about their subtopic is through videos.

Introduce a video on the general topic of study. Have students take notes on concepts in the video that will help them relate the concepts to their reading.

After the video, provide a selection of text on the general topic of study that relates in some ways to the video. Have students choose a partner to read the text selection with. They may alternate reading paragraphs aloud to each other or they may read silently and talk together about the text. Circulate among the partners to note how students chose to read the text selection.

After they have finished reading, ask students how the video helped them understand the text. Have students write an exit slip to tell you how the video helped them.

As time allows, have students move into their subtopic groups and continue exploring their choice of texts.

Assign homework to read their choice of text on the subtopic. Tell them they will use this reading to inform their small group the next day.

Day Four

Describe the **Circle of Voices** structure: Assign one person in the subtopic group to be the timer. Each person in the group has one minute to share something from the text they read for homework. After each person has shared, the group can ask questions, share additional information, or make connections between the texts.

Bring the whole class together. Use previously prepared models of culminating projects and explain each to the students. Ask for additional suggestions for culminating projects. The subtopic groups will decide on a culminating project and work on it together. Allow time in class for the groups to talk about projects.

Subsequent Lessons

Continue to focus on student-led groups, partner reading, and text choice as students complete their subtopic inquiries. Plan on time for completing the culminating projects to share what they learned with the class.

The example above illustrates collaborative inquiry groups that build shared understandings. Choosing topics and working together helps students to develop their understanding of both academic content and personal relationships. Through collaboration, students learn to listen to the perspectives of others that may differ from their own views. Considering the perspectives of others can help support the restructuring going on in adolescent brains.

Multiple Perspectives

> Five 10th grade students were seated at a table discussing social issues that were important to them. Terrell was emphatic about his stance toward animal abuse, saying, "My topic is animal abuse. Companies do tests on monkeys who unnecessarily die slowly."
>
> Jarod extended the animal abuse discussion, "Dog fighting, I disagree with that. I heard about a dog chained to a car and dragged."
>
> Lara ventured a different perspective saying, "I don't like dogs or cats."
>
> Jarod answered, "They don't need to be abused just because you don't like them."

Dialogue and interactions contributed to these students' understanding that different views exist in the minds of other people. Terrell, Jarod, and Lara were exposed to multiple perspectives by reading news articles and watching television newscasts. The teacher understood the importance of sharing multiple perspectives, so class time was provided for discussing social issues.

Small group discussions help students develop friendships and social experiences that are necessary to their developing brain networks. But what happens when students have differences of opinion? Students come to school with moral perspectives gleaned from their families and communities. These moral perspectives play a role in how people act, what they like, and how they see the world.

Moral perspectives, also called **moral preferences** are social preferences concerned with justice, harm, and human rights. Studies of the neural mechanisms of moral decision-making provide some insights that may help teachers understand the stances students take on social issues. One study identified neural processes involved in assigning value to human lives. Assigning value to human life involved different neural processes than assigning value to money (Ugazio, 2022). Value for human life involved unique mental processing.

Literacy instruction can provide opportunities for students to explore their moral preferences and compare them to those of others. Reading, reflecting, and discussing literary works with themes such as peace, war, survival, judgment, suffering, and justice compel students to take a moral stance.

Young children can discuss books such as *The Giving Tree* by Shel Silverstein. This book presents the perspectives of the tree and the boy. Children can discuss each perspective as the boy takes apples from the tree and later cuts it down. Adolescents can discuss books such as *The Hate You Give* by Angie Thomas. This book presents two worlds, one affluent and one underprivileged. It raises discussions about social justice and the judicial system. Children's and young adult authors continue to produce new books that are excellent resources for developing and understanding moral perspectives.

In the following instructional example, the teacher pulls together multiple texts that address an essential question. An **essential question** is genuine and meaningful. It is open-ended and generates additional questions. It leads to an ongoing inquiry. This example focuses on eliciting students' divergent views (Kim et al., 2017).

Discussing Divergent Views

Preparation

Select a short story for its ability to promote discussion (for example, *Eleven* by Sandra Cisneros; *I Want My Hat Back* by John Klassen). The story should contain at least one of the following:

- Ambiguous story characters
- Unexpected plot developments
- Contrasting positions

Create an essential question based on the short story that can be related to other stories and novels as well as real-world events (for example, Do our possessions define us? When do people mean what they say?).

Collect other texts that relate to the essential question.

Goals

Read and discuss short texts to build background knowledge and confidence for longer texts.

Talk about texts and divergent views that arise from the texts.

Develop personal stances on texts.

Partner Reading

Direct students to choose a partner for reading and a text they will read together.

- Discuss the title and cover art with a partner
- Read the first page or so then turn and talk (Encourage students to express personal perspectives and elicit divergent perspectives on what was portrayed on those pages)
- Continue to read then stop and talk about the book or story

The teacher circulates to listen and take notes. Note divergent views that could be raised in the whole class discussion.

Exploring Other Texts

Whole class: Introduce the essential question then read a short story aloud. Ask students how the short story pertained to the essential question.

Independent reading: Direct students to other texts that further explore the essential question and divergent views.

Small groups: Arrange for small groups to discuss the views in a text. Encourage expressing divergent views.

Discussing divergent views of texts provides an opportunity for critical thinking and perspective taking. This is accomplished through reading a variety of texts and discussing an essential question. It also provides a social opportunity to listen to the views of others. These opportunities support and encourage engagement with students' social and physical worlds. The thought patterns that are generated in this type of environment help to organize brain development over time. Rich, engaging learning environments are conducive to growth, intelligence, and health (Immordino-Yang et al., 2018).

Social Meanings in Texts

> Ms. Katie sat at a small table with two third graders and introduced the book they would be reading, *Follow the Moon Home* by Philippe Cousteau. "Have you ever seen a sea turtle in real life?" Ms. Katie asked.
>
> "Not me," said Keith.
>
> "I have," said Ron.
>
> Although he had never seen one, Keith knew that sea turtles lay their eggs in holes in the sand. As they began to read the book, Ms. Katie engaged the boys by connecting their previous knowledge of sea turtles and discussing challenging words.
>
> "What do you think dehydrated means?" Ms. Katie asked.
>
> "It means you need to drink water." Keith replied.

In this scene, Ms. Katie connected the story and information to the children's background and vocabulary knowledge. Her goal was for the students to make meaning based on what they knew and their interest in the topic.

Forming meaning from reading and other experiences involves a semantic brain network consisting of multimodal areas (Figure 4.2).

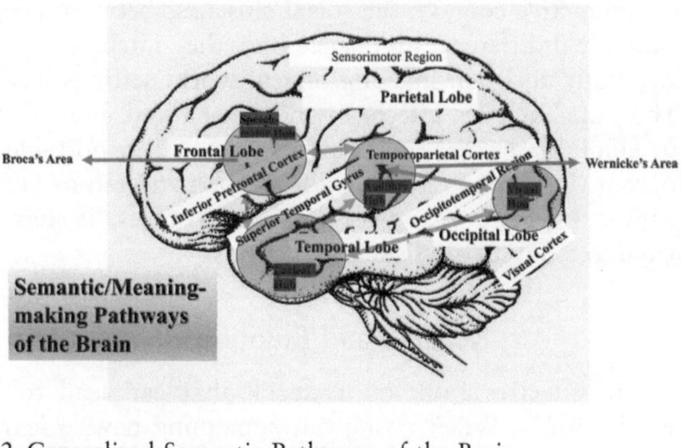

Figure 4.2 Generalized Semantic Pathways of the Brain.

Note: Adapted from Dual Pathway Language Model (Ueno & Lambon Ralph, 2013).

Sensory-motor and social information modulate the activation of the semantic network (Lin et al., 2018). The brain's **semantic network** represents one's accumulated, connected meanings including those in texts. Connected texts such as paragraphs, stories, and poems evoke social semantic activation to a greater extent than reading isolated words because of these accumulated meanings (Zhang et al., 2021). This area of brain research is promising for understanding the social aspects of reading. We know that words, sentences, paragraphs, and whole texts all have social meanings. As new research methods are developed, we will learn more about how we process the social meanings of texts.

New methods have emerged to study live social interactions in a scanner. One study found that social interaction in the presence of a live person (compared to a visually identical recording) resulted in the activation of multiple neural systems which may be critical to real-world social interactions but are missed in experiments that do not include live interaction (Redcay et al., 2010). Live interaction seems to elicit unique responses.

Neuroimaging methods are being developed to study dynamic real-world settings that include multiple participants in group learning contexts. Bevilacqua et al. (2019) captured the neural activity of students in a high school biology class. They looked at brain-to-brain synchrony between students and brain-to-brain synchrony between students and teachers. **Brain-to-brain synchrony** refers to a neural marker obtained by neuroimaging when there is social coordination of behavior between two or more individuals.

Bevilacqua found that social closeness with the teacher predicted greater brain-to-brain synchrony. Brain-to-brain synchrony is related to aspects of shared or joint attention. In social interactions, joint attention and mutual gaze seem to facilitate initiator and responder roles. There are also other factors that mediate brain-to-brain synchrony. The richness of the interactive context, the social closeness between people, and people's individual differences influence how they interact.

For now, studying brain imaging in real-world settings has its limitations. The data includes effects of movement and gestures that are difficult to eliminate in real social interactions. Also, portable electroencephalogram (EEG) equipment is not as sophisticated as laboratory-grade equipment. However, as technology advances, it may become more feasible to study naturalistic interactions.

Reading and Emotion

Emotion is an effective form of feedback that can lead to learning (Gruber et al., 2021). When trying out something new, a learner will look to a more experienced person for nonverbal or verbal feedback. A positive response lets learners know they are on the right track.

We consider the emotions of others in making decisions and assigning value to objects or events. For example, if a boy's peer group enthusiastically reads and views anime videos or manga books those positive emotions may induce the boy to choose a manga to read. Students are influenced by the emotional tone expressed by their peer group and their teachers. If a teacher or peer recommends a book, students are apt to choose to read the book.

Book talks are a simple way to recommend books in a classroom. One way to promote books is to collect a wide variety of genres such as fiction, informational texts, jokes, and poetry. Such a collection will include about ten books on differing topics. The teacher enthusiastically shows students the books one by one, reading the title and giving some tantalizing information about the book. After the book talk, these books tend to fly off the classroom library shelves. Students too can give book talks, which helps build a classroom community of avid readers. The following example describes self-selected books, another way to build enthusiasm for reading (Ivey & Johnston, 2013).

Self-Selecting Books

Preparation

This self-selected reading workshop eliminates whole-class assigned texts. Books are student-selected, and students pace their own reading.

Obtain 150–200 different titles. Rotate in new books when necessary to maintain student access to new books. Include books dealing with issues and concepts of high interest to students, primarily contemporary young adult fiction.

Goals

To increase student engagement in reading

To increase student agency in reading

Reading Workshop

Explain the reading workshop to students including how you will conduct reading conferences and how students will be assessed.

Start with a series of book talks and have students note the titles of books they might want to read. Periodically give a book talk on a new title at the beginning of class.

Students choose a book and read independently for an extended amount of time. Monitor student's for engagement and if a student is not engaged, schedule a reading conference with them (if possible, the conference can be initiated right away).

As students read, conduct short reading conferences with open-ended questions, following the student's lead. For example, "How do you like your book?"

In the reading workshop, you can also include other engagements such as teacher read-aloud. Discussions related to the read-aloud should stimulate and follow students' own questions and wonderings. If writing is included in the reading workshop, it should not take away from the agency for reading. Therefore, you should not require summaries or analytical essays on students' self-selected books.

Writing and Emotion

The process of writing involves many moving parts, so it is difficult to study writing using neuroimaging methods. Handwriting and spelling have been studied, but there are not many studies that focus on aspects of composing. In school, children and adolescents write for many purposes such as to demonstrate their learning or to develop writing skills. Reading and writing are deeply connected in literacy instruction. For example, teachers may ask students to respond in writing to a book, poem, or short story.

Students may also write for creative or emotional expression. Writing is even used as a form of therapy in clinical settings. In one of these studies, gratitude writing was associated with greater and lasting neural sensitivity to gratitude (Kini et al., 2015). This suggests that emotions such as gratitude can be influenced by writing. Writing is another experience that shapes brain networks.

Reading, writing, and emotion together contribute to learning. For example, in learning about traumatic material such as the Holocaust, students must grapple with their emotions during reading. Students can write to explore their emotions while making connections between texts, identity, and power in societies (Simon et al., 2022). The following example of instruction involves reading and writing with visual narratives, also known as graphic novels or comics.

Reading and Writing Visual Narratives

Students and teacher read and discuss the graphic novel *Maus* by Art Spiegelman. Include discussions of current connections to the history of the Holocaust.

Invite a guest comic maker or use a video source to present information on composing a comic such as ways of showing emotions, points of view in comic panels, placement of speech bubbles, and the process of storyboarding.

Teacher and students make an initial drawing of themselves in animal form reflecting the style used in *Maus*.

Use the storyboard to write and sketch a four-panel plot sequence that depicts how they interacted with the novel *Maus*. Include a question either to Spiegelman or a broader audience.

Use quick-drawing exercises to practice sketching rather than detailed drawings. Use pencil on the storyboard panels then go over the final draft in pen.

When students read, write, and think about historical events such as the Holocaust, they expand their perspectives and develop empathy. Empathy involves affective processes in the brain. **Affective processes** are engaged when witnessing emotions in others based on shared emotional, motor, and body sensations. Neuroscience research suggests that cognitive and affective processes are activated in understanding others' mental states (Schurz et al., 2021).

Major Brain Networks of Emotion

Brain networks involving intelligence, memory, mental flexibility, health, and attention coordinate to navigate real world contexts (Menon & Uddin, 2010; Niendam et al., 2012). To orchestrate this integration, three major networks of the brain are recruited, namely, the executive control network, the default mode network, and the salience network (Immordino-Yang et al., 2018).

The **executive control network** facilitates attention, holding information in the mind and strategizing approaches to complete tasks while ignoring distractor information and impulses (Beaty et al., 2015). This network is associated with creativity and the production of ideas. This network seems to inhibit irrelevant information and instead provides the attention control needed to manage complex search processes, supporting creative thought.

The **default mode network** focuses on the interpretive and reflective aspects of thinking primarily in relation to past experiences, future events, or deliberating on abstract thoughts (Immordino-Yang et al., 2012). Therefore, broadly speaking, the default mode network helps with social and cognitive processing. This network is engaged when task-oriented behavior and externally directed perception and attention are reduced and during tasks involving introspection, emotion, and processing information relevant to oneself.

The **salience network** helps with emotional relevance and perceived importance; it facilitates switching between states of mind supported by the other two networks (Goulden et al., 2014). The salience network, therefore, recruits from multiple modalities and helps maintain homeostasis during cognitive and emotional processing.

The three networks work together in processing emotion. This can help teachers understand that learning is embodied within the larger constructs of emotional, behavioral, and social interrelationships. Our daily cultural and social experiences play a vital role in human interaction and the development of the "emotional brain".

Although brain development has a typical trajectory there is an amount of variability in the way certain regions of the brain develop given the individual's social, emotional, cultural, cognitive, and physical context. Literacy instruction can support students in this development. Reading can foster social-emotional development as shown in the following example of bibliotherapy (Tijms et al., 2018).

Bibliotherapy

Preparation

Gather six books that are matched to the students' reading skills and reflect their personal challenges, feelings, and interests. The books should contain a realistic and dynamic story and characters. The books should encourage discussion and offer coping or problem-solving strategies.

Goals

Increase reading attitudes, reading comprehension, and social-emotional competencies.

Procedure

Present six books to students, briefly explaining each one.

Students choose the book they prefer to read with five to seven students per book.

Form groups of students who have chosen the same book.

Set up group norms such as respect others' opinions, express your opinions and feelings, do not offend.

Students read part of the book on their own then meet with their group to discuss.

Students write their thoughts and feelings in a notebook as they read.

Provide suggestions such as, "What would you have done in this situation?"

Students meet with groups to discuss the book and how the book relates to their lives.

Parts of the book may be reread during the sessions to clarify its meaning.

At the end of each session, students determine how much should be read for the next session.

Book clubs and fictional reading can be an effective means for social and emotional learning. Students face a variety of challenges in their lives that require support from teachers, schools, parents, and communities. For example, continuous exposure to adverse childhood experiences (ACEs) activates stress related hormones, leading to disruption of healthy brain development (McLaughlin, 2016; Shonkoff et al., 2012). Further, aggressive and anxious tendencies are observed in children with ACEs, where neural circuitry and connectivity patterns that enable cognition, reasoning, and memory are compromised (Briggs-Gowan et al., 2015; Nelson, 2014). It is important for teachers to understand the behavioral and cognitive issues that children face in school settings related to learning.

Opportunities to explore one's experiences and feelings activate brain networks important to well-being. Reading about the experiences and feelings of others promotes empathy. Writing about one's own experiences and feelings promotes self-awareness. Literacy instruction helps support students' social and emotional development while also addressing academic goals. The following example of instruction taps into students' emotional experiences to better understand symbols in literature.

Symbols in Literature

Preparation

Select short texts such as poems and short stories that will support multiple literary interpretations.

Goals

Construct abstract connotations in relation to specific, concrete details while reading.

Ascribe a range of positive and/or negative values to language within texts.

Construct overall thematic inferences after reading.

Procedure

Discuss the connection between everyday interpretations. For example, How do you feel when you see a colorful sunset? What would you think if a book character saw a colorful sunset? Would the sunset convey a mood? Students write a T-chart. On one side they list everyday objects or occurances. On the other side, they list the feelings the objects evoke. For example, a freshly baked cookie, a hot shower, a cold swimming pool, a snake, a bird's song, a crack of thunder, fireworks, etc.

Discuss the effects of language using examples from headlines or print ads.

Ask students to read a short story and write notes on language that conveys feelings. Students share their notes in a small group.

Discuss language that conveys feelings as potential symbols.

Students refer to their notes from the short story to look for language that might be symbolic. Students discuss possible symbols in their small group.

Students read a novel excerpt that contains symbolism such as *Black Boy* by Richard Wright. Students note language that conveys feelings. Students write an interpretation of what the language symbolized.

To expand this concept, give students the lyrics to two pop songs with different styles but similar themes. Construct interpretations by comparing two texts with similar themes but different styles

For example, Pop songs: "I Will Follow Him" sung by Little Peggy March and "I Will Follow You Into the Dark" by Death Cab for Cutie

In small groups, students write a T-chart for each song that shows the language and feelings. Groups then discuss the symbolism in the language. Students write a comparison of the two songs based on what they found regarding the language, feelings, and symbolism in the songs.

Continue similar discussion and activities for interpretation of fiction excerpts or short stories for example: "Linoleum Roses" from *The House on Mango Street* by Sandra Cisneros; "Ysrael" by Junot Díaz.

Embodied Emotion

The notion of embodiment necessitates a deeper look at written and oral language processing to understand the role of emotion. Societal growth and development are contingent upon the idea of meaningful social relationships in a collaborative environment.

Our emotions are connected to our bodies and brains. Emotions are driven by a variety of factors including knowledge of the situation, assessing the situation, and bodily reactions to the situation. The body and mind are interdependent. Emotions such as sympathy, moral indignation, admiration, and compassion draw on structures in the brain that are involved in sensing and regulating internal states.

Immordino-Yang in her seminal book *Emotions, Learning, and the Brain* (2016) tries to bridge the complex connection between learning and emotions. The book revolutionizes the field of educational praxis by showing how the power of emotions can be harnessed for learning within a meaningful context to provide better educational outcomes for children. Emotional processes should be leveraged in educational settings to further understand the student-teacher dynamic in a classroom and create a conducive environment for learning and instruction.

Learning is embodied within the larger constructs of emotional, behavioral, and social interrelationships. Our daily cultural and social experiences play a vital role in human interaction and the development of the emotional brain (Immordino-Yang & Gotlieb, 2017). Although brain development follows a general trajectory, there is a high amount of variability in the way certain regions of the brain develop given the individual's social, emotional, cultural, cognitive and physical context. For example, children's positive and negative emotional experiences have an impact on brain development.

Adverse Experiences and Resiliency

Humans experience positive, negative, and conflicting emotions. However, continuous exposure to adverse childhood experiences activates stress related hormones, leading to disruption of healthy brain development (McLaughlin, 2016; Shonkoff. et al., 2012). Traumatic experiences can compromise neural circuitry and connectivity patterns that enable cognition, reasoning, and memory (Briggs-Gowan et al, 2015; Nelson, 2014).

Resilience is the process of overcoming negative outcomes over time (Yao & Hsieh, 2019). Cognitive flexibility is crucial to resilience. This involves overlapping brain areas involved in adapting behavior when facing adverse events. Cognitive control, emotion regulation, physical pain perception, and cognitive functions are integral to positive adaptation.

The impact of emotional experience in childhood is an area of research that needs rigorous interrogation for us to be able to understand the behavioral and cognitive issues that children face in school settings. We can safely assume that brain functioning and development are a product of an individual's social, physical, and emotional development. Further, community and environmental factors play a significant role in the development of children and adolescents. Adverse experiences around issues of equity, poverty, racism, bullying, substance abuse, foster care, and academic stress can affect development (Luthar et al., 2021). Research on adverse experiences shows that brain networks are supported by overall behavioral, physical, mental, and psychosocial wellbeing.

Social and Emotional Learning

Social and emotional learning is a normal part of development that begins early in life as the infant begins to build secure attachments and a sense of safety. This includes being able to process cues from caregivers and parents. With the help of these social and interpersonal interactions children derive physical comfort and affection which creates a sense of safety and fascilitates regular communication and responsiveness in making sense of their environment (Immordino-Yang et al., 2018; Shonkoff et al., 2012).

Emotion is an effective form of feedback that can lead to learning (Gruber 2021). Our ability to monitor the emotions of ourselves and others and to use this information to guide our thinking and actions is called emotional intelligence (Salovey & Mayer, 1990).

Social and emotional learning has been developed as a framework that can be used within schools and other settings. Well-designed programs have resulted in positive effects on social-emotional competencies about self, others, and school and have enhanced student behavior and academic achievement (Durlak et al., 2011). Program goals include establishing a safe, caring environment and opportunities for students to contribute to their community.

Food for thought

Social Emotional Learning (SEL) involves teaching children self-regulation, impulse control, empathy, and problem-solving skills. Research on SEL has shown that it helps children academically and with their personal lives. Children learn to make good decisions and SEL reduces negative behaviors. More information on SEL can be obtained from the Committee for Children. https://www.cfchildren.org/

Did You know?

Emotions are not just chemicals in the brain, rather they are electrochemical signals that travel in the form of peptides and carry messages across the brain and the body, changing the electro/neurochemistry of every individual cell and sending vibrations to other people (Pert, 2007). We can look at the neurobiological evolution of emotion not as a product but a process. So, how does this information integrate the idea of embodiment and feeling the emotional states of another individual?

Bibliography

Adolphs, R. (2009). The social brain: Neural basis of social knowledge. *Annual Review of Psychology*, *60*(1), 693–716. 10.1146/annurev.psych.60.110707.163514

Arredondo, M. M. (2021). Shining a light on cultural neuroscience: Recommendations on the use of fNIRS to study how sociocultural contexts shape the brain. *Cultural Diversity and Ethnic Minority Psychology*. 10.1037/cdp0000469

Beaty, R. E., Benedek, M., Kaufman, S. B., & Silvia, P. J. (2015). Default and executive network coupling supports creative idea production. *Scientific Reports*, *5*, 10964. 10.1038/srep10964

Bevilacqua, D., Davidesco, I., Wan, L., Chaloner, K., Rowland, J., Ding, M., Poeppel, D., & Dikker, S. (2019). Brain-to-brain synchrony and learning outcomes vary by student–teacher dynamics: Evidence from a real-world classroom electroencephalography study. *Journal of Cognitive Neuroscience*, *31*(3), 401–411.

Briggs-Gowan, M. J., Pollak, S.h D., Grasso, D., Voss, J., Mian, N. D., Zobel, E., McCarthy, K. J., Wakschlag, L. S., & Pine, D. S. (2015). Attention bias and anxiety in young children exposed to family violence. *Journal of Child Psychology and Psychiatry*, *56*, 1194–1201. 10.1111/jcpp.12397

Bruneau, E., Dufour, N., & Saxe, R. (2013). How we know it hurts: item analysis of written narratives reveals distinct neural responses to others' physical pain and emotional suffering. *PloS One*, *8*(4), e63085. 10.1371/journal.pone.0063085

Durlak, J. A., Weissberg, R. P., Dymnicki, A. B., Taylor, R. D., & Schellinger, K. B. (2011). The Impact of enhancing students' social and emotional learning: A meta-analysis of school-based universal interventions. *Child Development*, *82*(1), 405–432. 10.1111/j.1467-8624.2010.01564.x

Falk, E. B., & Bassett, D. S. (2017). Brain and social networks: Fundamental building blocks of human experience. *Trends in Cognitive Sciences*, *21*(9), 674–690.

Gavrilov, Y., Rotem, S., Ofek, R., & Geva, R. (2012). Socio-cultural effects on children's initiation of joint attention. *Frontiers in Human Neuroscience*, *6*, 1–10.

Goulden, N., Khusnulina, A., Davis, N. J., Bracewell, R. M., Bokde, A. L., McNulty, J. P., & Mullins, P. G. (2014). The salience network is responsible for switching between the default mode network and the central executive network: Replication from DCM. *NeuroImage*, *99*, 180–190. doi:10.1016/j.neuroimage.2014.05.052

Gruber, T., Bazhydai, M., Sievers, C., Clément, F., & Dukes, D. (2021). The ABC of social learning: Affect, behavior, and cognition. *Psychological Review*. 10.1037/rev0000311

Guthrie, J. T., & Klauda, S. L. (2014). Effects of classroom practices on reading comprehension, engagement, and motivations for adolescents. *Reading Research Quarterly*, *49*(4), 387–416.

Hawley Turner, K., & Hicks, T. (2015). Connected reading is the heart of research. *English Journal*, *105*(2), 41–48.

Herold, D., Spengler, S., Sajonz, B., Usnich, T., & Bermpohl, F. (2016). Common and distinct networks for self-referential and social stimulus processing in the human brain. *Brain Structure & Function*, *221*(7), 3475–3485.

Immordingo-Yang, M. H. (2016). *Emotions, Learning, and the Brain: Exploring the Educational Implications of Affective Neuroscience*. W.W. Norton & Company.

Immordino-Yang, M. H., & Gotlieb, R. (2017). Embodied brains, social minds, cultural meaning: Integrating neuroscientific and educational research on social-affective development. *American Educational Research Journal*, *54*(1S), 344S–367S. DOI: 10.3102/0002831216669780

Immordino-Yang, M. H., Christodoulou, J. A., & Singh, V. (2012). Rest is not idleness: Implications of the brain's default mode for human development and education. *Perspectives on Psychological Science*, 7, 352–364.

Immordino-Yang, M. H., Darling-Hammond, L., Krone, C., & Aspen Institute, N. C. on S. E. & A. D. (NCSEAD). (2018). The Brain Basis for Integrated

Social, Emotional, and Academic Development: How Emotions and Social Relationships Drive Learning. Aspen Institute.

Ivey, G., & Johnston, P. H. (2013). Engagement with young adult literature: Outcomes and processes. *Reading Research Quarterly*, *48*(3), 255–275.

Jones, R. M., Somerville, L. H., Li, J., Ruberry, E. J., Powers, A., Mehta, N., Dyke, J., & Casey, B. J. (2014). Adolescent-specific patterns of behavior and neural activity during social reinforcement learning. *Cognitive, Affective & Behavioral Neuroscience*, *14*(2), 683–697.

Kim, J. S., Hemphill, L., Troyer, M., Thomson, J. M., Jones, S. M., LaRusso, M. D., & Donovan, S. (2017). Engaging struggling adolescent readers to improve reading skills. *Reading Research Quarterly*, *52*(3), 357–382.

Kini, P., Wong, J., McInnis, S., Gabana, N., & Brown, J. W. (2016). The effects of gratitude expression on neural activity. NeuroImage, 128, 1–10. 10.1016/j.neuroimage.2015.12.040

Lagercrantz, H. (2016). Connecting the brain of the child from synapses to screen-based activity. *Acta Paediatrica*, *105*(4), 352–357.

Levine, S. (2014). Making interpretation visible with an affect-based strategy. *Reading Research Quarterly*, *49*(3), 283–303.

Lin, N., Wang, X., Xu, Y., et al. (2018). Fine subdivisions of the semantic network supporting social and sensory–motor semantic processing. *Cerebral Cortex*, *28*(8), 2699–2710.

Luthar, S. S., Ciciolla, L., & Suh, B. C. (2021). Adverse childhood experiences among youth from high-achieving schools: Appraising vulnerability processes toward fostering resilience. *American Psychologist*, *76*(2), 300–313. 10.1037/amp0000754

Menon, V., & Uddin, L. Q. (2010). Saliency, switching, attention and control: A network model of insula function. *Brain Structure and Function*, *214*(5), 655–667.

Nelson, C. A. (2014). Romania's Abandoned Children. Harvard University Press.

Niendam, T. A., Laird, A. R., Ray, K. L., Dean, Y. M., Glahn, D. C., & Carter, C. S. (2012). Meta-analytic evidence for a superordinate cognitive control network subserving diverse executive functions. *Cognitive, Affective & Behavioral Neuroscience*, *12*(2), 241–268. 10.3758/s13415-011-0083-5

Pert, C. (2007, January 6). The physics of emotion: Dr. Candance Pert on the mind body connection and feeling Go(o)d. *Six Seconds*. The Emotional Intelligence Network. https://www.6seconds.org/2007/01/26/the-physics-of-emotion-candace-pert-on-feeling-good/

Redcay, E., Dodell-Feder, D., Pearrow, M. J., Mavros, P. L., Kleiner, M., Gabrieli, J. D. E., & Saxe, R. (2010). Live face-to-face interaction during fMRI: A new tool for social cognitive neuroscience. *NeuroImage*, *50*(4), 1639–1647.

Salovey, P., & Mayer, J. D. (1990). Emotional intelligence. *Imagination, Cognition and Personality*, *9*(3), 185–211. 10.2190/DUGG-P24E-52WK-6CDG

Sebastian, C., Viding, E., Williams, K. D., & Blakemore, S.-J. (2010). Social brain development and the affective consequences of ostracism in adolescence. *Brain and Cognition*, *72*(1), 134–145.

Schurz, Matthias, Radua, Joaquim, Tholen, Matthias G., Maliske, L., Margulies, D. S., Mars, R. B., Sallet, J., & Kanske, P. (2021). Toward a hierarchical model of social cognition: A neuroimaging meta-analysis and integrative review of empathy and theory of mind. *Psychological Bulletin*, 147, 293–327. 10.1037/bul0000303

Shonkoff, J. P., Richter, L., van der Gaag, J., & Bhutta, Z. A. (2012). An integrated scientific framework for child survival and early childhood development. *Pediatrics*, *129*(2), e460–e472. 10.1542/peds.2011-036

Simon, R., Gallagher, B. ,& Walkland, T. (2022)."Swirling a Million Feelings into One": Working-through critical and affective responses to the holocaust through comics. *Research in the Teaching of English*, 56(4), 385–410.

Spence, L. K. (2009) Developing multiple literacies in a website project. *The Reading Teacher*, 62, 592–597.

Spence, L. K., Bastos, P., & Cullars, A. (2022). "They're killing our imaginations": dialogue and reflexive writing development in historically marginalized students. *Reading Research Quarterly*, *57*(2). doi:10.1002/rrq.449.

Tijms, J., Stoop, M. A., & Polleck, J. N. (2018). Bibliotherapeutic book club intervention to promote reading skills and social–emotional competencies in low SES community-based high schools: A randomised controlled trial. *Journal of Research in Reading*, *41*(3), 525–545. 10.1111/1467-9817.12123

Turner, K. H., Hicks, T., & Zucker, L. (2020). Connected reading: A framework for understanding how adolescents encounter, evaluate, and engage with texts in the digital age. *Reading Research Quarterly*, *55*(2), 291–309.

Ueno, T., & Lambon Ralph, M. A. (2013). The roles of the "ventral" semantic and "dorsal" pathways in conduite d'approche: A neuroanatomically-constrained computational modeling investigation. *Frontiers in Human Neuroscience*, 7, 1–7.

Ugazio, G., Grueschow, M., Polania, R., Lamm, C., Tobler, P., & Ruff, C. (2022). Neuro-computational foundations of moral preferences. *Social Cognitive & Affective Neuroscience*, *17*(3), 253–265.

Wertsch, J. V. (1991). *Voices of the Mind: A Sociocultural Approach to Mediated Action*. Harvard University Press.

Wycoco, V., Shroff, M., Sudhakar, S., & Lee, W. (2013). White matter anatomy: What the radiologist needs to know. *Neuroimaging Clinics of North America*, *23*(2), 197–216. 10.1016/j.nic.2012.12.002

Yao, Z. & Hsieh, S. (2019). Neurocognitive mechanism of human resilience: A conceptual framework and empirical review. *International Journal of Environmental Research and Public Health*, *16*, 1–21.

Zhang, G., Xu, Y., Zhang, M., Wang, S., & Lin, N. (2021). The brain network in support of social semantic accumulation. *Social Cognitive and Affective Neuroscience*, *16*(4), 393–405. 10.1093/scan/nsab003

5

MULTIMODAL BRAIN

Do you use your phone to text, search the internet, and read? How are these forms of literacy involved in teaching and learning? Is there a difference between reading books and reading online? Are video games helpful or harmful to literacy? Does technology affect the brain?

In this chapter, we explore the multimodal nature of literacy. **Multimodality** is the way different modalities such as voice, text, and images come together to communicate ideas. Both neuroscience and multimodality involve multiple sources of information that are orchestrated by the reader. This chapter describes neuroscience findings related to written modalities and internet use.

Managing Information

Reading and writing in the 21st century pose unique challenges due to new ways of presenting and sharing information via the internet and other technologies. Teachers can help students find information, determine its trustworthiness, and organize the information for use. Most importantly, information must be readable and understandable. Teachers have a larger role in finding readable and trustworthy texts for younger students. Older students can learn to use apps and strategies to help them manage information.

Student writing can be impacted by many factors such as muscle control, idea generation, writing self-image, phoneme processing, vocabulary, and prior knowledge. To deal with these issues, educational researchers have robustly studied writing and effective teaching methods. Let's start with a classroom description of multimodal reading and writing (Spence, 2009b).

> A group of second graders entered the media center and began searching for information on their individual topics. The media center had a computer cart and shelves of informative books. The computer screens contained icons for child-friendly websites and an electronic encyclopedia. Several children rushed to the computers, while others began browsing through the non-fiction bookshelves.

DOI: 10.4324/9781003256199-6

Other children took paper folders of collected information to the tables and began organizing their project notes.

The children in this scene read, wrote, and illustrated using a variety of media including computers, books, and paper. They read texts and viewed photos, diagrams, and videos. Their tools included keyboards, icons, pencils, and markers. K-12 students are increasingly relying on a hybrid collection of media for reading and writing. Some teachers and administrators promote technology for learning, while others emphasize the benefits of paper. Which is better?

Managing Information

When we use our smartphones or other computers, we engage in lots of clicking, scrolling, and jumping from topic to topic. Researchers have explored how this multi-tasking affects our thinking. Some studies have found that digital multitasking is not beneficial and may decrease the ability to multi-task in other situations because of a reduced ability to ignore incoming distractions (Firth et al., 2019).

Digital media tends to be read in fragmented ways, which makes certain demands on the brain. In internet reading, we may search for information, randomly surf, or receive links from others. We may glance at a text, save a text, or read it more carefully. Turner et al. (2020) found that fragmented approaches to reading digital texts are not as productive as reading connected texts. For example, in Turner's study, students had access to an abundance of texts through the internet yet did not have skills beyond simple searching and then searching again to find a previously read text. Since multitasking and fragmented text can be counterproductive to students' research and writing, we should encourage work habits that enhance students' ability to focus on a task.

Learning to seek out, catalog, and share digital texts and information can build the literate habits necessary in our digital age. The following example from a high school study illustrates one way to teach students to manage information sources during their research (Turner & Hicks, 2020).

Managing Digital Information

Preparation

Find and become familiar with applications that will help students manage information by

- Blocking advertisements from Web pages (e.g., AdBlock)

- Converting webpages into clutter-free pages (e.g., Evernote)
- Accessing Web pages from a smartphone for later reading (e.g., Pocket)
- Preparing an outline and creating bibliographies (e.g., Citelighter)

Goals

Use digital tools to manage resources prior to reading and writing informative texts.

Procedure

Demonstrate how to install the apps on students' digital devices.

Demonstrate how to use each app to manage information sources.

Monitor students as they collect sources and capture information on their topics.

Managing digital information allows students to focus on reading and writing, rather than jumping from webpage to webpage and taking notes in a haphazard way. When high school students used apps to organize and de-clutter information, they could then read the texts in a continuous block without the distraction of advertisements, links, and unneeded information.

Younger students can also be taught to focus when they use digital sources. First, the teacher can help students find trustworthy, readable web pages and scaffold their reading. Next, students can be taught to read a portion of the digital text and then turn away from the screen to write the information in their own words on a piece of paper. Finally, students can organize their notes for a report or essay (Spence, 2009a).

Teachers scaffold instruction to help students read many different types of texts in different subject areas. Students expand their abilities with increasingly complex texts while reading texts just beyond their current ability level. Throughout their schooling, students engage with new vocabulary, new ideas, and new forms of digital texts.

Our society has become increasingly dependent on technology. Rather than letting our students sink or swim in the digital ocean, we can teach them how to manage information. Managing information decreases multitasking and allows students to focus on what they are reading and writing. We can help students read internet-based texts by teaching them how to manage information and by discussing the aspects of a text that support them as readers. Understanding text organization can help students read and can help them write well-organized cohesive texts.

Texts that Support Reading

There are several aspects of texts that support reading comprehension (Fesel et al., 2018). Whether they are internet-based and digital, or linear print, a more easily comprehended text has the following characteristics:

- An organized structure with logical sections
- The ideas across the whole text are linked together cohesively
- If there is a graphical overview of the text, it is clear and easy to navigate

When a text is organized and cohesive, it supports the reader. With internet texts, the reader can choose different reading routes. In some texts, those reading routes take the reader on an organized path. In other texts, the result may be a less organized reading experience and the reader will need more working memory to navigate through it.

Internet-based reading also involves navigating hypertext. **Hypertext** is a link on the computer screen that can access related information and graphics. Hypertexts can increase scanning and browsing behaviors, which draw the reader's attention away from the main text. Internet-based texts seem to promote scanning information quickly, then searching for more information. This behavior does not promote thinking deeply about the previous material or synthesizing ideas (Peng et al., 2018). In contrast to internet text, linear print texts are relatively fixed and allow for more synthesis of the information. **Synthesis** involves combining ideas together to see how it all fits together into a whole.

Sometimes we want students to read straightforward texts that are easier to comprehend. But students also must learn to navigate complex texts. **Complex texts** have unfamiliar language, implicit meanings, or unconventional structures. Both literature and internet texts may have some of these features. The following example of instruction supports students in thinking, discussing, and writing about complex texts (Leighton et al., 2019).

Discussing Complex Texts

Preparation

Gather books on historical change-makers such as Susan B. Anthony, Eleanor Roosevelt, Mary McLeod Bethune, Jackie Robinson, Rosa Parks, Martin Luther King Jr., and Cesar Chavez.

Choose one book to read aloud to the whole class. Choose conceptually rich vocabulary to preview, for example, courage. Prepare guided questions for interactive read-aloud.

Craft an overarching question. For example, What is a trouble-maker, and is it ever OK to be one?

Goals

Discuss books on historical change-makers.
Discuss conceptually rich vocabulary.
Talk and write about ideas related to change-makers.

Procedure

Introduce students to the guiding question and encourage discussions between partners or small groups.

Prior to the read-aloud, record conceptually rich vocabulary on anchor charts as you preview the words through whole-class discussions. **Anchor charts** are large-format papers adhered to the classroom walls. They are left on the walls for the duration of the unit so that students can refer to them in their work.

Build students' background knowledge on the timeframe, setting, and other important aspects of the book.

Read the book aloud, stopping for discussion of guided questions and pertinent student noticing and wondering.

After reading, discuss the book including connections to the overarching question, and connections to target vocabulary.

Provide extended time for students to discuss their ideas with a partner or small group and to write. Talk and writing can center on how the book made them feel, connections to their experiences, or connections to other books, movies, etc.

Use additional books on historical change-makers for additional read-aloud, guided reading, or independent reading.

As shown above, discussions of complex texts within a unit of study provided a cognitively rich environment for learning. This environment included teacher demonstration, interactions between teacher and students, student-student interaction, and time for individual reflection. These activities provided students with multiple perspectives.

As students engage with new concepts, their brains flexibly adapt to the demands, domains, and properties of the task (Passiatore et al., 2021). For example, a task demand might be unknown vocabulary. An example of task domain might be the historical time period, and a property of the task might be the format of the text, either print or digital.

We can teach students strategies for reading complex texts. Planning an extended unit of study with multiple instructional configurations allows for long-term memory to be built. New concepts are taken in during teacher demonstrations then concepts are internalized as students talk to each other and individually reflect through thinking and writing.

Writing

Writing is important to thinking and learning as students engage in a reflexive process. This involves considering, discussing, and deciding how to use ideas in their writing. **Reflexive writing** involves reflecting on interests, values, beliefs, and power in relation to ideas or purposes. Writing contributes to the ongoing development of the self by forcing a person to grapple with ideas and experiences they may not have previously expressed. Impressions of life, social interactions, and political events are clarified through dialogue and writing.

As you can imagine, writing involves many different brain processes working together. Auditory, semantic, short-term memory, long-term memory, and motor processes are all involved in writing (Purcell et al., 2011). Even when students speak and read quite well, writing may be difficult because of the cognitive demands involved.

As children progress from their earliest scribble-writing to more and more conventional writing, they exercise multiple literacy skills. As a result, writing strengthens memory and speaking skills. As children observe the written language that surrounds them, they begin to understand the many purposes for writing. As a result, young children can develop their own purposes for writing.

Emergent Writing

Children's early writing practices emerge from their growing understanding of the goals of different kinds of writing events in the home or school. Children use this knowledge about writing as a system for representing things with marks (Rowe, 2008). When children speak multiple languages, they make comparisons and notice differences between scripts such as Korean and Farsi (Choi, 2021). Children also use their knowledge of when, how, and by whom writing occurs.

Children may begin experimenting with writing at around two years old. Their first writing may include mock handwriting that resembles a horizontal English script. Writing may include other characteristics of conventional writing such as letter-like shapes, forward and backward letters, and numbers (Figures 5.1, 5.2, and 5.3).

Figure 5.1 Emergent Writing with Horizontal Mock-handwriting, the Letter P, and the Number 5.

Along with letter-like marks, children represent things and people using drawings in their emergent writing. This involves a range of cognitive processes. To draw, a person must integrate many systems to make a mental representation and coordinate a series of motor commands. Thus, the process of drawing is associated with a wide brain network (Raimo et al., 2021).

In the emergent writing examples above, the teacher provided a purpose and social context for the children's development as writers. The children were given blank journals, crayons, and pencils each day. They were free to choose their writing topics and talked about their writing with their peers and teachers. In these discussions, the teachers often asked, "What did you write about today?" This reinforced that the children's marks are a form of communication. Early experiences

Figure 5.2 Emergent Writing with Letter-like Shapes.

such as these help children build neural connections linking language to print.

Writing involves orchestrating multiple brain processes even for the basic skills of handwriting and spelling. Writing complexity increases when forming ideas for composing an extended text. Because of the multiple processes involved, students sometimes face roadblocks to their writing. Understanding how the brain processes during writing can help teachers understand students' writing progress.

Handwriting and typing require long-term memory, working memory, and other central processes. Related processes are also needed for their associated motor actions (Purcell et al., 2011). To write by hand, a person must retrieve the word and spelling forms from long-term memory or sound-to-letter conversion. One must also coordinate

Figure 5.3 Roberto's Emergent Writing of the Letter R.

neuromuscular processes to produce the graphic script (Planton et al., 2013). This involves nerve impulses that cause the release of a chemical messenger into the junction of the nerve cell and the muscle cell (Figure 5.4).

Mastering handwriting takes time and depends on the development of fine motor skills (Dinehart, 2015). When young children write a letter, interconnected brain areas are engaged in activating working memory, motor coordination, decision-making, and eye-hand coordination (Vinci-Booher, 2020).

Young children's handwriting contributes to their recognition of letters as they learn to read. Teachers may help children make the sound-letter connection by asking the child to dictate a word or sentence. The teacher may say and point to the correct letter on an alphabet strip, helping the child to produce each word. This helps the

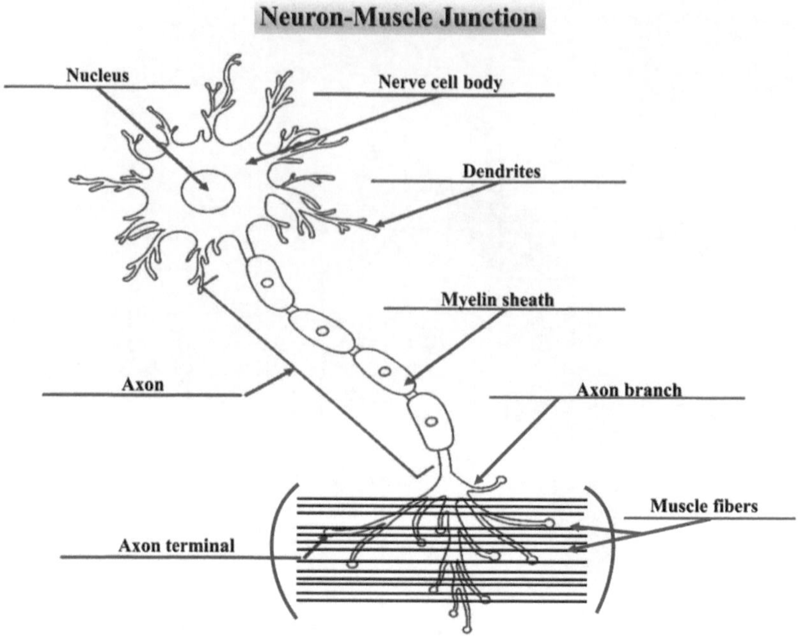

Figure 5.4 Junction of Nerve Cell and Muscle Cell.

Note: Adapted from: Wikimedia Commons.

child to build the brain's reading network. Print displays in classrooms are resources for developing reading and writing. **Word walls** display a collection of words that are important to the class. Posters with songs or poems, name tags, book titles, and labels on objects are other examples of classroom print that allow children to see that print can represent people and objects.

Teaching children to write legibly is important for developing connections among motor areas of the brain. Children who are more fluent in handwriting and spelling have developed more neural efficiency and connectivity than less fluent hand writers and spellers (Costa et al., 2022). Handwriting and spelling skills are still used in schools and society even though computer programs and smartphones auto-correct spelling for us. So how important is spelling?

Spelling

Spelling is still important in today's world. Spelling influences reading and writing skills and is necessary for employment and business. Spelling affects how writing is perceived by others and how writers perceive their own writing (Pan et al., 2021). You may have been taught spelling through receiving a weekly word list, writing the words in sentences, and taking a test at the end of the week. However, there are other effective ways to teach spelling that engage multiple brain processes.

The brain processes involved in spelling include working memory, long-term memory, phoneme-grapheme conversion, and executive functions.

We store knowledge of how to spell a word in our long-term memory. If we do not know the spelling of a word, we can use long-term memory to access similar words or parts of words. We also can convert the sounds in a word to the letters that represent it. Our working memory is needed to organize all this information for physically writing the word.

Effective learning strategies for spelling include the following (Pan et al., 2021):

- Segmenting words into sounds
- Sorting words according to patterns
- Studying rules for plurals and adding suffixes
- Self-corrected tests
- Study-copy-cover-compare method
- Grouping words that are related in some way

Strategies such as these can help students to build white matter connections across the brain because the strategies involve the reading network, working memory, and building long-term memory for spelling. They are effective strategies for learners of all ages. The following is an example of how to work with young children to develop their phonemic awareness and active exploration of words (Levin & Aram, 2013).

Spelling patterns

Preparation

Give a pretest to determine what spelling patterns the child needs to learn. Choose five target words for each 10–15-minute session.

Obtain magnetic letters and steel board and prepare the board with boxes on the bottom so that each letter or phoneme can fit into one box. Put a bank of magnetic letters at the top. The child will use the bottom portion of the board to spell words.

Goal

Use phoneme segmentation to spell words.

Procedure

Use the pretest to determine word patterns to explore.

Ask the child to spell a word using the magnetic letters then ask the child to return the letters to the top of the board.

Tell the child it is your turn to spell the word, but first you will segment it with your fingers.

Hold up a finger for each sound.

Explain that a letter is needed for each sound. Say the sound while selecting the letter and placing it in the first square at the bottom of the board. Repeat this for each sound.

Wait a few seconds for the child to look at the correctly spelled word then return the letters to the top of the board.

Tell the child to spell the word again by segmenting it with fingers. If the child makes a mistake, assist the child in segmenting the sounds with fingers. Then tell the child to spell the word with the magnetic letters.

Make sure the word is spelled correctly and then have the child write the word on a card that can be kept on a ring of cards for later reading practice.

Continue this procedure with the remaining four words.

In the example above, the teacher guided the child in invented spelling. **Invented spelling** is the attempt by a child to spell a word that is not stored in their long-term memory or their phonetic memory. The child uses what they already know along with their working memory to order information while writing the word.

The example also illustrated **phonemic segmentation**, which is the ability to separate words into their individual sounds. The teacher can demonstrate this with an individual child, small group, or whole class by holding up one finger for each sound. Some words require two or more letters that make one sound. Using Elkonin boxes helps the child apply this concept to new words. **Elkonin boxes** are drawn by the teacher so that one box is large enough for a letter or letters that make up a sound. For example, the word "through" would have a double letter-sized box for "th," a single letter-sized box for "r," and

Figure 5.5 Elkonin Box for the Word "through."

a four-letter-sized box for "ough." Three boxes for three sounds "th-r-ough" as shown in Figure 5.5.

It is important to develop fluency in handwriting, typing, and spelling, but children do not need to master these before they begin writing meaningful messages. Writing to convey meaning begins with a child's first emergent writing attempts. Parents and early childhood teachers reinforce the function of writing to communicate when they look at the child's marks and emergent writing and ask, "What does this say?" Engaging the child in a conversation about their writing encourages oral and written language development.

Writing Process

The process of writing an extended text involves planning, drafting, and revising. These tasks involve similar processes as handwriting and spelling but are even more demanding of executive control functions and processes. Elementary through secondary writing instruction often uses a workshop structure. Writing workshop is modeled after an artisan workshop, where people work on individual or group projects, receive feedback on their work in progress, and incorporate feedback into their creations.

In a **writing workshop**, the teacher usually plans a brief mini lesson and then circulates among the students as they work on their writing projects. Students usually choose their own writing topic, which is highly motivating because students have a purpose and an audience in mind. Students write drafts and revisions as they talk through their writing with peers and the teacher. Their final written product is shared with each other, teachers, and the intended audience. Table 5.1 includes elements of effective writing instruction including aspects of the writing workshop.

The findings from the writing research above support students' dynamic changes in brain network structures. These changes occur incrementally across time as students orchestrate the many skills needed to engage the cognitive processes involved in written composition. The brain is a complex system and is made up of interactions between small and large-scale networks (Figure 5.6). Challenging cognitive processes depend on the brain's executive function and regions across the brain that exchange information at hyperefficient speed (Liu et al., 2021).

Table 5.1 Effective Writing Instruction Roles for Teachers and Students (Graham, Harris, & Beard, 2019)

Teachers	*Students*
Establish routines for a positive and supportive writing environment and consistent time for writing.	Actively engage in writing.
Implement a process approach to writing.	Gather ideas, write drafts, read drafts, revise and edit.
Encourage students to compose together and provide feedback on writing.	Provide and receive feedback from other students.
Make sure students have goals for writing.	Develop clear and specific goals for writing.
Teach elements of different types of texts.	Gather and organize possible writing content.
Provide students with good models of texts.	Study models of texts such as an example of a genre or the way a particular author crafted a text.
Provide consistent time and motivation to write.	Write frequently and stay motivated.
Teach sentence construction and vocabulary.	Write drafts, reread them, and revise.
Teach spelling, handwriting, typing, and technological supports.	Use technological supports for editing.
Use writing as a way to support content learning.	Write within content areas such as science, math, arts, physical education, and social studies.

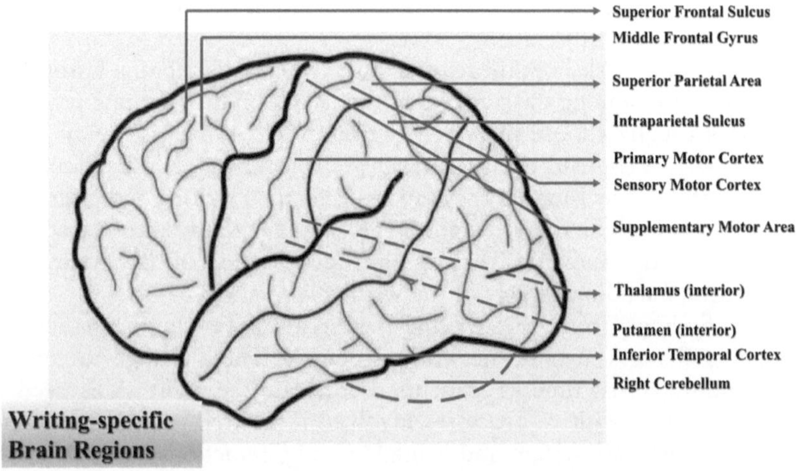

Figure 5.6 Writing Brain Regions.

Note: Regions of Interest to Writing (See Metanalysis, Planton et al., 2013).

A metacognitive theory of the writing process is supported by emerging neuroscience. The memory system, language processing, working memory functions, and semantic integration are involved in writing (Shah et al., 2013). Ideas are generated from stored memories. Language structures and words are chosen to represent those ideas. The writer uses working memory to add or delete as needed. And the meaning of the text must be carried through.

Metacognitive theory helps us understand how a writer controls and monitors the following processes:

- Control strategies are used to produce thoughts
- Monitoring strategies are used to observe how the thoughts are being produced
- The writer uses strategies to achieve their writing goals

Control strategies include generating ideas, drafting ideas, revising ideas, and choosing words to represent the ideas. Monitoring strategies include reading what has been written, rereading, reflecting, and reviewing. These are just some of the control and monitoring strategies used during writing (Hacker, 2018).

We have discussed emergent writing, spelling, and the writing process. We must also discuss how writing has been impacted by new technologies. Writers can use internet searching, speech recognition, and spelling and grammar checking. Writers can easily combine writing with other modalities such as pictures, audio, and video. How does all this technology impact the brain processes of writing?

Digital Tools

> Mr. Colter stood in front of the class drawing a T-chart on the white board with the title "Elements of Drama." The eighth graders copied the T-chart in their notebooks and then suddenly looked up at the large screen at the front of the class. A video had appeared on the screen.
>
> Mr. Colter said, "Write some examples from the clip. Ready, Ms. Lara?"
>
> Lara replied, "I'm on the last one." The video played and the students attentively watched a clip from the movie, *Major Payne* (Castle, 1995). They began to chuckle a little, then reacted with more and more laughter.
>
> When the clip ended, Mr. Colter said, "Six minutes to think about what you saw and fill in the T chart."

> After a discussion of elements of drama, the students wrote a paragraph about how one of the character's personalities might be similar to their own. Lara wrote, "... Major Payne because when the little boy was down, he went and cheered him up. And when people are down, I cheer them up too."

In the classroom example above, Mr. Colter had two goals. He wanted the students to learn about the elements of drama and he wanted them to connect with the moral implications depicted in the movie scene. Like Mr. Colter, almost all the students in this class were African American, so Mr. Colter chose a movie with an African American family. He chose a comedy that would thoroughly engage his students.

It is not surprising that videos are increasingly viewed by young people as videos circulate across different media. Videos have a tremendous impact on viewers, and both negative and positive effects have been documented. On the positive side, videos that include admiration for moral virtue can lead to positive behavioral changes. This finding can be leveraged in the classroom because brain activation while watching these morally edifying videos is very consistent among viewers (Englander et al., 2012). Listening to audio dramas also produces consistent brain activations across listeners (Boldt et al., 2013). Given the constant exposure to video and audio, we can speculate that students are viewing, listening to, and creating videos and audio for a variety of purposes.

In one high school English class, students used video, digital drawing tools, and screen capture, among other resources (Schwartz, 2014). The students wrote within a wiki, which allowed them to reach a broad audience. **Wikis** are sites that allow users to make changes and update content. The high school students used digital tools to create a portfolio of three essays. A **portfolio** is a collection of student work that exemplifies development and can be used to assess student progress. As a result of this project, students leveraged their identities, interests, and practices to present compelling arguments to a broad audience. The following example details instruction for this multi-part project.

Researching Your Identity

Preparation

Choose digital tools such as screen capture, drawing tools, and wiki.

Explore student-generated wikis such as Writers' Wonderland.

Goals

Use multiple modalities to collect representations of one's identity on a wiki.

Write a persuasive essay that explores the concept of identity.

Conduct interviews, analyze, and write a research report.

Create a multimodal argument.

Procedure

Part 1: Exploring Identity—Essay

Familiarize the students with the digital tools and wiki.

Discuss issues of identity as a whole class.

Repurpose images, text, and other modalities from students' social media and internet sources to curate a wiki page.

In small groups, discuss the meaning of identity.

Write an essay supporting their definition of identity.

Post the essay on the wiki page.

Part 2: Community Social Issue—Report

Collaboratively brainstorm and decide on research questions that connect to identity issues impacting their community.

Use community networks and social media to conduct interviews based on the research question.

In small groups, co-analyze the interviews and co-write a research paper within the wiki.

Part 3: Multimodal Argument—Essay

As a whole class discuss social issues that relate to identity projects.

Develop a stance on a social issue.

Collect and create texts, images, voice, music, etc., to inform, persuade, or motivate their audience to consider their stance on the social issue.

Portfolio

Collect writings in a portfolio. Return to each piece to reflect and self-assess writing development.

In the example of instruction above students created multimodal texts. Some modalities used in the wikis were video, screen capture, doodles, songs, and texts. This multimodal project shows how students can make use of current technology to meet academic requirements.

Another digital tool that impacts writing is voice recognition. Voice recognition allows a person to write by talking. This removes the need to type or handwrite one's thoughts. **Voice recognition** technology converts speech to characters on the computer or device screen. Some software programs require training for the recognition of a specific voice. This software is more accurate than more common voice recognition available on smartphones or tablets. Regardless of the program used, the writer must do some physical typing to correct mistakes made during speech conversion. Some writers immediately correct these errors as they arise. Other writers wait until their text is complete (Leijten et al., 2010).

Speech recognition software has benefited students who have difficulty with handwriting or typing. Smartphones, tablets, and notebook computers have also been used by young children to translate between languages (Rowe, 2020) and in drafting texts (Baker, 2017). An example lesson using voice recognition for writing a patterned text follows.

Voice Recognition for Patterned Text

Preparation

Gather several short books with patterned text such as "Five Little Monkeys." Include these books in the independent reading center.

Prepare digital devices for voice recognition and determine internet connectivity.

Goals

Use voice recognition as an assist during the drafting phase of writing.

Compose a patterned text.

Make the patterned text into a book.

Read and share the book with an audience.

Procedure

Teacher and students engage in a shared reading of patterned books. Discuss the illustrations and text pattern.

Brainstorm ideas for students to write their own patterned text.

Demonstrate by orally composing using voice recognition in front of the students. Discuss the accuracy of the voice-generated text, encouraging students to notice and comment on mistakes. Have fun with this, while using the mistakes to learn about phonemics.

The next step is to transfer the digital text to handwritten text. The teacher writes on chart paper to demonstrate how to write a draft. The teacher might demonstrate how to work out the spelling of a word. Be open to taking writing recommendations from the students.

Provide digital devices for the students to use as they draft their own patterned texts in the writing center. They will write using pencil and paper, as demonstrated by the teacher on the chart paper.

On ensuing days, use your demonstration text to revise the text to make it better. For example, discuss the rhythm of the patterned text. Demonstrate editing strategies such as deciding on where to insert punctuation.

Help students with their revisions and edits over several days until the desired result is achieved.

Demonstrate how to make a book including text and illustrations for each page. Demonstrate how to make a title, cover, and the binding process (for example stapling the pages together).

Help students make their own books from their individual texts.

Find an audience for students to read and share their books.

In the example lesson above, the teacher did not completely rely on voice recognition for the children's composition of their patterned text. Instead, she used it as a tool to help students make the voice-to-print connection. Representing spoken language with text helps children build the brain's reading network.

As new technological tools are developed, reading and writing are becoming more and more multimodal. Visual and audio aspects of communication seem to be outpacing the written word and the internet has become our most important tool for gathering information. Meanwhile, neuroscientists and psychologists are studying problems associated with internet use such as video game addiction and reduced cognitive control (Kühn & Gallinat, 2015).

A longitudinal study of children and adolescents found that a higher frequency of internet use was associated with a decrease in verbal intelligence and smaller increases in grey and white matter volume in widespread brain areas. These areas were related to language processing, attention, executive functions, emotion, and reward (Takeuchi et al., 2018). Research is still ongoing and study replication will be necessary to draw conclusions about the effect of internet use on the brain.

Neuroscience findings can provide a greater understanding of multimodal literacies including reading, spelling, writing, digital texts, visual texts, and internet use. Our role as teachers is to provide students with a variety of tools and materials for communication, to support students in using the tools and materials, and to teach students to make good decisions about what to use and how to use them.

Did You know?

Multimodal literacy involves combining two or modes of literacy. Combining modes comes easily to children as they combine art, text, music, movement, and sound. The National Council of Teachers of English summarizes major concepts for teaching multimodal literacy.

https://ncte.org/statement/multimodalliteracies/

Food for Thought

Multimodal literacies involve forms of communication, whereas multisensory instruction involves the human senses of vision, hearing, sight, touch, and smell. Multisensory instruction is often used for students who have learning differences. Instruction includes the use of color for highlighting text, student-created images, audio books, music, puzzles, real objects, and games involving movement.

Bibliography

Baker, E. A. (2017). Apps, iPads, and literacy: Examining the feasibility of speech recognition in a first-grade classroom. *Reading Research Quarterly*, *52*(3), 291–310. 10.1002/rrq.170

Boldt, R., Malinen, S., Seppä, M., Tikka, P., Savolainen, P., Hari, R., & Carlson, S. (2013). Listening to an audio drama activates two processing networks, one for all sounds, another exclusively for speech. *PLoS ONE*, *8*(5), 1–10. 10.1371/journal.pone.0064489

Castle, N. (Director). (1995). Major Payne [Film]. Universal Pictures.

Choi, J. (2021). Demystifying simultaneous triliteracy development: One child's emergent writing practices across three scripts focusing on letter recognition, directionality and name writing. *Journal of Early Childhood Literacy*, *21*(4), 614–636. 10.1177/1468798419896064

Costa, L.-J. C., Spencer, S. V., & Hooper, S. R. (2022). Emergent neuroimaging findings for written expression in children: A Scoping review. *Brain Sciences*, *12*(3), 406, 2076–3425. 10.3390/brainsci12030406

Dinehart, L. H. (2015). Handwriting in early childhood education: Current research and future implications. *Journal of Early Childhood Literacy*, *15*(1), 97–118.

Englander, Z. A., Haidt, J., & Morris, J. P. (2012). Neural basis of moral elevation demonstrated through inter-subject synchronization of cortical activity during free-viewing. *PLoS ONE*, *7*(6). 10.1371/journal.pone.0039384

Fesel, S. S., Segers, E., & Verhoeven, L. (2018). Individual variation in children's reading comprehension across digital text types. *Journal of Research in Reading*, *41*(1), 106–121.

Firth, J., Torous, J., Stubbs, B., Firth, J. A., Steiner, G. Z., Smith, L., Alvarez-Jimenez, M., Gleeson, J., Vancampfort, D., Armitage, C. J., & Sarris, J. (2019). The "online brain": How the Internet may be changing our cognition. *World Psychiatry: Official Journal of the World Psychiatric Association*, *18*(2), 119–129.

Graham, S., Harris, K. R., & Beard, K. (2019). Teaching writing to young African American male students using evidence-based practices. *Reading & Writing Quarterly*, *35*, 19–29.

Hacker, D. J. (2018). A metacognitive model of writing: An Update from a developmental perspective. *Educational Psychologist*, *53*(4), 220–237.

Kühn, S., & Gallinat, J. (2015). Brains online: Structural and functional correlates of habitual Internet use. *Addiction Biology*, *20*(2), 415–422. 10.1111/adb.12128

Leighton, C. M., Ford-Connors, E., Proctor, C. P., & Wyatt, J. (2019). Engaging second-grade English learners in complex texts, topics, and tasks. *Literacy Research and Instruction*, *58*(4), 272–294.

Leijten, M., Janssen, D., & van Waes, L. (2010). Error correction strategies of professional speech recognition users: Three profiles. *Computers in Human Behavior*, *26*(5), 964–975. 10.1016/j.chb.2010.02.010

Levin, I., & Aram, D. (2013). Promoting early literacy via practicing invented spelling: A comparison of different mediation routines. *Reading Research Quarterly*, *48*(3), 221–236. 10.1002/rrq.48

Liu, M., Backer, R. A., Amey, R. C., & Forbes, C. E. (2021). How the brain negotiates divergent executive processing demands: Evidence of network reorganization in fleeting brain states. *NeuroImage*, *245*, N.PAG. 10.1016/j.neuroimage.2021.118653

Pan, S. C., Rickard, T. C., & Bjork, R. A. (2021). Does spelling still matter—and if so, how should It be taught? Perspectives from contemporary and historical research. *Educational Psychology Review*, *33*(4), 1523–1552. 10.1007/s10648-021-09611-y

Passiatore, R., Antonucci, L. A., Bierstedt, S., Saranathan, M., Bertolino, A., Suchan, B., & Pergola, G. (2021). How recent learning shapes the brain: Memory-dependent functional reconfiguration of brain circuits. *NeuroImage*, *245*. 10.1016/j.neuroimage.2021.118636

Peng, M., Chen, X., Zhao, Q., & Zhou, Z. (2018). Attentional scope is reduced by Internet use: A behavior and ERP study. *PLoS ONE*, *13*(6), 1–12.

Planton, S., Jucla, M., Roux, F.-E., & Démonet, J.-F. (2013). The "Handwriting brain": A meta-analysis of neuroimaging studies of motor versus orthographic processes. *Cortex: A Journal Devoted to the Study of the Nervous System and Behavior*, *49*(10), 2772–2787. 10.1016/j.cortex.2013.05.011

Purcell, J. J., Turkeltaub, P. E., Eden, G. F., & Rapp, B. (2011). Examining the central and peripheral processes of written word production through meta-analysis. *Frontiers in Psychology*, *2*. 10.3389/fpsyg.2011.00239

Raimo, S., Santangelo, G., & Trojano, L. (2021). The neural bases of drawing: A meta-analysis and a systematic literature review of neurofunctional studies in healthy individuals. *Neuropsychology Review*, *31*(4), 689–702. 10.1007/s11065-021-09494-4

Rowe, D. W. (2008). Social contracts for writing: Negotiating shared understandings about text in the preschool years. *Reading Research Quarterly*, *43*(1), 66–95.

Rowe, L. W. (2020). Hey Siri: Exploring the potential for digital tools to support heritage-language use in English-dominant classrooms. *Language Arts*, *97*(6), 363–375.

Schwartz, L. A. (2014). Challenging the tyranny of the five-paragraph essay: Teachers and students as semiotic boundary workers in classroom and digital space. *Literacy*, *48*(3). 124–135.

Shah, C., Erhard, K., Ortheil, H.-J., Kaza, E., Kessler, C., & Lotze, M. (2013). Neural correlates of creative writing: An fMRI study. *Human Brain Mapping*, *34*(5), 1088–1101. 10.1002/hbm.21493

Spence, L. K. (2009a). Inquiry based writing workshop. *Teacher Librarian*, *37*(1), 23–27.

Spence, L. K. (2009b) Developing multiple literacies in a website project. *The Reading Teacher*. *62*(7), 592–597.

Takeuchi, H., Taki, Y., Asano, K., Asano, M., Sassa, Y., Yokota, S., Kotozaki, Y., Nouchi, R., & Kawashima, R. (2018). Impact of frequency of internet use on development of brain structures and verbal intelligence: Longitudinal analyses. *Human Brain Mapping*, *39*(11), 4471–4479. 10.1002/hbm.24286.

Turner, K. H., Hicks, T., & Zucker, L. (2020). Connected reading: A framework for understanding how adolescents encounter, evaluate, and engage with texts in the digital age. *Reading Research Quarterly*, *55*(2), 291–309. 10.1002/rrq.271

Vinci-Booher, S., & James, K. H. (2020). Visual experiences during letter production contribute to the development of the neural systems supporting letter perception. *Developmental Science*, *23*(5), 1–17.

6

MAKING MEANING

> "Miguel is excited to read and teach others about topics he is learning about or that he has prior knowledge of. For example, he could explain to me how each dinosaur won a battle in the *Dinosaur Versus* series. And he was fascinated at the new things he learned about sharks in a passage about great whites." (Teacher reflection)

Miguel's teacher described how her student used his prior knowledge of dinosaurs to comprehend a fictional story. When students read, they access their long-term memory and build white matter connections to new learning. The dinosaur story was easier for Miguel to understand because he knew some of the facts about dinosaurs. His interest in sharks motivated him as he read a nonfiction book about the great white shark. Miguel's experiences show us that reading comprehension involves not just skills and cognitive processes, but also background knowledge, experiences, and interests. Our comprehension depends on the type of text we are reading, our life experiences, our interest in the topic, and our vocabulary.

Reading comprehension is the process of making meaning as we read. We are actively making meaning at the word, sentence and paragraph level, and the whole text. If we do not continually make meaning in these ways, our understanding of the text eventually breaks down. That is why we teach students to monitor the meaning of a text as they read. We teach strategies, such as using the context to figure out a word or going back to re-read if they have lost the thread of meaning.

Some types of texts are easier for us to understand, and others are more difficult. A scientific research article may contain too many unknown words, or a historical novel's lengthy descriptions might lose one's interest. Think about your own reading experiences. When you read an informative article, you have a different experience than when you read a short story. Reading a biology textbook is not the same as reading a fitness blog. Reading comprehension always involves a range of understanding of different texts.

DOI: 10.4324/9781003256199-7

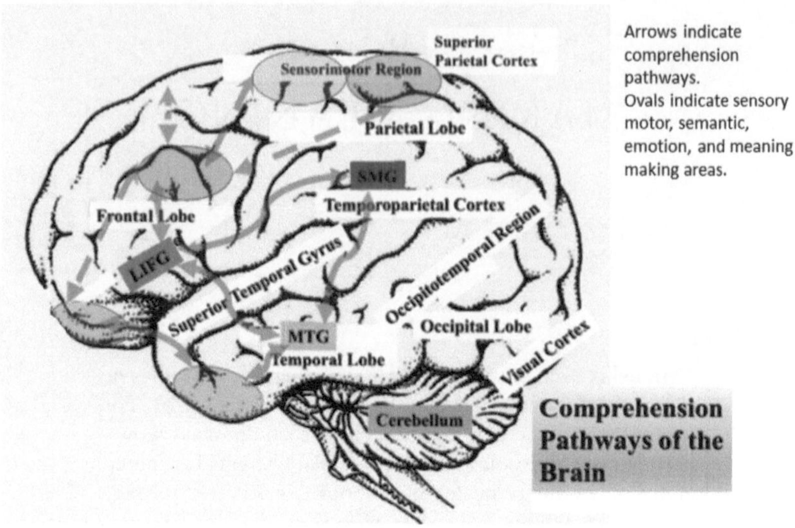

Figure 6.1 Comprehension Pathways in the Brain.

Note: The figure above shows the left hemispheric comprehension pathway of the brain (Hruby & Mitra, in press); however, recent research also indicates the involvement of the right hemisphere. The right hemisphere is no longer seen as just a compensatory pathway for comprehension but instead as a region of interest for language comprehension in typically developing readers (Horowitz-Kraus et al., 2014).

Multiple areas of the brain are involved in distributed networks needed for reading comprehension. Young children seem to use a wider range of neural connectivity in reading, for example, more processing in the right hemisphere of the brain. As children mature and gain linguistic and scholastic experience, the brain becomes more specialized for reading and more associated with the left hemisphere (Meyler et al., 2007), although the right hemisphere remains active. Additionally, comprehension entails a large-scale cortical network across different areas of the brain (Figure 6.1). This large network indicates that reading comprehension is a complex cognitive task (Aboud et al., 2016; Landi et al., 2013).

This chapter will explore how memory, metacognition, and word knowledge contribute to reading comprehension. Along the way, we will explore brain functions related to reading comprehension.

Prior Knowledge

Have you noticed when reading a book that you have constructed a mental picture? Then when you watch a movie adaptation of the book, it may not match the movie you made in your mind. When we read or watch a movie, we must construct meaning, forming a mental representation that makes sense. We integrate what we are reading or watching with our existing knowledge, which is stored in long-term memory. As we continue to read or watch, our mental representation is monitored, updated, and confirmed.

Some models of reading comprehension include these three functions that operate together, not in sequence:

- Putting words together into meaningful units
- Using knowledge of one's language syntax
- Linking together sentences and paragraphs to put together a complete picture of the whole text.

The brain's executive functions maintain and organize all this information. Executive functions coordinate many areas of brain function. Task-specific networks are formed within and outside of the language network to perform these multiple functions (Aboud et al., 2016).

The reading comprehension of children and adolescents varies from person to person. Some children enter school already reading simple words like "mom, dad, brother, love, house." They use their life experiences such as making birthday cards or drawing and labeling pictures. However, some children have rich life experiences but may not havemade the sound-to-print connection by the time they enter school.

Life experiences impact reading comprehension in the classroom. Experiences like bedtime reading, storytelling, language games, and family conversations encourage the growth of language networks. To build on home language experience, teachers can make links to reading instruction. For example, if the reader has a pet, comprehending a book about pets will come more easily than reading about the sinking of the Titanic. Background knowledge plays an important role as the reader constructs mental models based on meaning cues, linguistic cues, and relevant background knowledge (van Moort et al., 2020).

Throughout elementary school and adolescence, children are exposed to many different texts and their comprehension will vary. Stories, informative articles, novels, and textbooks each present their own challenges. Topics, text organization, and vocabulary become increasingly complex as children progress through school. As they grow, their vocabulary expands through consistent reading and instruction. Their life experiences and exposure to ideas also develop. As concepts become more abstract throughout the school years, children must make connections to abstract ideas and infer the meanings of complex texts.

Adolescents also differ in their comprehension of literature and textbooks. A student who has grown up in a family of thespians may thoroughly enjoy and connect with *Romeo & Juliet* while the rest of the class struggles to make sense of the archaic dialogue and plot. Students who read many books over time, both at school and at home, develop their comprehension through this exposure. Broad experience with many kinds of books serves to develop large vocabularies and intuitive understandings of literary elements and text features.

The example of instruction below comes from a study of knowledge-building during reading. Reading a collection of informational texts helped build students' general knowledge and content knowledge (Wright, 2022). These collections are known as text sets. A **text set** is a collection of materials that are focused on a specific topic. Some text sets include a range of materials such as books, articles, fiction, nonfiction, photographs, video, audio, maps, art, and primary documents. In the example that follows, the teachers used written texts.

Text Set

Preparation

Gather a set of at least six texts that are conceptually related, for example, several books about birds (how they fly, feathers, bird life cycle, raptors, songbirds, sea birds). Make sure the books include important words about the topic. Plan for at least three days to read about one topic.

Goals

Develop general knowledge and vocabulary through reading and discussion.

Develop content-specific knowledge through reading and discussion.

Procedure

Each day, introduce two of the texts highlighting information the students will be learning. During the discussion, allow students to mention information they already know. Point out important words for understanding the topic and make sure they know how to pronounce them.

Students then read the two texts. They may read independently, with a partner, or in a small group guided by the teacher.

After reading, engage students in a discussion about the information learned from the books.

Continue reading books that address the same concept for at least three days. On subsequent days and weeks, students could read other, related topics, or the class might move on to another topic.

In the example of instruction above, students built concepts and vocabulary through reading conceptually related texts. This develops a memory basis that students can use for reading and writing in the future. They develop prior knowledge and a representational schema by reading a variety of texts.

Memory

The importance of memory in reading is clear. Educators have highlighted the importance of memory in accessing prior knowledge during reading. Memory is also involved in creating schema, which is a mental representation of a situation. **Prior knowledge** and **schema** are terms educators use to describe the process of building on what one already knows while integrating new information.

As new information is taken in, the brain's semantic system integrates it with previous information built over time. Integrating information through the semantic system allows us to build meaningful representations of our world. However, when we infer an abrupt change in the semantic context, we may have to revise our representation or build a new representation (Branzi et al., 2020). This knowledge base of semantic memory is accessed as we read.

Engaging memory is important for visualization during reading. Actions, emotions, and concrete details can be visualized based on experience. In reading complex texts, readers must make connections within a text. For example, they must connect a character's actions early in the novel with a consequence that occurs later. Readers also may connect events, actions, or emotions within a text to their own experiences or to other texts.

As readers make sense of a text, they draw upon their background knowledge and the context of what they are reading. As they proceed through the text, they continuously monitor the emerging meaning. Both context and background knowledge influence the construction of a mental representation of the text.

Scientists are trying to pinpoint areas and functions of the brain that are involved in monitoring for meaning. One imaging study found a large network of regions involved in knowledge-based monitoring during reading, a smaller network involved in text-based monitoring, and a number of interacting regions (van Moort et al., 2020). This means that reading is much more involved than a simple input of letters to an output of word meaning.

Context and background knowledge help the reader anticipate what a word will be (Chow, et al., 2014; Kutas & Federmeier, 2000). Readers predict upcoming words in a sentence based on context, experience, and prior knowledge. The reader encodes the incoming word, recognizes its meaning, and integrates the word into the unfolding sentence. The meaning of that sentence becomes integrated into the reader's existing knowledge so that the reader will feel a sense of familiarity when the sentence is read again (Pu et al., 2020). This process involves multiple networks in the brain yet happens quickly.

During reading, the language comprehension system seems to quickly use all the information it can to efficiently search semantic memory to predict the most likely word or words (Benjamin & Gaab, 2012). This predictive strategy is efficient when the prediction makes sense. However, if the prediction does not make sense, additional strategies are used for information maintenance and integration with working memory. Some educators use the term **automatic processes** when discussing the rapid language comprehension process. **Control processes** can be thought of as how readers apply conscious attention to read words and make sense of the text.

Metacognition

In addition to the rapid processing describe above, readers also consciously monitor some aspects of reading. Effective readers exercise knowledge and control over their thinking and learning. They employ strategies to make meaning and overcome problems during reading. Comprehension monitoring is an important metacognitive activity. **Metacognitive** activities are conscious cognitive or affective experiences that accompany intellectual work (Flavell, 1979). A reader's self-regulation when comprehension stalls is a metacognitive activity. Teachers can encourage metacognitive strategies to improve students' reading comprehension.

Cognitive Strategies

> Ms. Hope gathered her four-year-old students on the rug at the front of the classroom. She sat on the rocking chair and showed the children the front of a picture book, *Swashby and the Sea* by

Beth Ferry. "Look at the cover illustration, what do you see?" Ms. Hope asked.

"I see a girl."

"I see a boat."

"A man." The children called out their observations.

"Where are they? Where are the girl and the man and the boat?" Ms. Hope asked

In the example above, Ms. Hope was helping the children sample elements from the book to make predictions about what they would be reading. They were sampling the pictures on the cover, just like they would learn to sample words and letters as beginning readers. The pictures helped them make predictions, an important reading strategy.

The term **reading strategies** refers to the actions and cognitive activities that readers use to process information during reading. These are the strategies readers use to work toward a goal, such as solving problems during reading. For example, when a reader comes to an unknown word while reading, they may predict based on what they have read so far or based on their background knowledge. The reader may substitute a word with similar meaning. Or they may make an unacceptable substitution and then correct it. These predictions can be **lexical** (letter-sound relationship), **syntax** (sentence grammar), or **semantic** (meaning) as defined in Table 6.1.

Readers often predict a word based on the sentence structure, or syntax. They also use lexical knowledge such as letter-sound relationships or whole words. They may use the semantic, or meaning of the word within the context of the passage to solve an unknown word. Thus, readers use syntax, lexical, and semantic cues to monitor their understanding as they work their way through a passage or a whole book.

Table 6.1 Cues for Reading with Each Cue's Definition

Cues for Reading	*Definition*
Syntax	The predictable pattern in which words are put together to form phrases, sentences, and longer texts.
Semantics	The meaning of a word, sentence, or longer text.
Lexical	Elements of a word, such as letter-sound correspondence and meaningful word parts such as prefixes and endings.

As language is processed, prediction occurs at multiple levels of specificity. Syntactically, words are put together in predictable patterns. Semantically, meaning develops as the speech or text progresses. Lexically, words or word parts are retrieved from memory (Colenbrander et al., 2022). Prediction of these different types of information is generated by unique brain networks and occurs rapidly in response to ongoing linguistic input (Carter et al, 2019). Prediction is essential for language processing so we teach prediction as a strategy starting in prekindergarten. We continue to teach prediction in elementary through high school as texts become more complex.

Next, we will see how readers control their reading process using strategies described by Goodman, Watson, and Burke (2005).

- Initiate, sample, select

  The reader initially decides to read something. Then the reader samples information that might be letters, words, illustrations, or diagrams. The reader selects information that is needed to make sense of the text.
- Predict, infer

  The reader retrieves background knowledge and experiences. The reader uses what they have read so far, as they continue through the text.
- Confirm, disconfirm, correct

  If the reader's prediction is appropriate to the emerging meaning, the reader confirms their prediction was correct. Alternatively, their prediction may be disconfirmed, and the reader will usually try to correct it.
- Integrate background knowledge

  The reader integrates what they are reading with what they already know to construct the meaning of the text.
- Terminate reading

  The reader considers whether to continue reading. Just as a reader decided to initiate reading, they may also decide to stop reading for a variety of reasons. Beginning readers may need to learn to terminate reading if a text is too difficult and frustrating.

Reading Strategy Example

To illustrate the cognitive reading strategies, we present a first grader living in the southeastern United States, Alex. Alex learned to recognize letters and their sounds at home and in kindergarten. In first grade, he used these skills but still needed to practice monitoring his comprehension. We will look at two pages followed by Alex's reading. The book was in the fantasy genre and the main character was a young dragon. It is important to note that the book was written and set in Scotland, which impacted Alex's comprehension. Here are two pages of the book, *Dylan the Dragon and the Playground Ride*, by Zani Mathoo.

> When he was hungry he would
> go home to his cave where
> mummy dragon would have hot
> soup ready for his dinner
> "Wash your wings and get ready for tea.
> I've made your favourite today, darling,
> peas and toad soup." said mummy dragon.

On the first page, Alex sampled and predicted accurately until he came to the word "dinner." He said, "dr, dr ..." perhaps predicting "dragon." Alex turned away from the book and thought about it. At that moment, he was not using print cues, but instead drew upon his prior knowledge to infer the word was "dinner." The context of the story and his prior experience provided cues for solving the word.

Alex used semantic memory to associate the visual look of the word, the syntax of the sentence, and the meaning within the context of the story. He tapped into his conceptual understanding of dinner. Neuroimaging studies have shown an incremental influence of both semantic and syntactic context that guides semantic processing. These different sources of information simultaneously contribute to the unfolding neural dynamics of comprehension (Payne et al., 2015). Reading and making meaning involve complex, interconnected systems including the semantic system and memory. Alex engaged these automatic processes when he read the following.

> Wash your wings? Wash your wings and get ready for tag.

Alex asked, "Wash your wings?" and looked up at his teacher. This question shows he was actively making meaning and tapping into his prior knowledge. He had heard the phrase, "Wash your hands" but "wings" did not fit with his expectation of how the sentence should read so he repeated the phrase and continued reading.

Alex read the sentence again but substituted "tag" for "tea." He was using automatic sampling and predicting. He sampled the T sound and the length of the word. However, he could not engage his background knowledge because he did not think of tea as a meal, as it is in Scotland.

As Alex continued to read, he encountered more problems with the next sentence.

> Each, take, you, mum, he said" instead of, "Peas and toad soup, said mummy dragon."

As shown in the underlined portions, Alex sampled letters, vowel digraphs, and words. However, he became frustrated at this point because the story as he read it was not making sense. He terminated reading because his sampling was not effective, and he was not making meaning.

Alex's teacher saw that he needed to learn the strategy of confirming or disconfirming a prediction. This would help him revise his plan for reading and learn to inhibit information that is not relevant or helpful. A sentence that says," Each take you mum" is not relevant to the meaning he constructed on the previous page. Rather than relying on automatic processes, Alex needed to confirm, disconfirm, and self-correct to solve his difficulties. Alex also needed to revise his plan for reading. His current plan was to sample letters and words regardless of syntax and semantics.

Planning is an **executive function** of the prefrontal cortex. This area involves networks associated with working memory and cognitive control, which may enable comprehension despite problems with decoding (Patael et al., 2018).

When Alex confirmed, disconfirmed, and corrected his predictions for the words, "Peas and toad soup" Alex could revise his plan for reading and control additional reading strategies. Alex's reading shows us the importance of developing cognitive reading strategies that will help children actively read for meaning and help them make decisions when reading becomes difficult.

It would also help for Alex to read books that would make better use of his background knowledge to predict unknown words. "Dylan the Dragon" was free via the internet, but it was written and set in Scotland. The language differences and fantasy genre overwhelmed Alex's automatic processing. This shows the importance of choosing books carefully for young readers. Books that connect to readers' lives or experiences can more easily engage semantic memory.

Selecting Texts for Reading Instruction

As students progress through school, they may become avid readers, or they may abandon reading for pleasure. When students enjoy reading, they read more, and their reading comprehension improves. How can teachers promote reading for enjoyment? Reading interviews are a good way to start. The interview can be either written or verbal. Reading interviews help students to think about their reading process and attitudes toward reading. They also provide teachers with information on student progress.

Reading Interview

What are your hobbies and interests outside of school?

What do you like best?

Books
Short stories
Informative articles
Websites
Social media

What was the last book you read?

What was the best book you ever read?

What would you like to read next?

What do you do when you come to a word you do not know?

How do you know that you understand what you are reading?

What makes reading fun?

What is easiest about reading?

What is difficult about reading?

How did you learn to read?

Interviewing students about their attitudes toward reading provides teachers with insights into the range of student reading. Factual as well as fiction books are of interest to students of all ages and should be encouraged. When children learn to differentiate factual books from fictional books, they use this knowledge to guide their comprehension strategies.

An interesting neuroimaging study found that factual texts elicited mental simulation of actions and outcomes of actions in the brain's motor area, the same brain area that is active when physically moving one's body (Figure 6.2). Fictional texts appeared to elicit mental simulation of motives behind the action of a story's protagonist (Altmann et al., 2014). Students need opportunities to read both factual and fictional texts to engage in different, but equally important ways of thinking.

Comprehension Strategies

Some students mainly engage in the automatic processing of words. However, they can also benefit from using comprehension strategies to

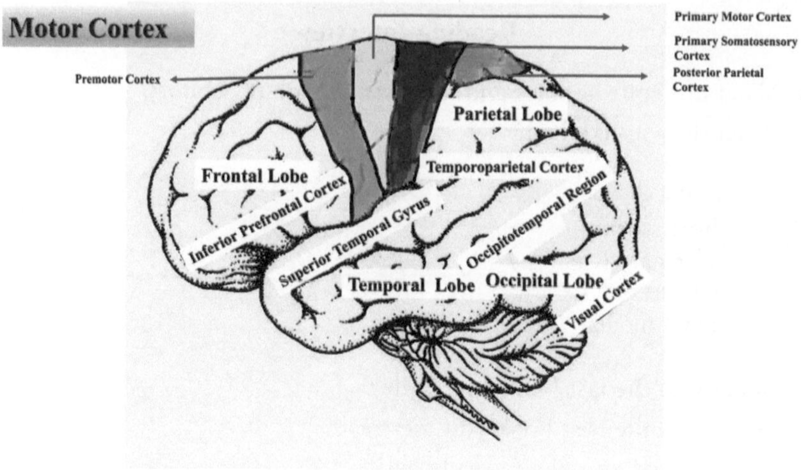

Figure 6.2 Brain Motor Cortex.

increase reading fluency. Fluent reading activates networks of brain regions extremely rapidly. For example, word meaning is activated less than half a second after seeing a word (Tarkiainen et al., 1999). Comprehending longer texts involves multiple brain networks that also coordinate rapidly during reading.

Scharlach's (2008) classroom research described a method of scaffolding students to internalize the following comprehension strategies:

- Predicting/inferring
- Visualization
- Making connections
- Questioning
- Main idea
- Summarizing
- Checking predictions
- Making judgments

These comprehension strategies can be demonstrated one at a time during a teacher's read-aloud. Then students can practice the strategy during their self-selected reading. **Self-selected reading** is time set aside for students to read books that they have chosen. Teachers often keep a well-stocked classroom library for this purpose. Let's look closely at each reading comprehension strategy.

Asking questions during reading is a useful strategy. Questioning something in a text may cause a reader to pause and think. Or the reader may go back to a previous page to reread a section for better understanding. Questioning is automatic for some readers, but some readers may need to learn how to question and reflect when they don't understand something.

Determining the main idea of a reading selection is often taught in language arts classes. However, it is not as widely taught as a metacognitive strategy. Students can learn to think about the main idea as they progress through their self-selected reading. A reader might say to themself, "The most important thing is ..." Similarly, a reader can pause to summarize during reading. A reader might think, "Basically, the text is saying ..." Students can learn to monitor their comprehension through questioning the text when necessary and periodically summarizing what they are reading. However, the goal is for these strategies to become automatic processes, so that thinking about reading does not impede rapid processing.

Just as younger readers learn to confirm and disconfirm their predictions and inferences, more advanced readers also check their predictions. As a reader moves through the text, they may notice a misconception. For example, in reading the word, "sister" a student thought two characters were related. Later, when the sister went to the convent, the student checked her prediction and realized the sister was a religious nun and was not a sibling of the other character. Checking predictions can be taught as a metacognitive strategy, but over time, it will become part of the automatic reading comprehension process.

Readers make judgments about their texts. They may enjoy a book, be offended, or be disappointed. They may relate to the content or find it strange. Many types of judgments can be made about a text. Judgments can be made about the character's actions, the writing style, the length of the book, or the type of vocabulary used. The reader may agree or disagree with an argument or opinion.

Students can learn to judge the texts they are reading. Some teachers have students keep a reading journal or write comments on notes that stick to the pages of a book. These notes are excellent conversation points that students can use during book discussions.

To teach each of the strategies described above, the teacher first demonstrates one strategy while reading aloud. As the teacher reads aloud, students are activating their listening comprehension. Neurobiological studies of skilled reading comprehension indicate a largely overlapping language circuit for both reading comprehension and listening comprehension (Landi et al., 2013). This suggests that demonstrating reading strategies during read-aloud may activate brain areas needed for reading comprehension.

During read-aloud, the teacher pauses to explain when and how to use a strategy. For example, determining the main idea could rely on searching the text or may require inferring an implicit main idea. Once a strategy has been demonstrated, the students are asked to try out the strategy as they continue to read independently. On subsequent days, each of the strategies is introduced separately, while the teacher continues to model the previous strategies during read-aloud sessions. By continued demonstration of the strategy and students' independent use, students increase their use of metacognitive comprehension strategies to monitor their automatic use and fluency.

Another example of reading comprehension instruction involves guiding students through pre, during, and post-reading activities (White et al., 2014).

Before, During, and After Reading

Preparation

Determine students' reading interests and abilities by providing several different books and asking them to page through them. Then ask them which would be too easy, just right, or too challenging. Ask them if any of the book topics interest them or what other topics they would like to read about.

Choose a text for a group of students such as a guided reading group based on their interests and matched to their reading ability.

Pull a list of vocabulary words from the book that represent the major events (narrative books) or concepts (informational books).

Goals

To successfully read, understand, learn from, and enjoy a book.

Before Reading

Prediction activity. The teacher reads the word list and explains that the words will be used to make a prediction about what the book will be about. Students can write their story prediction, or this can be done orally as a group prediction.

During Reading

As students read, demonstrate and teach strategies that would best help students understand the book. Listed are five comprehension strategies but use only those that pertain to the reading.

- Reread to clarify understanding of a word, sentence, or passage
- Predict what will happen based on what has been read
- Ask questions when unsure of something or just wondering
- Make connections between the events, characters, actions, or concepts
- Summarize occasionally during reading

After Reading

Ask open-ended questions based on students' wonderings and follow students' lead in discussing the book.

Encourage students to use comprehension strategies on their own when reading independently.

Pre-, during-, and postreading activities can be used with read-aloud or guided reading. Once students have learned the strategies, they can practice them on their own during silent reading of a whole class text or during self-selected reading. Pre-, during-, and postreading activities allow students to use their background knowledge and make connections while reading. This involves networks within the brain that coordinate long-term memory, working memory, and reading networks, among other functions. Comprehension strategies thus have the potential for engaging multiple components of the reading process.

Teachers support students' development as avid readers by providing a classroom environment that strongly encourages reading engagement. Relevance and student autonomy are especially important for engaging adolescent readers. In a classroom study, teachers designed a relevant and autonomous classroom using the following ideas (Ivey & Johnston, 2013):

- Provide a wide variety of texts that deal with issues and concepts of high interest to students
- Provide for discussion that follows students' lines of inquiry
- Allow students to choose their texts and read at their own pace
- Eliminate assignments associated with the texts
- Encourage students to read at home
- Do not assign additional homework

By participating in the self-selected reading of high-interest books, the students shifted their self-perception as readers and increased their reading engagement both in class and at home (Ivey & Johnston, 2013).

Self-selected reading and access to high-interest books allow students to engage emotionally in choosing books and during the process of reading. Because emotion is linked to learning, students develop as readers when they read books that interest them. Relevant books allow students to access emotion, their prior experiences, and vocabulary to make sense of their reading.

Word Meanings

Readers need to know the meaning of words critical to what they are reading. They use word knowledge along with concepts, social, and cultural background to integrate information from the text. This allows the reader to form connections and make inferences as they read.

Semantic systems in the brain are important to learning new vocabulary. At the same time, other systems are involved in understanding the meaning of a word. Task demand and lexicality are part of the meaning-making process. Task demand involves the context in which the word appears. Lexicality involves the phonological and morphological make-up of the word. Task demand and lexicality in combination contribute toward making meaning while reading (McNorgan et al., 2015).

The context of the text, meaning of the words, and structure of the words are all important aspects of vocabulary instruction. New vocabulary is learned when embedded in scenarios and connections among words and sentences (Chilton & Ehri, 2015; Coulson et al., 2005). The following examples from grade six and grade one illustrate how two teachers address these aspects of vocabulary.

Grade Six Example

Ms. Green, a sixth-grade teacher listens to her students as they talk and socialize before school, in-between classes, and after school. She also listens to their discussions during novel studies. Ms. Green described how the students made connections between their experiences and vocabulary encountered in the book.

> "During the read-aloud and discussion of definitions, students had an idea about what most of today's words meant. They recognized the word *brutal* from a popular song that they have heard. They recognized the word *heirloom* from a video game as an object that could be unlocked in the game. I think

> acknowledging prior knowledge of the words works really well with my students and I am going to continue that in the next lesson."

Ms. Green also knew that these students' social interactions were becoming more important to them. She incorporated partner and group work because it made their studies more interesting and motivating. As they studied vocabulary together, they developed an enthusiasm for investigating words.

> "Students finish their work faster when they work with a partner and collaborate. Students prefer working together over completing the work individually. As the students worked, I heard them discussing the correct definition for the words."

Ms. Green's class was reading the novel, *The Crossover* by Kwame Alexander. Her goal was for the students to better comprehend the story by investigating the words and to become more fluent when reading new vocabulary. Ms. Green introduced the book and vocabulary study by reading parts of the book aloud as the students followed along. She stopped and defined words that she thought were unfamiliar. She also pointed out word parts and she demonstrated making connections to the words.

The next day, students previewed the upcoming pages of their novel, briefly scanning each page for words that were unfamiliar. They made a list of these words in their notebooks and worked with partners to come up with definitions using their choice of the dictionary, internet, prior knowledge, or the novel's context clues. The partners also collaborated on writing sentences using the words. Next, they created semantic maps to make connections with each word. After this thorough exploration of unfamiliar words, the students began reading the assigned pages of *The Crossover*.

Grade One Example

Ms. Lee felt it was important to develop her students; motivation to read. At the same time, Ms. Lee was trying out new vocabulary learning strategies. So when Brandon chose the book, *Let's Look at Emergency Vehicles* she took photos of Brandon holding his book and posted his picture on the bulletin board. Ms. Lee and Brandon engaged in a shared reading of the book over three days during small group reading instruction time.

First, Ms. Lee previewed the book with Brandon who located three words that he wanted to explore through vocabulary study: *snowblower*,

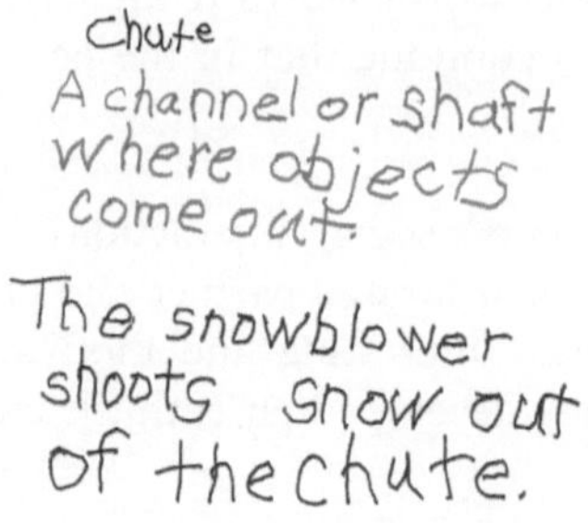

Figure 6.3 Brandon's Vocabulary Study Definitions.

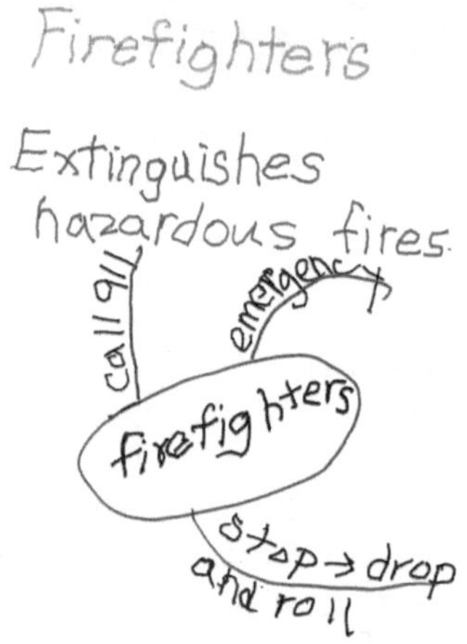

Figure 6.4 Brandon's Vocabulary Study Semantic Map.

firefighters, and *chute.* Ms. Lee wrote the words on a small erasable board. Ms. Lee helped Brandon write the definitions (Figure 6.3), then together, they discovered the prefixes, suffixes, and compound words.

Brandon made a semantic map of *firefighters* to generate related words and phrases (Figure 6.4). That led to acting out what a person needs to do if their clothes catch on fire. As they explored the text, they found more compound words. Ms. Lee used that opportunity to reinforce the concept of two words together. She noted that the student understood how the compound words were formed but did not know they were called compound words.

Next, Ms. Lee and Brandon orally generated sentences for *snowblower, firefighter*, and *chute.* Using the erasable board, they took apart the word *snowblower* to look at the similar and different sounds. One common sound for both words was *ow* making the long *o* sound. After

Ms. Lee and Brandon completed their shared reading of the book, Brandon dictated a sentence telling what the book was about and Ms. Lee wrote his sentence on the erasable board. Finally, Brandon typed his sentence under the digital photo of himself holding the book.

Brandon was so proud that he chose and read his book with assistance. Ms. Lee could see his confidence level building and his self-efficacy becoming more positive. She felt they were accomplishing more and overcoming Brandon's reading difficulties through flexible and focused vocabulary instruction.

The following example of instruction describes a sequence that is similar to Ms. Lee's vocabulary lesson (Silverman et al., 2014).

Building Vocabulary

Vocabulary study can take place at the beginning of guided reading, read-aloud, reading workshop, or content area reading such as science, math, and social studies.

Preparation

Based on the text that students will read, choose 1–3 vocabulary words that will need to be explicitly taught.

Prepare 2–3 sentences using the word. The sentence must use the words necessary to understand the target word. The sentence must be about a scenario familiar to the students.

Students will need a notebook or personal dictionary pages on which to write new words, related words, and sentences.

Goals

To learn and remember new vocabulary

To read the new words when encountered in the text

Instruction

Provide a definition: This can be written on the board, or it can be projected. Students write it in their notebooks.

Present the words within sentences based on familiar scenarios: The sentences must use words that are necessary to understand the target word. Encourage students to contribute their own sentences using the word.

Connect to related words or phrases: Give students one related word and ask if they can think of other related words. These words can be written on the board and in student notebooks

Break down morphological units (if any helpful units are in the word): **Morphological units** are meaningful word parts. For example, "pre" means "before." The teacher may need to break down words, initially, but over time students will be able to do this when the teacher asks, "what parts can you find in this word?"

Example vocabulary word: *prepare*

Definition: To make something ready.

Sentences: I will prepare spaghetti for my family's dinner tonight. Lisa will prepare for the math test tomorrow. We put on sunscreen to prepare for the hot day at the beach.

Related words or phrases: get ready, before, ahead, make something, prepare food

Morphological units: pre-before

After teaching the words, you may preview other aspects of the text, such as using the title and cover to predict what a book will be about. Then the students will read the text.

Vocabulary study builds students' background knowledge and develops a schema for making sense of texts they read in school and their future reading. Students build connections within long-term memory and other functional networks in the brain. Learning metacognitive strategies helps students work their way through texts using all the available cues, rather than relying on only phonetics or sight words. The **multicomponential model** of the reading brain goes beyond discreet skills and recognizes components, such as orthographic, phonological, syntactic, and semantic processing. Working with all the components of reading, students can learn strategies that will help them when they encounter unknown words or when something they read doesn't make sense.

Through building background, vocabulary study, and using strategies, students strengthen the reading networks in their brains and add to their long-term memory for words and text structures. The role of the teacher is to be a guide and model. Teachers guide students through pre, during, and post-reading activities. They demonstrate semantic, syntactic, and lexical reading strategies. Ultimately, the teacher releases the responsibility for these actions to the students, who become fluent readers that comprehend increasingly complex texts.

Food for thought

Is there coactivation in the motor region of the brain when a child is reading a sentence about playing a basketball game? Does the semantic or the reading comprehension network of the brain communicate with the motor network because of the use of action verbs in the sentence? Neurophysiological research implicates the motor cortex not only for action execution but also action recognition and understanding. By extension, the motor cortex has been found to share co-activations with the semantic network of the brain while processing written and spoken action-related words and sentences (Hauk et al., 2008). What does that say about the spread of the reading network across the brain? Does this indicate that meaning making is integrated within the entire reading network and is manifested in different regions of the brain depending upon the content/context?

Did You know?

An article in The Reading Teacher clarified the difference between reading strategies and skills.

"Reading strategies are deliberate, goal-directed attempts to control and modify the reader's efforts to decode text, understand words, and construct meanings of text. Reading skills are automatic actions that result in decoding and comprehension with speed, efficiency, and fluency and usually occur without awareness of the components or control involved" (Afflerbach, Pearson, & Paris, 2008, p. 368).

Bibliography

Aboud, K. S., Bailey, S. K., Petrill, S. A., & Cutting, L. E. (2016). Comprehending text versus reading words in young readers with varying reading ability: Distinct patterns of functional connectivity from common processing hubs. *Developmental Science*, *19*(4), 632–656.

Afflerbach, P., Pearson, P. D., & Paris, S. G. (2008). Clarifying differences between reading skills and reading strategies. *Reading Teacher*, *61*(5), 364–373.

Altmann, U., Bohrn, I. C., Lubrich, O., Menninghaus, W., & Jacobs, A. M. (2014). Fact vs fiction—how paratextual information shapes our reading processes. *Social Cognitive & Affective Neuroscience*, *9*(1), 22–29.

Benjamin, C. F. A., & Gaab, N. (2012). What's the story? The tale of reading fluency told at speed. *Human Brain Mapping*, *33*(11), 2572–2585. 10.1002/hbm.21384

Branzi, F. M., Humphreys, G. F., Hoffman, P., & Lambon Ralph, M. A. (2020). Revealing the neural networks that extract conceptual gestalts from continuously evolving or changing semantic contexts. *NeuroImage*, *220*, 1–16.

Carter, B. T., Foster, B., Muncy, N. M., & Luke, S. G. (2019). Linguistic networks associated with lexical, semantic and syntactic predictability in reading: A fixation-related fMRI study. *NeuroImage*, *189*, 224–240.

Chilton, M. W., & Ehri, L. C. (2015). Vocabulary learning: Sentence contexts linked by events in scenarios facilitate third graders' memory for verb meanings. *Reading Research Quarterly*, *50*(4), 439–458.

Chow, W.-Y., Lago, S., Barrios, S., Parker, D., Morini, G., & Lau, E. (2014). Additive effects of repetition and predictability during comprehension: Evidence from event-related potentials. *PLoS One*, *9*(6), 1–11.

Colenbrander, D., Parsons, L., Bowers, J. S., & Davis, C. J. (2022). Assessing the effectiveness of structured word Inquiry for students in grades 3 and 5 with reading and spelling difficulties: A randomized controlled trial. *Reading Research Quarterly*, *57*(1), 307–352

Coulson, S., Federmeier, K. D., Van Petten, C., & Kutas, M. (2005). Right hemisphere sensitivity to word- and sentence-level context: Evidence from event-related brain potentials. *Journal of Experimental Psychology: Learning, Memory, and Cognition*, *31*(1), 129–147.

Flavell, J. H. (1979). Metacognition and cognitive monitoring: A new area of cognitive-developmental inquiry. *American Psychologist*, *34*(10), 906–911.

Goodman, Y., Watson, D., & Burke, C. L. (2005). *Reading miscue inventory: From evaluation to instruction (2nd ed.)*. Richard C. Owen Publishers, Inc. ISBN-13: 978-1572747371

Hauk, O., Shtyrov, Y., & Pulvermüller, F. (2008). The time course of action and action-word comprehension in the human brain as revealed by neurophysiology. *Journal of Physiology, Paris*, *102*(1–3), 50–58. 10.1016/j.jphysparis.2008.03.013

Horowitz-Kraus, T., Wang, Y., Plante, E., & Holland, S. K. (2014). Involvement of the right hemisphere in reading comprehension: A DTI study. *Brain research*, *1582*, 34–44. 10.1016/j.brainres.2014.05.034

Hruby, G. G., Mitra, A. (2023) A naturalized view of literacy education: What the neuro- and life sciences may offer language and literacy research. *International Encyclopedia of Education (4th ed.)*. Elsevier.

Ivey, G., & Johnston, P. H. (2013). Engagement with young adult literature: Outcomes and processes. *Reading Research Quarterly*, *48*(3), 255–275.

Kutas, M., & Federmeier, K. D. (2000). Electrophysiology reveals semantic memory use in language comprehension. *Trends in Cognitive Sciences*, *4*(12), 463–470

Landi, N., Frost, S. J., Mencl, W. E., Sandak, R., & Pugh, K. R. (2013). Neurobiological bases of reading comprehension: Insights from neuroimaging studies of word-level and text-level processing in skilled and impaired readers. *Reading and Writing Quarterly*, *29*(2), 145–167.

McNorgan, C., Chabal, S., O'Young, D., Lukic, S., & Booth, J. R. (2015). Task dependent lexicality effects support interactive models of reading: A meta-analytic neuroimaging review. *Neuropsychologia*, *67*, 148–158.

Meyler, A., Keller, T. A., Cherkassky, V. L., Lee, D., Hoeft, F., Whitfield-Gabrieli, S., Gabrieli, J. D. E., & Just, M. A. (2007). Brain activation during sentence comprehension among good and poor readers. *Cerebral Cortex*, *17*(12), 2780–2787.

Patael, S. Z., Farris, E. A., Black, J. M., Hancock, R., Gabrieli, J. D. E., Cutting, L. E., & Hoeft, F. (2018). Brain basis of cognitive resilience: Prefrontal cortex predicts better reading comprehension in relation to decoding. *PloS One*, *13*(6), e0198791. 10.1371/journal.pone.0198791

Payne, B. R., Lee, C.-L., & Federmeier, K. D. (2015). Revisiting the incremental effects of context on word processing: Evidence from single-word event-related brain potentials. *Psychophysiology*, *52*, 1456–1469. 10.1111/psyp.12515

Pu, Y., Cheyne, D., Sun, Y., & Johnson, B. W. (2020). Theta oscillations support the interface between language and memory. *NeuroImage*, *215*, 1–12.

Silverman, R. D., Proctor, C. P., Harring, J. R., Doyle, B., Mitchell, M. A., & Meyer, A. G. (2014). Teachers' instruction and students' vocabulary and comprehension: An exploratory study with English monolingual and Spanish-English bilingual students in grades 3–5. *Reading Research Quarterly*, *49*(1), 31–60

Scharlach, T. D. (2008). START comprehending: Students and teachers actively reading text. *Reading Teacher*, *62*(1), 20–31.

Tarkiainen, A., Helenius, P., Hansen, P. C., Cornelissen, P. L., & Salmelin, R. (1999). Dynamics of letter string perception in the human occipitotemporal cortex. *Brain*, *122*, 2119–2132. 10.1093/brain/122.11.2119

van Moort, M. L., Jolles, D. D., Koornneef, A., & van den Broek, P. (2020). What you read versus what you know: Neural correlates of accessing context information and background knowledge in constructing a mental representation during reading. *Journal of Experimental Psychology. General*, *149*(11), 2084–2101.

White, T. G., Kim, J. S., Kingston, H. C., & Foster, L. (2014). Replicating the effects of a teacher-scaffolded voluntary summer reading program: The role of poverty. *Reading Research Quarterly*, *49*(1), 5–30.

Wright, T. S., Cervetti, G. N., Wise, C., & McClung, N. A. (2022). The Impact of knowledge-building through conceptually-coherent read alouds on vocabulary and comprehension. *Reading Psychology*, *43*(1), 70–84. 10.1080/02702711.2021.2020187

7
PHONOLOGY

> I enjoyed listening to Ayan Mitra's presentation on the reading brain. It makes sense to me that emergent readers use more phonological processing during reading, while more experienced readers use whole word recognition. Young readers are exposed to new, unfamiliar words each day and therefore must use phonics strategies to decipher not only how to say specific words, but to also determine their meaning. This makes me wonder if more experienced readers who are focusing on whole word recognition have stronger comprehension because they don't have to focus on those beginning phonics skills like the younger readers do?

The question the pre-service teacher asked is a perfect segue into our next section on understanding the different subskills, phonology, orthography, lexicality, and semantics that are involved in the reading process. This chapter focuses on instructional methods for teaching phonics and phonemic awareness that have been shown to be effective through educational research studies, while corroborating recent findings from neuroimaging studies of the brain.

Child Development

Early childhood literacy educators understand the importance of developing children's speech-to-print connections at home and in early school experiences. Speech-to-print concepts are developed through reading stories, playing alphabet games, exploring writing, drawing, and writing down children's words for them to read.

As children progress, they are invited into ever-expanding print experiences. Different genres and reading materials such as narrative stories, informational and procedural texts, poetry, songs, play scripts, and websites teach children how to navigate, enjoy, and understand different types of reading material. Yet, these materials make different demands

 DOI: 10.4324/9781003256199-8

on the reader (McNorgan et al., 2015). Wide reading, independent choice and reading discussions become increasingly important in children's literacy development.

By the time children reach adolescence, they are generally fluent readers. Interestingly, fluent readers take no more than half a second between the time they see a word and comprehension of its meaning. This ability to rapidly recognize words or word parts is developed in late childhood or adolescence.

Phonics

Phonics is a method for teaching people to read and write. Within this method, the sounds associated with letters are taught beginning with initial consonants, such as *d* in *dog*. Bear et al. (2012) describe a developmental sequence for how children learn to manipulate phonemes to spell words. **Phonemes** are the distinct units of sound that make up words, including *d* in *dog* and *sh* in *shop*. An adaptation of Bear et al.'s (2012) developmental spelling sequence is shown in Table 7.1.

As children experiment with English writing and are guided by teachers and family members, they first learn to represent words with beginning consonants. Often, the first letters children learn are the beginning consonants of their own name or the initial letter of words like *mom* and *dad*. People and experiences that are important to children become their topics for writing. Children often spontaneously write the sentence, *I love my family,* accompanied by a picture of all the members of the family including a pet if they have one. Children have heard and

Table 7.1 Developmental Spelling Sequence (Adapted from Bear et al., 2012)

Emergent & Letter Name Spelling Stage				
Spelling pattern	Beginning consonant	Final consonant	Short vowels	Diagraphs
Example	d (dog)	g (dog)	o (dog)	sh (shop)
Within Word Patterns Spelling Stage				
Spelling Pattern	Blends	Long vowels	Other vowels	
Example	sp (spin)	i – e (fine)	ar (car)	
Syllables & Affixes Spelling Stage				
Spelling pattern	Inflected endings	Syllable junctures	Unaccented final syllables	
Example	ed (glued)	tt (little)	le (little)	
Derivational Relations Spelling Stage				
Spelling pattern	Harder suffixes	Bases or roots		
Example	tion (position)	phon (phonograph)		

spoken these names many times. We know that language networks in the brain are used for the development of reading networks. This may be why children easily learn to read and write the names of people that are close to them. Emotion may also be connected to this learning. Emotions mediate thoughts, language, and behavior as they contribute to neuronal networks (Šimić et al., 2021).

When young children are given the tools for writing, such as crayons and paper, they will experiment with writing and drawing without direct instruction. Children mimic print found in their life experiences including business signs, cereal boxes, and television, among many other sources of environmental print. They also mimic the writing and texting of family members. Many children have valuable lap reading or bedtime reading experiences, which expose them to aspects of writing such as forms of print, print direction, and sound-print relationships (Clay, 2005). These literacy experiences build a wealth of knowledge that impacts reading, writing, and spelling development.

As children gain experience with letters, they begin to apply the **alphabetic principle**. This is the understanding that words are composed of letters that represent sounds and using this knowledge to spell or read unknown words. This provides the child with a self-teaching strategy for sounding out even unknown words with the help of a letter-by-letter progression for decoding. This adds to a register of words that the child may be able to recognize by sight. As children learn to read, they learn to associate letters, sounds, and the meaning of words.

Despite being an alphabetic language, English has a **deep orthography**, meaning that it is highly irregular and inconsistent in the relationship between letters and sounds. This is why children learning to read in English must learn to recognize some words by sight. The common storybook phrase, "once upon a time" is difficult to read based on the alphabetic principle alone. *Once* is highly irregular and the vowels in the rest of the phrase are associated with more than one sound. Also, the word "time" contains the letter E, which is not sounded at all.

Once children have learned the basics of decoding written words, they recognize many words without the need for slow decoding, saying each sound individually. Instead, they quickly retrieve the word from memory. Long-term memory is organized by networks of connections and it is important to the developing reader. In this way, readers use prior experiences to predict what a word will be (Price & Devlin, 2011).

Teaching Beginning Readers

Beginning readers need to know that print is used for communication and there are certain conventions that are used to make sure people understand what is written. Children must develop fluency with the alphabetic principle and learn about other cues that will help them read because the phonological network emerges in early childhood (Yu et al. 2018). Teachers provide supportive opportunities for students to develop these understandings in both structured and unstructured reading contexts as exemplified below (Scanlon & Anderson, 2020).

Learning to Read

Materials

Prepare a phonics inventory to assess students' phonemic knowledge.

Gather interesting, and meaningful books with few words on each page. Choose a book that highlights a letter or letters students need to learn or practice. This will be the focus book.

Prepare centers or stations around the classroom where children can read or work on tasks independently while the teacher works with a small group.

Goals

Use letters to represent the beginning sounds of words.

Use a pattern, picture, or beginning letter to predict a word from a focus book.

Spell target words from the focus book.

Procedure

Whole Group Lesson

Introduce the focus letter or letters to the whole class. Teach the letter name and sound or sounds it represents.

Read an enlarged version of the focus book, encouraging students to join in when they can read a word or phrase. Have fun with this.

Discuss how the pattern, picture, or beginning letter of a word helps their reading. The cues (pattern, picture, or beginning letter) depend on the cues the focus book contains.

Explain how the book will be used either in small groups for guided reading or in the library corner for independent reading.

Guided Reading

Gather a small group of children and give them each a copy of the focus book. Discuss the book based on what they remember from the whole group lesson.

As you listen to the children reading the book, help them use the strategies they learned in the whole group lesson.

Give the children magnetic letters, so they can arrange the letters to spell a word from the book. After the children try it, the teacher spells the word with the magnetic letters.

Finally, have the children write the word on paper.

In the lessons above, children receive explicit phonics instruction while also reading for meaning and enjoyment. They recognize cues in the text that help them read so they are not solely dependent on sounding out each letter one at a time. They have an opportunity to discuss the book orally, which helps them develop their verbal reasoning abilities.

The Reading Network

As children begin to learn sound-print relationships, the brain's reading network begins to develop (Alcauter et al., 2017). The reading network continues to build and become robust through associating words, letters, and meanings (Fischer-Baum et al., 2017). As children connect symbols on the page with meaningful words, the reading network becomes more organized, and children move away from phonetically decoding word parts. They develop a rapid ability to extract word meaning from their memory. Additional exposure to reading builds a reading network of increasing strength. Chapter 1 included models of reading with a generalized illustration of the brain's reading network.

The reading network integrates multiple areas of the brain needed for reading tasks. Visual processing, phonology, orthography, morphology, and semantics work together as required for different tasks. When we read a book for pleasure that has familiar vocabulary, our eyes scan the pages quickly, processing whole words to gain meaning. However, when we read a textbook with unfamiliar content or new vocabulary, we may have to decode some of the words and work harder to make meaning based on meaningful word parts (morphemes). Children draw upon phonological decoding and visual word form processing as needed (Twomey et al., 2015).

The reading network is not a linear progression from grapheme-phoneme processing to word recognition and comprehension. Both beginning and proficient readers use both phonology and semantics

(Jobard et al., 2011). As readers use phonology to solve unknown words, they are also using semantics to attach meaning to those words. These meanings provide information that helps the reader predict what the next word will be. Readers use meaning information along with phonological processing to understand the words within the written context to construct the meaning of the passage.

Early Writing

Meaningful contexts are important to early development of the reading network and higher-order processing. We illustrate this through the four-old kindergarten classroom of Ms. Hope.

Figure 7.1 shows the drawing of a four-year-old boy, Ramon, who is beginning to develop his reading network. Ramon used his knowledge of a video game to draw and write about the characters Luigi and Mario. L and M were among the first letters he produced in his writing.

Figure 7.1 Four-Year-Old Writing with Initial Consonants Written on Hats.

Ramon's teacher provided a classroom environment that encouraged experimenting with print. Ms. Hope dedicated the first 30 minutes of the school day to book browsing, when parents brought their children to school and the bus was arriving. After signing their name at the door, the children entered the classroom and went to the bookshelves and bins to choose books. They found a comfortable place to sit and began looking at illustrations. They made up storylines and talked to their friends and teacher about the stories.

Ms. Hope also provided a station with abundant writing materials: paper, envelopes, crayons, markers, pencils, and stickers. The children were encouraged to use this station to write letters to their friends and deposit them in the classroom mailbox. They also experimented with forms of writing such as shopping lists, recipes, and other types of writing seen at home or demonstrated by Ms. Hope.

Stations, also called centers, are an essential part of early childhood classrooms. These spaces allow children to explore instructional materials at their own pace while interacting with other children. Engaging in stations allows children to follow their interests, manage time, socially engage, and develop self-regulation (Berk & Meyers, 2013). Teachers carefully plan and design spaces for three to four children to work together. Some teachers like to have children follow a rotation from station to station. Other teachers allow students to move freely among the stations. Some common early childhood stations include book browsing, writing, building, dramatic play, art, and science. Ms. Hope also included a center for digital gameplay.

In addition to Ms. Hope's writing center, the children engaged in free writing every day. The children retrieved their journals from a bin and sat at tables with room for about six to eight. Ms. Hope and her assistant circulated among the children, asking, "What did you write today?" The teachers commented on the children's ideas, drawings, and texts. The teachers sometimes wrote the child's verbal description on the page. In this way, Ms. Hope demonstrated the concept that spoken words can be written down and read. Each day, the page was stamped with the month, day, and year, which allowed the journals to be assessed for progress.

After writing, Ms. Hope chose a child or two to share their writing. She used a document projector and computer software to capture additions made to the page during the sharing time. Classmates offered questions, comments, and suggestions. Ms. Hope wrote the young author's words on the page while the other children watched via the projection system. Here is an example sharing time dialogue.

Classmate (pointing to page projected on the screen):	"Who is that?"
Author:	My dad.

Teacher: Your dad! I'll write *dad* by his picture. *d-aaa-d.*

By sounding the letters while writing, Ms. Hope demonstrated phoneme-letter relationships. Over the school year, the children had many demonstrations of phoneme-letter correspondence, and they began to use more and more letters and whole words in their journal writing (Spence et al., 2012). The children engaged in writing and sharing every day, with all children having a chance to share and discuss their ideas with classmates.

As children learn the alphabetic principle, they develop both as writers and readers. Opportunities to interact with books and other texts are essential to this development. Book browsing, freewriting, and sharing in Ms. Hope's classroom provided children with a literacy-rich environment for learning concepts of print. Extensive literacy opportunities are continued as children move into elementary school.

Phonemic Awareness

Phonemic awareness is the ability of an individual to reflect and manipulate the sound structure of spoken words. Some researchers describe a hierarchical pattern to the progression of phonological awareness where children first isolate larger units like words or syllables, then intermediate units like onsets and rimes, and then finally smaller units like phonemes (Treiman & Zukowski, 1996). The **onset** is the first consonant or consonant blend in a word and the **rime** is the rest of the word after the initial consonant(s). For example, in the word *fright*, *fr-* is an onset, and *-ight* is a rime. If you ask a child to take off the *fr* in *fright*, and ask, "What is left?" The child will answer by saying, "-ight."

Increasing Phonemic Awareness and Word Reading

Children learn at varying paces, so within a classroom, students will need many types of books and other texts at different levels of difficulty. Motivation and interest are very important when selecting books. Sometimes children will work extra hard to read a book that is difficult yet interesting. Conversely, a child may be interested in the topic of a book that is quite easy to read. Allowing students to make book choices acknowledges and encourages self-reliance and interest in reading. Reading enjoyment is important because, through wide reading, children are exposed to spelling, sight words, ideas, structures, and vocabulary.

Throughout children's early reading experiences, they are exposed to words containing consonant blends, long vowels, and other vowels such as the r-controlled vowels found in words like *car, fork,* and *hurt.* In these words, the vowel sound changes from the usual short vowel sound in *at, off,* and *up.* Children need guidance in understanding these nuances of the English language. English originated through a mixture of Germanic, Norse, and Norman French. Later, French, Latin, and Greek words were added. Indigenous and African languages have also contributed to English vocabulary. Because of these influences, children are sure to encounter words that are difficult to decode. English words contain phonemes, affixes, and roots that arose from the melding of languages that became modern English.

As students move into the upper elementary grades, they will encounter new words from the content they are studying in math, science, and social studies. Greek and Latin affixes and roots such as *hemi-*, *hyper-*, *sub-*, *-able*, and *-logue* can be found in many English words. By studying affixes and roots, children can become word detectives or word collectors, searching for patterns in words and collecting lists of similar words. One way to engage in this word work is through the joint development of wall charts as collection points for words with similar patterns. Children can also make spelling notebooks to collect words for later use in their writing. Another method for working with words is interactive writing (Jones & Reutzel, 2015) as described in the following example.

Interactive Writing

Preparation

Large chart paper and marking pens will be needed for group writing. White masking tape can be used to cover mistakes so that the correct letters can be written on the tape.

Goals

Use print concepts, phonological awareness, letter knowledge, and sentence construction to generate a meaningful text.

Procedure

With the students seated close to the chart paper, make a group decision on a topic for writing. A shared experience or academic content can provide a topic.

Discuss the topic with students, prompting them to plan the writing. "Let's talk about what should be at the beginning, the middle, and the end."

Ask questions to prompt students in generating the first sentence. "How should we start?"

As a child volunteers a sentence, and everyone agrees, repeat what the child said and count the words in the sentence.

Analyze the letter-sound correspondence in the words, listening to each sound and asking the children what letters represent the sounds. Also, use children's spelling knowledge when offered.

The teacher can start writing on the chart paper, but at certain points, offer the marking pen to students who want to write letters or words.

Prompt children to identify word parts and letter clusters. Prompt connections to similar words and word parts in the text and other resources such as a word wall or their memories.

Monitor the writing and provide correct spelling if someone makes a mistake on the chart paper. Use white masking tape to cover over the mistake and write the correct spelling on the tape.

After the writing is completed, ask the group to read it orally.

Ask students if the writing is clear and makes sense. Keep the finished writing in a convenient place for the children to re-read multiple times.

As shown above, interactive writing is a method that can improve student reading and writing through scaffolded instruction at the phoneme, word, and meaning stages through guided, authentic writing. Interactive writing can be implemented with the whole class, in small groups, or individually to develop children's phonemic knowledge and spelling skills. The following example shows a teacher working individually with a child.

> A first-grade boy, Sye, who spoke Chinese at home was rapidly learning English. Ms. Kelly saw that Sye had written a list of words in his notebook. She asked him what else he would like to write. As Sye dictated a sentence, Ms. Kelly helped him transfer his idea to paper.
>
> Sye wanted to write *I like* but started to write *like* without leaving a space, so Ms. Kelly helped him erase and leave a space. She helped him write correct sentences in this way until they

came to the word *dribble.* Because of the consonant cluster, *bble*, Ms. Kelly wrote a series of lines to segment the sounds, *d-r-i-bb-le.* Then she guided Sye in writing the letters on the lines (Figure 7.2).

When Sye's mother and father came to pick him up, Sye eagerly read his notebook to them. He read four sentences, "I like to run dribble and shoot," "I swim in a race," "I win the race," "I can swim fast."

Interactive writing sessions may not always result in every word spelled perfectly; however, it is important to strive for correct writing because the interactively written text will be read and re-read to gain reading fluency. In the first-grade example, Sye read sentences from his journal to his parents. Students may also read their interactive texts to themselves, classmates, the teacher, and family members. In Sye's interactive writing, he combined letters, sounds, word parts, whole words, and meanings.

You may wonder how it is possible for a teacher to work individually with children in a busy classroom. Next, we describe classroom structures that support students in developing phonemic awareness, and phonetic skills.

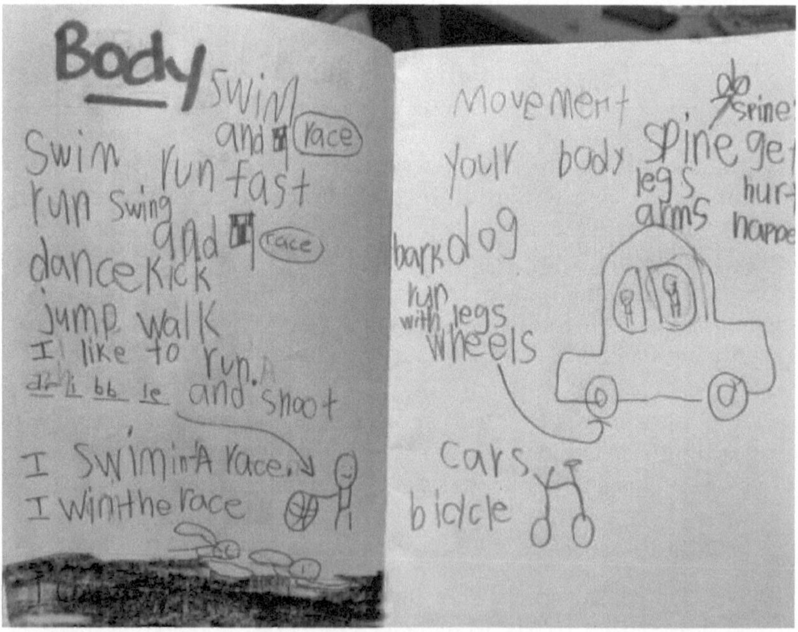

Figure 7.2 Sye's Interactive Writing Notebook.

Shared, Guided, and Independent Reading

Shared reading is one way to help children develop phonemic awareness and word reading (Flack et al., 2018). **Shared reading** supports children's reading through the use of a common text such as an oversized, "big" book, a book projected on a screen, or individual copies of the same book or short text. As the teacher reads softly, his voice supports the children as they read along. The teacher and students work together to solve problem words as they arise. The teacher might plan ahead by covering a word with paper. When they come to that word, the teacher can reveal it letter by letter, helping the children to see how to use the meaning and grammar of the sentence along with the beginning, middle, and end of a word to solve the covered word. The goal of shared reading is to provide children with tools for making meaning and solving unknown words on their own. Shared reading can also influence children's narrative skills (Gámez et al., 2016).

Guided Reading

Children should be provided with opportunities to solve their own problems as they read with the teacher's support (Iaquinta, 2006). **Guided reading** supports children as they practice reading strategies on their own. This involves children reading the text as the teacher listens, ready to provide guidance if needed. Guided reading allows teachers to assess whether individual children are transferring reading strategies they have learned during shared reading.

Independent Reading

Providing opportunities for independent reading in the classroom allows the teacher to assess if children use word-solving strategies on their own. It is important that students self-select their books and other texts for independent reading because they are more likely to be motivated, focused, and self-aware when they choose their own reading material (Scharlach, 2008).

Table 7.2 describes how shared reading, guided reading, and independent reading gradually shift the responsibility for using reading strategies to the children. The table is followed by an example of shared, guided, and independent reading.

> Mr. Andre had written a fun poem by Shel Silverstein on a large piece of chart paper. He chose the poem, *Snowball* to talk about the *ow* digraph. A **digraph** is a combination of letters that represent one sound. See Table 7.3 for more examples of diagraphs.

Table 7.2 Responsibilities during Shared, Guided, and Independent Reading

Instructional Method	*Teacher Instruction*	*Teacher Support*	*Student's Role*
Shared reading	The teacher usually chooses text and plans to discuss the words and meaning of the text.	The teacher reads softly while the children also read.	The students read with the teacher's voice support.
Guided reading	The teacher usually chooses text and plans to listen while a child reads. Support is given through questioning and strategy suggestions.	The teacher helps with unknown words to reinforce strategies. Meaning making is monitored as the child reads.	The students read independently unless unable to solve an unknown word or the meaning breaks down.
Independent reading	The teacher sets a routine and guidelines for independent reading time. A well-stocked classroom library is provided.	The teacher encourages student choice of texts. Reading behaviors are observed and noted.	The students choose texts and read independently, solving their own problems.

First, Mr. Andre read the poem to the children, who enjoyed the humor and playful language. Then he invited the children to read the poem along with him, while he pointed at each word. He asked the children, "Who can find the words that have the *ow* sound?" Mr. Andre gave a marking pen to one child to underline each instance of *ow* in the poem. Then they all read the poem again before moving on to independent reading. To conclude, Mr. Andre asked the children to look for *ow* words in the individual books they would be reading. Over time, the children collected these words on a wall chart near the classroom library.

While the children were reading their individual books, Mr. Andre gathered a small group of children who were reading fluently at their grade level yet needed help maintaining the meaning of the books they read. He asked them, "Do you ever finish a page and think, 'I don't get it?'

Table 7.3 Examples of Vowel and Consonant Digraphs

Vowel Diagraph	ow	snow	show	blow	crow
	ou	ouch	count	pouch	pound
	ai	pain	faint	train	wait
Consonant digraph	sh	show	shine	shell	short
	ch	chair	choose	charm	chin
	wh	when	why	whether	what

> Sometimes that happens to me. One strategy for understanding a book is to stop and think. Let's try it today. After each page, stop and think about what you read, then tell what you think." Then Mr. Andre listened to each child read a page including stopping to think and telling their thoughts. In this way, Mr. Andre guided the children toward better comprehension.

Shared reading, guided reading, and independent reading are structures that provide instructional support in reading while moving children toward greater independence.

When the children stopped to think while reading their books, they developed associations between the words on the page and the meanings they represented. By talking about their thinking, they reinforced and expanded their understanding.

Below we provide another example of guided reading (Rodgers et al., 2016). In this example, children are introduced to a new story they have not read before.

Scaffolding a New Story

Using Comprehension Strategies

This teaching method can be used in guided reading or tutoring.

Preparation

Determine the student's instructional level for reading. For example, provide several books and ask the student to look through each of them, then choose one they could read successfully. Then ask the student to choose one that would be interesting. Ask about other interests the student would like to read about.

Choose a book that is on the student's instructional level and would be interesting to the student.

Goals

Read a book using meaning, structure, or visual information to solve unknown words.

Enjoy reading about an interesting topic.

Procedure

Introduce the topic of the book. Ask the student to page through the book, looking at the pictures. Point out phrases or language structures that may be difficult for the student. Look at one or two words and talk about the structure of the words.

Ask the student to begin reading the text, starting with the title.

Do not interrupt the reading unnecessarily.

When the student comes to an unknown word, and it becomes clear that they need help solving it, use these suggestions:

- Notice the information the student is using to try to solve the word
    - Meaning: story background, information from pictures, the meaning of a sentence or word.
    - Structural: parts of speech, the structure of sentence or passage
    - Visual: letter-sound correspondence, word length, familiar word parts
- Decide what information the student is not using. Meaning? Structural? Visual?
- Prompt the student to use a new source of information to solve the word, either meaning, structural, or visual.
- Provide a lower level of help when the student's response to the first prompt was closer to solving the word. Provide more help if the student's response was not close or was moving away from solving the word.

When the student finishes reading, you can ask them to retell the story in their own words, or ask about their personal connections to the story.

The book will be read again in the next lesson.

Over time, the teacher will raise the reading level of the books to more complex material.

Early literacy experiences are important for developing the reading network. The brain's neural networks seem to have more plasticity in the first years of school and increases in the volume of the reading network have been found during the early stage of reading (Phan et al., 2021). This is why, it is important for parents and early years teachers to encourage literacy with enjoyable games, rhymes, and wordplay.

Word Sorts, Games, Rhyming, and Word Play

Children enjoy the challenge of games and can benefit from word sorts, games, rhyming, and wordplay. Bear et al. (2016) have developed word sorts and word games for the developmental spelling levels of children. For example, with a stack of word cards with different endings, children are encouraged to sort the words in any way they choose. The child may decide to sort according to ending such as *at, bat, cat, sat* and *it, sit, bit.* Or the child may decide to sort according to the initial consonant. By encouraging children to sort according to their own preferences, the children must analyze the words and make decisions. This is more engaging and motivating for the child than being told they must sort a certain way. It also requires higher-level thinking processes.

Games also benefit children's literacy development. Board games and card games can be easily developed for wordplay. For example, the card game, *Go Fish* is easy to make and play. A double set of playing cards can be made with words on each card. The children must ask if their partner has a certain word contained in the child's hand. If the card is obtained, the pair is kept by the child. If the card is not in the partner's hand, the partner says, "Go fish" and the child must draw a card from a pile. The child with the most pairs wins the game. This is an enjoyable game for practicing phonemes, roots, or affixes.

Rhymes and prosody aid in developing phonemic awareness. **Rhymes** involve similar word endings and **prosody** involves patterns of rhythm and sound. When children learn rhymes in poetry or songs, they make connections between words that sound the same (Woods, 2003). Patterns of rhythm and sound support children's literacy development because of prosody's role in language acquisition (Holliman et al., 2014) and can enhance phonics instruction. For example, the old favorite, *Twinkle, Twinkle Little Star* is an excellent song for teaching r-controlled vowels.

Mr. Manny printed the song lyrics on a large poster, illustrated with shiny stick-on stars.

Twinkle, twinkle little star
How I wonder what you are.
Up above the world so high
Like a diamond in the sky.
Twinkle, twinkle little star
How I wonder what you are.

As the children sang the song, Mr. Manny pointed to each word with a pointer. After singing, Mr. Manny pointed to the word *star* and explained that the A in *star* has a different sound than the A in *cat* or the A in *make*. This is because the R influences the sound of A. Mr. Manny asked the children if they could find another word in which the R influences A. The children were quick to point out the word *are*.

There are many rhyming poems and songs that have been favorites throughout the generations and new ones are constantly being written. When choosing poems and songs, look for literary quality and a melodious sound. Fun, lovely, lyrical, or silly, songs and poems are well-remembered and repeated often. Children sing these songs at home once they have learned them at school and when the songs and poems are shared with parents, they can join in the fun.

Wordplay is also beneficial for children. One parent engaged her children in a word train. Lana began with a word she had chosen, *mint*. Bo had to think of a word that starts with the last letter of *mint*, so he chose *tank*. Mother chose the word *kiss*. Then it was Lana's turn again and she chose the word, *silly*. The family continued to take turns until they could not think of any word that would fit. Bo liked to keep a count of how many words each person chose, and announced the winner, the person who had chosen the most words using the correct letter.

I Spy is another game that can be used for wordplay. The first player chooses something in the room and says, "I spy with my little eye. I see something that starts with *ch*." The other players must look around the room until they find the object that starts with *ch*. In this way, children develop phonemic awareness by connecting the sounds of letters to words. These word games can be used in school or teachers might encourage families to play the games at home.

Involving parents and families in phonemic awareness activities will benefit the children in your classroom and the other children in the family. Teachers can provide ideas for games and can send home books and interactive writing notebooks for children to read to their family members. This extends the learning of reading beyond the school day and provides information for families on fun and engaging reading activities. Rather than sending worksheets for homework, enjoyable reading and phonemic awareness activities can become a valued part of family recreational time.

Research-based instructional practices such as interactive writing, learning centers, shared, guided, independent reading, and wordplay can help children develop a strong reading network. This network begins to develop early as children begin making connections between words they hear and the text that represents oral language. Soon, children recognize whole words, reducing the need to phonetically decode each word. The direct and indirect reading routes are activated as needed depending on the text being read, thus areas of the brain interact during the reading process. Instruction that highlights meaning, demonstrates phonemes and builds word memory will build connections between areas of the brain used for visual, phonological, and semantic processes.

Dyslexia

Educators and researchers do not always agree on how to define dyslexia. We present the view, that dyslexia is not a condition that causes a reading problem. Dyslexia is a label. This label describes the lower end of a continuum of reading ability. Across individuals, there is variation in reading development. The label **dyslexia** is used for an unexpected difficulty learning to read despite adequate opportunity and instruction. Dyslexia is not used for individuals with hearing, visual, or significant intellectual disabilities. Dyslexia is not used when the person has not received adequate instruction in reading (Catts & Petscher, 2022).

Neuroscientists studying dyslexia have found that some people do not adequately develop the dorsal or indirect route for reading. Instead, the person may develop compensatory mechanisms and greater development of the ventral or direct route for reading and increased white matter pathways in the right hemisphere of the brain (Pugh et al., 2001; Zuk, et al., 2021). Dyslexia continues to be explored through neuroimaging. Yet because reading development is influenced by many factors that interact in complex ways, no single deficit has been consistently associated with identifying dyslexia (Catts & Petscher, 2022).

Recent findings in studies of dyslexia have identified possible risk factors. A reader could exhibit problems with phonological awareness, rapid automatized naming, oral language, visual processing, or attention (see Table 7.4). There also may be genetic factors involved, however, there is no one gene that determines dyslexia. Rather, multiple genes working together may constitute a risk factor.

Even when risk factors are present, positive factors can promote resilience and allow an individual to avoid the label of dyslexia (Table 7.5). Positive factors include high-quality reading instruction that includes explicit phonics instruction and the development of verbal reasoning skills. Another

Table 7.4 Dyslexia Risk Factors

Phonological awareness	Impeded ability of an individual to reflect and manipulate the sound structure of spoken words.
Rapid automatized naming	Impeded ability to name words, letters, pictures, or objects quickly and automatically.
Oral language	Impeded ability to articulate sounds, word parts, sentences, vocabulary, or social language use.
Visual processing	Impeded ability to perceive, analyze, and think with visual patterns.
Attention	Impeded ability to focus on certain environmental features, while ignoring other aspects.

positive factor is persistence through difficulty and social-emotional resilience. Students who are hopeful, goal-oriented, and take control of their learning can reduce the effects of risk factors (Idan & Margalit, 2014).

This chapter has stressed the importance of high-quality instruction that can help children develop positive factors for reading success. High-quality instruction involves teaching the alphabetic principle through explicit instruction. An understanding of children's spelling development can guide teachers as they implement phonics instruction, shared reading, guided reading, interactive writing, and wordplay. These activities help children develop their phonemic awareness as they manipulate sounds within words. Reading instruction that includes meaningful reading, writing, speaking, and listening opportunities develops children's verbal reasoning skills and goal-oriented learning.

Table 7.5 Positive Factors for Resilience

High-quality reading instruction	Instruction that includes explicit phonics instruction and the development of verbal reasoning skills.
Persistence	The ability to remain highly engaged in tasks even when confronted with failure.
Social-emotional resilience	The ability to cope with learning challenges.

Did You Know?

You can design learning centers and stations that are successful for all students. A useful guide for planning and developing learning centers and stations was created by the Center for Research on Education, Diversity & Excellence, US Department of Education.

http://manoa.hawaii.edu/coe/crede/wp-content/uploads/Hilberg_et_al_20031.pdf

Food for Thought

Neuroscientific studies have shown that reading is not accomplished in a step-by-step process of phoneme, word, and meaning. How does the reading network integrate processes during reading?

Think about yourself as a reader. Do you sound out every word? What do you do when you encounter an unknown word? What do you do when you lose track of the meaning of a text? How can knowing your own reading process impact how you teach reading?

Bibliography

Alcauter, S., Garcia-Mondragon, L., Garcia-Tabuenca, Z., Moreno, M. B., Oritz, J. J., & Barrios, F. A. (2017). Resting state functional connectivity of the anterior striatum and prefrontal cortex predicts reading performance in school-age children. *Brain and Language*, *174*, 94–102.

Bear, D. R., Invernizzi, M., Templeton, S., & Johnston, F. (2016). *Words Their Way: Word Study for Phonics, Vocabulary, and Spelling Instruction (6th ed.)*. Pearson.

Bear, D. R., Negrete, S., & Cathey, S. (2012). Developmental literacy instruction with struggling readers across three stages. *New England Reading Association Journal*, *48*(1), 1–9.

Berk, L. E., & Meyers, A. B. (2013). The role of make-believe play in the development of executive function: Status of research and future directions. *American Journal of Play*, *6*(1), 98–110.

Catts, H. W., & Petscher, Y. (2022). A cumulative risk and resilience model of dyslexia. *Journal of Learning Disabilities*, *55*(3), 171–184. 10.1177/00222194211037062

Fischer-Baum, S., Bruggemann, D., Gallego, I. F., Li, D. S. P., & Tamez, E. R. (2017). Decoding levels of representation in reading: A representational similarity approach. *Cortex: A Journal Devoted to the Study of the Nervous System and Behavior*, *90*, 88–102.

Flack, Z. M., Field, A. P., & Horst, J. S. (2018). The effects of shared storybook reading on word learning: A meta-analysis. *Developmental Psychology*, *54*(7), 1334–1346.

Gámez, P. B., González, D., & Urbin, L. M. (2017). Shared book reading and English learners' narrative production and comprehension. *Reading Research Quarterly*, *52*(3), 275–290.

Glezer, L. S., Eden, G., Jiang, X., Luetje, M., Napoliello, E., Kim, J., & Riesenhuber, M. (2016). Uncovering phonological and orthographic selectivity across the reading network using fMRI-RA. *NeuroImage*, *138*, 248–256.

Hall, A., Toland, M., Grisham-Brown, J., & Graham, S. (2014). Exploring interactive writing as an effective practice for increasing head start students' alphabet knowledge skills. *Early Childhood Education Journal*, *42*(6), 423–430.

Holliman, A., Critten, S., Lawrence, T., Harrison, E., Wood, C., & Hughes, D. (2014). Modeling the relationship between prosodic sensitivity and early literacy. *Reading Research Quarterly*, *49*(4), 469–482.

Iaquinta, A. (2006). Guided reading: A research-based response to the challenges of early reading Instruction. *Early Childhood Education Journal*, *33*(6), 413–418.

Idan, O., & Margalit, M. (2014). Socioemotional self-perceptions, family climate, and hopeful thinking among students with learning disabilities and typically achieving students from the same classes. *Journal of Learning Disabilities*, *47*(2), 136–152. 10.1177/0022219412439608

Jobard, G., Vigneau, M., Simon, G., & Tzourio-Mazoyer, N. (2011). The weight of skill: Interindividual variability of reading related brain activation patterns in fluent readers. *Journal of Neurolinguistics*, *24*(1), 113–132.

Jones, C. D. & Reutzel, D. R. (2015). Write to read: Investigating the reading-writing relationship of code-level early literacy skills. *Reading & Writing Quarterly*, *31*(4), 297–315, DOI: 10.1080/10573569.2013.850461

McNorgan, C., Chabal, S., O'Young, D., Lukic, S., & Booth, J. R. (2015). Task dependent lexicality effects support interactive models of reading: A meta-analytic neuroimaging review. *Neuropsychologia*, *67*, 148–158.

Phan, T. V., Sima, D., Smeets, D., Ghesquière, P., Wouters, J., & Vandermosten, M. (2021). Structural brain dynamics across reading development: A longitudinal MRI study from kindergarten to grade 5. *Human Brain Mapping*, *42*(14), 4497–4509.

Price, C. J., & Devlin, J. T. (2011). The interactive account of ventral occipitotemporal contributions to reading. *Trends in Cognitive Sciences*, *15*(6), 246–253.

Pugh, K. R., Mencl, W. E., Jenner, A. R., Lee, J. R., Katz, L., Frost, S. J., Shaywitz, S. E., & Shaywitz, B. A. (2001). Neuroimaging studies of reading development and reading disability. *Learning Disabilities Research & Practice*, *16*(4), 240–249.

Rodgers, E., D'Agostino, J. V., Harmey, S. J., Kelly, R. H., & Brownfield, K. (2016). Examining the nature of scaffolding in an early literacy intervention. *Reading Research Quarterly*, *51*(3), 345–360.

Sandak, R., Mencl, W. E., Frost, S. J., & Pugh, K. R. (2004). The neurobiological basis of skilled and impaired reading: Recent findings and new directions. *Scientific Studies of Reading*, *8*, 273–292.

Scanlon, D. M., & Anderson, K. L. (2020). Using context as an assist in word solving: The contributions of 25 years of research on the interactive strategies approach. *Reading Research Quarterly*, *55*, S19–S34. 10.1002/rrq.335

Scharlach, T. D. (2008). START comprehending: Students and teachers actively reading text. *Reading Teacher*, *62*(1), 20–31.

Šimić, G., Tkalčić, M., Vukić, V., Mulc, D., Španić, E., Šagud, M., Olucha-Bordonau, F. E., Vukšić, M., & R Hof, P. (2021). Understanding emotions: Origins and roles of the amygdala. *Biomolecules*, *11*(6), 823. 10.3390/biom11060823

Spence, L. K., DeFord, D., & Reardon, H. (2012). Spanish speakers writing in an English-language pre-kindergarten. In Dunston, P., Fullerton, S., Bates, C. C., Headley, K., & Stecker, P. (Eds.), *61st Yearbook of the Literacy Research Association* (pp. 105–118). Literacy Research Association.

Treiman, R., & Zukowski, A. (1996). Children's sensitivity to syllables, onsets, rimes, and phonemes. *Journal of Experimental Child Psychology, 61*, 193–215. 10.1006/jecp.1996.0014

Twomey, T., Waters, D., Price, C. J., Kherif, F., Woll, B., & MacSweeney, M. (2015). Identification of the regions involved in phonological assembly using a novel paradigm. *Brain and Language, 150*, 45–53.

Woods, C. S. (2003). Phonemic awareness: A crucial bridge to reading. *Montessori Life, 15*(2), 37–39.

Yu, X., Raney, T., Perdue, M. V., Zuk, J., Ozernov, P. O., Becker, B. L. C., Raschle, N. M., & Gaab, N. (2018). Emergence of the neural network underlying phonological processing from the prereading to the emergent reading stage: A longitudinal study. *Human Brain Mapping, 39*(5), 2047–2063.

Zuk, J., Dunstan, J., Norton, E., Yu, X., Ozernov-Palchik, O., Wang, Y., Hogan, T. P., Gabrieli, J. D. E., & Gaab, N. (2021). Multifactorial pathways facilitate resilience among kindergarteners at risk for dyslexia: A longitudinal behavioral and neuroimaging study. *Developmental Science, 24*(1), 1–18.

8
LANGUAGING

> One month into the school year, Miguel joined Ms. Bradley's second-grade class. Ms. Bradley spoke English and was learning Spanish. Recently arriving from Mexico, Miguel spoke Spanish fluently and was beginning to learn English. The class was busy writing about non-fiction topics using internet sources and bilingual library books. They each had chosen a topic. Miguel joined right in, choosing sharks as his topic.
>
> Miguel liked to talk and was not at all shy. He used his emerging English constantly as the children researched and wrote. After writing, revising, and editing, the children wrote a final copy with several pages of text and illustrations. They wrote book titles, made covers and illustrations, then stapled the books together. They wrote a paragraph about themselves as authors for the back cover.
>
> Once the books were complete, parents, family members, friends, and siblings were invited to the classroom and each child read their book. Miguel had written his book in English. He read it proudly as the audience listened with amazement that he had progressed so rapidly. Miguel looked up expectantly as he finished reading and everyone burst into vigorous applause.

In the scene above, Miguel, his classmates, and his teachers were **languaging.** This refers to using any of one's available linguistic resources to communicate with others and function in a social context (Garcia & Wei, 2014). The brain's language networks are capable of integrating multiple languages for communication. Through speaking, listening, and reading in both Spanish and English, the class was using all their available linguistic resources to write their books.

Do you or someone you know speak both English and an additional language? The authors of this book, Spence and Mitra, are fascinated with the languages of the world and are currently learning one or two. Many of Spence's friends and students in Arizona grew up bilingually.

DOI: 10.4324/9781003256199-9

It is common for people in the southwestern United States to speak both English and Spanish. Mitra grew up in India, speaking English, Hindi, and Bengali. Many people in India grow up multilingually, speaking the local languages as well as English.

Bilingual and **multilingual** refer to people's regular use two or more languages. A shorthand way of referring to a person's language is L1, the first language a person learns, and L2, the second language a person learns. L1 is sometimes called a **heritage language** because it is passed down from parents and the culture. Some children learn two or more languages simultaneously because their parents are multilingual. Some people speak more than two languages and so the terms L1 and L2 do not precisely describe them. **Emergent bilinguals, English learners,** and multilingual learners are other labels used for those who are learning English as a new language.

Over the past two decades, a growing area of neuroscience research has been in bilingual language processing. Factors such as age when a language is acquired, amount of exposure to a language, and knowledge of a language can all impact brain structure and function. Yet the effects of these factors and other differences in bilingual experiences are debated and much work is needed to form a complete picture of the brain's representation of two or more languages (Sulpizio et al., 2020).

This chapter discusses the benefits of multilingualism and bilingual education, followed by what we have learned about how languages are learned and the effects on brain development over the lifespan. This information is illustrated by examples of instruction for multilingual learners.

Benefits of Multilingualism

Learning a new language can seem intimidating to many people, yet it could be argued that everyone has smatterings of multiple languages they have learned. We learn some of this in school, yet often feel we are not "fluent" enough to use it. You may know how to count and recite the days of the week in the language you learned in school. Traces of multiple languages are also embedded in American culture. A fun festival, *Cinco de Mayo* is Spanish. Some favorite desserts, *crème brulé* and *croissant* are French. *Karaoke* and *sushi* are Japanese. Let's celebrate our knowledge of languages!

About 50% of people worldwide are bilingual or multilingual and their language practices vary considerably. This means that bilingualism is not a situation where either you are, or you are not. Bilingualism is complex and must be seen as a spectrum on which there is a variety of contextual factors at play (Di Pisa, 2021). Did you grow up speaking two languages every day? Did you learn a second language as a child or as an adult? Did you grow up in a foreign country, then return to your parent's heritage language community? Do you speak two or more languages only at school or all the time? The answers to these and other questions reflect the spectrum of bilingualism.

The language network in the brain activates in the same ways across languages, as shown in a study of 45 diverse languages. Across languages, the network is strongly integrated across components and supports broadly common features of language (Malik-Moraleda et al., 2022).

Language is acquired through social interactions with our families, school, and society, so people should not be afraid of learning a language. However, misconceptions about language learning persist. For a long time, people thought two languages would interfere with each other. As a result, languages different from the school language were suppressed. This still takes place today in some schools and language restrictive policies have been codified into law in some states in the United States. Teachers like Ms. Bradley are helping to reverse these misguided practices.

The main benefit of learning a new language is the ability to communicate with so many more people. When one speaks two or more languages, all languages are simultaneously active in the brain. That is why people can switch from one language to another when needed. Knowing what language to use at a given time requires additional cognitive control. Moving between languages places demands on executive and language control networks. Because of this increased demand, the brain seems to develop improved executive control functions and increased efficiency in task performance over time (Di Pisa et al., 2021). As discussed in previous chapters, executive and language networks are essential to literacy development (Figure 8.1).

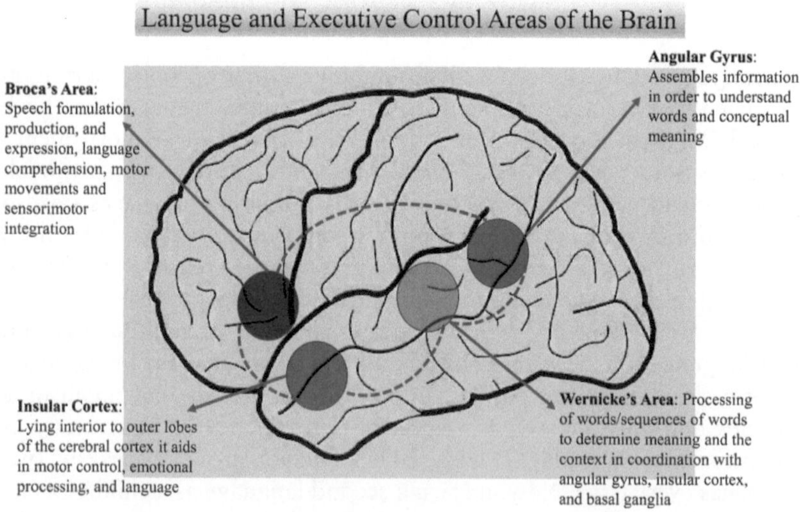

Figure 8.1 Language and Executive Control Areas of the Brain.

Given the neuroscience findings on the cognitive benefits of bilingualism, it is not surprising that bilingual programs contribute to better family communication, improve students' literacy skills, and result in improved English reading scores (Alvear, 2019; Steele et al., 2017). Dual-language students' mathematics and science skills remain on par with students in traditional classrooms while students gain skills in the target language (Thomas et al., 1993). Let's look at some of these bilingual programs in detail.

Bilingual Education

Bilingual School Models

In US schools, bilingualism has an extensive history because immigration has always brought multiple languages into classrooms (Crawford, 2004). In the 1800s, students in various communities grew up speaking German, Dutch, French, and Spanish. These languages were often accepted within those communities. However, in some places, languages were discriminated against. Asian, Indigenous, and some Spanish-speaking people's languages were devalued in schools. Around the 1900s, as additional immigration continued, an English-only ideology arose in the United States. English-only ideology in the United States reflects the belief that the country is monolingual, and it is assumed that everyone in the country should speak English. This is despite the fact that a variety of languages have always been spoken in the United States.

Because of English-only ideologies, students who come to school with languages other than English are often thought of as lacking. This is called a **deficit perspective.** On the other hand, schools are increasingly offering enrichment programs that teach world languages to native English speakers. For example, one urban school offers half-day instruction in Mandarin or Spanish.

Instead of treating one group of students as lacking and another group as worthy of special treatment, schools should leverage the language experience of bilingual students. Bilingual students bring knowledge of two languages to school. The heritage language and English should both be developed and valued.

Most educators have moved beyond the idea that bilingualism is a deficit and instead consider it an asset. Many classroom teachers now encourage bilingual conversations in class, on the school grounds, and within the homes of their students. Parents increasingly understand the benefits of bilingualism and use their heritage language and literacies at home to help children retain bilingualism and promote brain development. Administrators and policymakers also wish to reap the benefits and as a result, bilingual programs such as dual-language immersion are now proliferating across the United States.

There are several school models for providing instruction in two or more languages, but each program does not place equal value on speakers of languages other than English. First, we will discuss programs that focus on these students.

Bilingual Programs

Bilingual instruction allows students to learn academic content in their heritage language while they develop English for everyday communication. This can be accomplished in a variety of ways. In a **transitional bilingual** model, the class is made up of all heritage language speakers and all instruction is in the heritage language. This continues through the primary grades and incrementally transitions to all English in later grades when heritage speakers are in mixed classes with native English speakers. In bilingual maintenance models, half the students in a class speak a heritage language that is prevalent in the community. The other half of the class are native English speakers. The goal is for all students to become fully literate in two languages. The following scene illustrates a group of students who are transitioning from Spanish to English instruction in fourth grade.

> Ms. Pacheco is walking among four tables that are covered with paper flowers. Each table seats five or six students who are making the flowers for an upcoming Mexican holiday celebration. The teacher and students are chatting quietly, enjoying the break from math class. The whiteboard in the front of the classroom is covered with division exercises that have been completed by the students. Ms. Pacheco explained the division process using English, clarifying the concepts in Spanish. She demonstrated division using both US and Mexican methods. Many of the students were familiar with the Mexican method, which involves fewer steps to solving a division problem.

In the classroom example, Ms. Pacheco used Spanish to clarify math concepts. This was important because the students had been learning math in Spanish since kindergarten. By presenting the concepts first in English and then using Spanish to clarify them, she made sure the concepts were understood. Ms. Pacheco also included the students' cultural knowledge of math. This was important for completing homework with help from their parents. The students and parents needed to speak the same math language.

Studies have found that bilingual education can help promote bilingualism without sacrificing English proficiency and can lead to improved performance on standardized reading and math tests (Padilla et al., 2013; Slavin et al., 2011). These results may be explained because the brain processes both languages through the same language network. Language involves phonology, word meanings, and grammar in speaking any language. As a person learns a non-native language, the volume of grey matter in regions involving language increases and white matter connections are strengthened. This expansion reverts back to normal if language learning stops, but continuous exposure to the new language enhances structural connectivity in the brain (Pliatsikas, 2020).

Dual-Language Immersion

Another model of bilingual education is **dual-language immersion.** In dual-language schools, the school day is split between languages, immersing students in academic content such as math and science in a world language for a half day each. Dual-language schools may offer instruction in Spanish, Mandarin Chinese, French, German, or other world languages. In these schools, English speakers learn a world language while continuing to learn in English for half the day. Dual-language schools tend to be promoted in affluent, native English-speaking communities (Chang-Bacon, 2021). This contrasts with language ideologies that extinguish heritage languages through neglect. Dual-language schools have the potential to be extremely beneficial to heritage language speakers by leveraging the strength of their home language for multilingual achievement. The following scene illustrates a teacher, originally from France, and her second-grade students who are all native English speakers. One child's family also spoke Spanish at home and one child's mother spoke French.

> Mme. Dupont was seated on a low chair and the children were seated in front of her on a brightly colored rug. She held up the book, *Lave-Toi Les Maines*, which showed the procedure for washing hands. This was a health topic that Mme. Dupont had been teaching. The children listened and looked at the illustrations as Mme. Dupont turned each page. Some children scooted forward to see the pictures more clearly. Other children glanced at each other, smiling. After reading, Mme. Dupont encouraged the children to verbalize the information in French. Several children responded by repeating phrases from the book.

In this classroom example, the mainly middle-class English-speaking children were novices at speaking French. They understood classroom

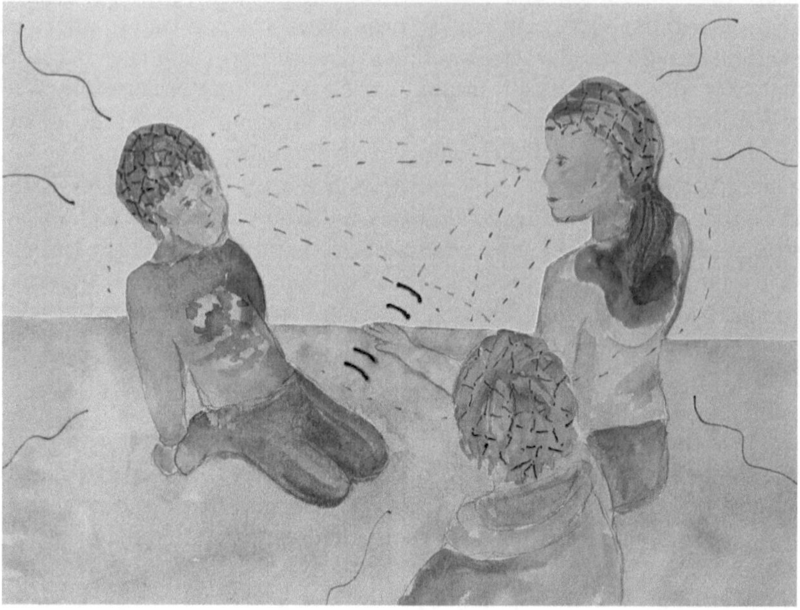

Figure 8.2 Artist's Impression of English Speaking Children Discussing the Physics of Motion in French, Activating Areas Across the Brain.

commands, such as "write your name on the top of your paper" and they repeated phrases they heard during instruction. They could write a few words and simple sentences in French.

The artist's impression (Figure 8.2) shows these English-speaking children engaged in conversation using their emerging French. Multiple brain areas across the brain are active. The children are taking in information from language, vision, gestures, and the environment as they discuss the physics of motion.

Although dual-language programs have become popular among middle-class English-speaking families, the dual-language immersion model is used rarely to maintain heritage languages in the United States. World languages are important assets for students, families, and society (Chang-Bacon, 2021). Rather than waiting until high school to teach a language, educators would do well to maintain and develop the languages that our students speak at home.

Program Models for L2 English Students

Students who are learning English have been given several labels over the years. In many settings these students are referred to as

English language learners. The term emergent bilinguals, on the other hand, highlights the advantage of becoming bilingual.

In addition to bilingual programs, there are many programs available to help K-12 emergent bilinguals develop English proficiency.

- **Sheltered English** programs teach academic content and language simultaneously. Teachers use methods that ensure students understand the language. Active learning, cooperative learning, visuals, simplified texts, models, and demonstrations are some ways to make sure that the content is understood.
- **English as a Second Language (ESL)** programs explicitly teach English language skills with a focus on developing English proficiency.
- **Content-based ESL** programs teach academic content as a means to develop language skills.

To summarize, different models of bilingual education exist in the United States. A major goal of bilingual education programs is to develop biliteracy and academic skills in the heritage language. Dual-language programs share this goal, with a parallel goal of developing English speakers' foreign language skills. Other programs for English learners pursue the goal of teaching English language and academic skills without trying to maintain or develop students' heritage languages.

Recent neuroscience research seems to point to enhanced structural connectivity in the brain with continuous exposure and learning in two or more languages. Bilingual maintenance and dual-language programs seem optimum for brain development. It will be important for bilingual educators and policymakers to follow brain research in this area, as the implications could influence their programing decisions.

Culturally Relevant Pedagogy for Emergent Bilinguals

Gloria Ladson-Billings (1994) introduced educators to the term culturally relevant pedagogy, which focuses on developing students academically and supporting their cultural competence. Culturally relevant pedagogy involves notions of capability, critique, and relationships as the core of teaching that supports marginalized students. Students' cultures and languages should also be maintained and sustained because students should not be expected to give up their cultures to succeed in school (Paris, 2012; Paris & Alim, 2014). The following scene illustrates how students' cultures and languages can be used to design inspiring and ambitious instruction.

> Fifth-grade students were gathered in a group surrounding an electronic tablet, listening to a rhythm and percussion app. They

> nodded and tapped as they planned a Civil War Reconstruction rap that would showcase their learning. In this diverse classroom, the students were Black, White, and Hispanic. Their teacher, Ms. Barrera was of mixed heritage. Later, students wrote responses to their social studies and language arts assignments on the classroom blog. When Ms. Barrera responded in Spanish to Spanish-speaking students, the others became interested and wanted to know what was going on. So, Ms. Barrera created a Spanish tutorial section on the blog.

Ms. Barrera's classroom illustrates how teachers can create culturally relevant pedagogy. This supports bilingualism by respecting and valuing the knowledge and cultural practices of students and their families. Students can be encouraged to use their heritage language when working on projects. Families can be welcomed into the school and classroom by providing heritage language materials and opportunities to collaborate with other families.

Reading

When children are learning to read in English, they must navigate an inconsistent orthography. Sound-to-letter mapping is inconsistent in English, while it is highly consistent in transparent languages such as Spanish and Italian. Because some languages are more or less transparent, there are differences in brain activation in readers of different languages. Positron emission tomography (PET) studies have shown greater phoneme processing activation in Italians than in English readers. English readers showed greater activation in areas associated with word retrieval (Paulesu et al., 2000). This suggests that we can expect Spanish readers to rely more on their phonetic knowledge. We can expect English readers to rely on a combination of phonetic knowledge and word knowledge.

Differentiation

Differentiating instruction means designing instruction to meet individual needs or the needs of a group of students. As a reading specialist and a teacher of English learners, Spence had to differentiate quite a bit. As a reading specialist, Spence had to assess what students could do. She often used the language experience approach and had students write about a personal experience, encouraging them to use what they knew of sounds, letters, or words as they wrote a rough draft. Spence scribed or typed the text into a booklet for them, which they then read. This activity revealed their zone of proximal development for phonics, spelling, sight words, and fluency.

We know that reading pathways are developing in children's brains and these pathways involve making sound-letter connections and accessing word meanings through memory. Engaging in reading and writing create specialized brain networks for orthographic processing. Engagement is key. Spence's students were interested in their booklet making because it was based on personal experience, and they had a purpose and audience when they read their booklets and took them home to read to family members.

Theories of reading and English learning are consistent with constructivist teaching. For example, Stephen Krashen's (1985) **comprehensible input** is similar to Vygotsky's Zone of Proximal Development (ZPD). With ZPD, the student learns skills just above the current skill level with the help of a teacher or more knowledgeable peer. An important difference between ZPD and comprehensible input is that communication with a language learner should be mostly at the learners' level of understanding, without intentionally communicating a bit beyond that level. We provide language input the student can understand when teaching academic content.

When English learners are engaged in productive activities, they use their new language to reach their goals. As a language teacher, Spence provided oral instruction and reading material that her students could comprehend. She provided language support such as pictures, photos, and videos to introduce new concepts and vocabulary.

All teachers must differentiate, whether in special programs like Spence taught, in self-contained elementary classrooms, or in a subject taught in middle or high school. There is a need for differentiation in all these settings. Interest and purpose are important in every educational setting and in any learning situation in or outside of school

Translanguaging

Some learners may be stronger in one of their languages, yet they can be seen as having a bank containing knowledge of multiple languages. This is called a **linguistic repertoire**. If you think of a musical repertoire, a person who is learning to play the piano can play some pieces very well, some less well, some simple pieces, and perhaps a few more complex pieces. This piano repertoire is like a linguistic repertoire. By building a linguistic repertoire, the knowledge gained in one language contributes to overall growth in communication skills.

As bilinguals use their widespread neural system to access word meanings, they must control the process of switching between different languages to produce words and grammatical structures. Researchers suggest that bilinguals use general executive functions to prevent competition from their stronger language, which allows them to be fluent in their other language (Sulpizio, 2020). This function is engaged differently depending on how well and how often the other language is used.

Executive control functions are high-level and complex mental processes that allow people to successfully monitor goal-directed behavior such as engaging in conversation. Whenever we need to consciously think about our behavior, we exert cognitive control. Our executive control functions help us control our attention, provide working memory, block unneeded information, and solve problems.

As children develop in multilanguage environments, they use two or more languages in speaking, reading, and writing. Emergent language users occasionally switch languages to express certain words. As they grow more proficient in the new language, they use different languages for a variety of situational and stylistic reasons (Gort, 2012). This often happens when speaking to a mixed-language group of friends or when writing about a personal experience.

The following narrative was written by Elena, an emergent bilingual third grader in a transitional bilingual program. This was drafted in her notebook, and she did not edit for punctuation or spelling.

> My first time making tortillas
> in my moms kitchin my tia was
> they're and she told me to first
> put arina then to put water
> but a little bit of water because
> it will not be good to eat my
> tia help me I got to put salt
> on the arina and my tia made
> the balls from the arina then
> me and my tia were turning on
> the fire then we started
> to cook the tortillas

In writing about her cooking experience, Elena used mostly English but included a few Spanish words that were meaningful within the story. *Tortilla* is a Mexican flatbread that really has no English translation. *Tia* means aunt. Elena used *tia* in her story because that is how she addresses her aunt. *Harina* means flour. Elena used this word at home and perhaps did not know the English word, flour. She spelled *harina* without an H, probably because she had not formally learned how to spell *harina* and the H is not voiced in Spanish. In these ways, Elena used her personal knowledge of Spanish to write an English narrative about her home life.

Home literacy plays an important role in developing heritage language and literacy development. For students to maintain their heritage language, they must speak and read in their heritage language at home. The heritage language does not interfere with English language development because vocabulary growth and reading skills in English continue to grow with English exposure and instruction in school (Ryan, 2021).

Moving between two languages is sometimes called code-switching, code-meshing, or translanguaging. **Translanguaging** is based on the idea that world languages are not isolated by social or political boundaries. Instead, individuals engage in languaging by using any of the linguistic resources available to them. Translanguaging involves the social, cognitive, emotional, and affective lived experiences of those involved in the communication. Translanguaging moves beyond the focus on two or more languages as separate, and views language as one encompassing repertoire (Garcia & Kleifgen, 2020).

Macbeth et al. (2021) looked at how the brain's executive control functions are activated when a person chooses a word from their language repertoire. White matter axons transmit information between areas of grey matter in the brain. Axons are projections of neurons, that typically conduct electrical impulses away from the nerve cell body. These axons connect areas of grey matter across the brain. White matter connectivity allows access to vocabulary in a second language that is stored in memory. White matter connectivity in the frontal lobe executive control area allows speakers to control which language they are accessing (Abutalebi & Green, 2016). The executive control system directs attention to one language and inhibits the other language as needed. For example, if a Spanish speaker wants to use the English word, aunt, the student must inhibit, or block the Spanish word, *tia* as they activate their memory for the English word.

People engage in translanguaging for a variety of reasons. If you studied Spanish or French in high school, perhaps you used your emerging language when ordering food in a Mexican or French restaurant. You may not know how to express everything you want to say to your server and move between your emergent language and English. In speaking casually with Indian friends and relatives. Mitra combines English, Hindi, and Bengali. In Spanish-speaking communities in the United States, students often translanguage as they help their parents negotiate parent-teacher conferences.

The concept of translanguaging is consistent with neuroimaging studies. There are no separate systems for separate languages, rather bilingual language users have been shown to have increased brain grey matter and neural connections (Pliatsikas et al., 2020). The neural systems activated in bilingual language use include executive functions for monitoring speech based on the context of the situation.

There might also be a benefit in bilinguals' executive control functions. Because bilinguals must shift between languages and monitor which language to use for a task, researchers have studied their executive control functions. It seems bilinguals may have an advantage over monolinguals in some functions such as inhibitory control and monitoring under certain conditions (Gunnerud et al., 2020).

The Reading Network

Whether reading in English or a heritage language, the same general reading network is developed in the brain (Paulesu et al., 2000). Readers of English and readers of Chinese engage the same reading network, although there may be subregions that are more highly activated for alphabetic scripts such as English or character scripts such as Chinese (Chen et al., 2002).

Languages have differences in orthographic depth. **Orthographic depth** refers to how well the sound of a language maps onto the spelling pattern. **Transparent orthographies** such as Spanish have one-to-one letter-to-sound mapping, such as the word, taco: t-a-c-o. Languages that have close letter-sound relationships activate more of the indirect route, from letter- to sound- to meaning. Once the reader accesses the sounds the letters represent, they access the meaning. However, even in these transparent writing systems, the reader may also go directly from word to meaning, using the most efficient route for the reading task. **Opaque orthographies** such as English rely largely on previously acquired word patterns (Paulesu et al., 2000). For example, the letter pattern ough, and words ending with a silent e must be learned beyond the sound of one letter.

Opaque languages more often activate a direct route from word to meaning. As described in the dual-route model, the direct route moves directly from the written word to meaning without the need to process the sound each letter represents (Pugh et al., 1997; Pugh et al., 2001; Sandak et al., 2004). However, even in opaque languages such as English, readers also use the indirect route of letter-sound correspondence, especially for words they are unfamiliar with. Because of the differences between transparent and opaque orthographies, some written languages require more memory activation during reading while other languages rely more on sounding out words (Das et al., 2011). As additional models of reading are developed and tested, neuroscientists are describing the ways that reading and other brain networks interact beyond decoding and whole word retrieval.

Reading Comprehension

Once students have learned to read, teachers continue to address English learners' reading comprehension. Reading comprehension can be assessed and developed by talking to students about their books or other texts. Literacy instruction that includes book clubs or literature circles gives students opportunities to talk to each other and learn from their peers. It is important to carefully plan student groups, putting students together who have different strengths. For example, a student who has knowledge of the content, but less English vocabulary can be paired with a student who is more proficient in English but has less knowledge of the content. The following scene illustrates peer scaffolding in a literature circle.

> Ms. Meyer taught 11th grade English. One class had 30 students, with 10 students designated as English learners. Ms. Meyer noticed that one student, Javier did not voluntarily engage in the class discussions as they read *The House on Mango Street* by Sandra Cisneros. If he was asked directly, he answered questions about the plot, characters, and setting. To help Javier join in open-ended literature discussions, Ms. Meyer designed literature circles of 4–5 students who would discuss the book together. First, Ms. Meyer demonstrated different question types. These were closed questions, open-ended questions, and leading questions. Next, the students created their own questions for the upcoming small group discussions. In the literature circles, Javier voluntarily answered both closed and open-ended questions. Creating his own open-ended questions continued to be challenging for Javier, so Ms. Meyer continued to provide and analyze examples of questions to prepare students for their literature circle discussions.

In this classroom example, Javier was given the tools and structure to move beyond answering closed questions about literature. Ms. Meyers supported Javier in contributing to academic discussions by demonstrating the types of questions that open a discussion. Academic discussions contribute to brain development by building vocabulary and content knowledge. Learning new skills expands grey matter volume and white matter connectivity. Once a skill is learned, the brain generally goes back to its normal state. This is because the most efficient pathways have been established through the process of growing and pruning that is a hallmark of brain plasticity (Pliatsikas, 2020).

Reading, language arts, and English classrooms should have a wide variety of books for students' varied interests and experiences. Fiction, non-fiction, graphic novels, picture books, joke books, magazines, newspaper articles, poetry, classics, pop culture, and many more options will give students something they can relate to and enjoy. English language books or articles with fewer words on the page are helpful for emergent bilinguals.

Bilingual books and heritage language books allow students to develop biliteracy. **Bilingual books** are written in two languages. Heritage language books are also known as foreign language books. These are books written only in the heritage language. Even if the teacher does not speak or understand the students' L1, the teacher can ask students to tell them about the heritage language books.

Retelling the story in the students' own words develops students' comprehension skills through thinking, reflecting, and translating, even when the retellings differ from the text (Kucer, 2015). When students retell in their own words, teachers' responses should acknowledge the thinking that goes into the retelling, while guiding the student back to the text to clarify any misunderstandings or to explain unknown vocabulary.

Reading in a new language involves some unique processing to gain meaning from the text. Readers may rely on translation if they are not able to access the meaning with direct processing. Emergent bilinguals need more processing time as they read because of the use of translation to make meaning. Proficient bilinguals can access meaning directly from words in both languages (Guo et al., 2012).

High-quality instruction promotes expansion and efficiency of grey and white matter in the brain as students engage in reading and discussion. Texts that are matched to readers and opportunities to discuss these texts are important to reading comprehension. It is also important for the student to think about their reading process. Teachers can help promote reading comprehension through cognitive reading strategies. When students are aware of reading strategies and practice the strategies, they strengthen their executive control functions.

The following example shows metacognitive strategy instruction that was used with emergent bilinguals (Teng, 2020).

Metacognitive Reading

Students engaged in a literacy workshop for their language arts instruction. The components of the workshop were: read aloud, guided reading, shared reading, interactive writing, shared writing, reading workshop, writing workshop, and word study. Within the workshop, students read for authentic purposes.

Preparation

Provide students with texts that have thought-provoking content, and the students can read independently.

Provide students with a list of metacognitive prompts.

Goals

Contemplate the meaning of the text.

Contemplate similarities and differences between texts.

Reflect on appropriate reading strategies.

Evaluate their reading process.

Procedure

During read-aloud, introduce the metacognitive strategies in Table 8.1.

Table 8.1 Metacognitive Reading Strategies and Prompts

Metacognitive Prompts			
Comprehension	Connection	Strategy	Reflection
What was the text about? What were the purposes of this text? What specific points did I find important in this text?	What were the similarities and differences between this text and those I have read in the past?	What strategies were appropriate for completing this text reading in time? What strategies were useful for grasping the gist of this text? What strategies were useful for inferring unknown words?	Did my strategies for reading make sense? Did I focus on all the details of the text? Did I consider all relevant information while figuring out the purpose of this text? What prevented me from achieving the correct answers? What did I do to understand as much of the text as possible?

Inform students of the usefulness of metacognitive prompts and introduce a list of metacognitive prompts.

During shared reading and guided reading, have students reflect individually on their use of metacognitive strategies. They can respond in a reading journal, handouts of printed prompts, or in other ways.

Monitor students' individual reflections and provide enrichment and remedial help as necessary.

Reading comprehension can be strengthened through learning and using cognitive reading strategies. Additional reading strategies are discussed in chapter 6. Bilingual students must deal with multiple cognitive demands as they read in L2 English. They may encounter unfamiliar vocabulary and concepts that are outside their experience. They must control their focus as they read, actively making meaning from the English words and sentences. Teachers can help their students with these demanding tasks by teaching them cognitive strategies and monitoring how they are using the strategies during reading. Next, we will discuss the equally demanding task of writing L2 English.

Writing

Writing involves many areas across the brain including language networks, reading networks, emotion, memory, and semantics. Bilingual children's writing development progresses like monolingual children. They understand that writing is a form of communication and demonstrate their emerging phonological development in two languages as early as preschool and kindergarten.

Young bilinguals move across languages as they talk about their writing, which helps them plan and compose (Williams & Lowrance-Faulhaber, 2018). The following scene illustrates one teacher's writing workshop approach to instruction. In the **writing workshop**, students choose their topics and progress at their own rate as they generate ideas, research information, write drafts, revise their work, and carefully edit their work to produce a final written product.

> Third-grade students collected their writing folders from a basket on a table and began working on their projects. Ms. Cortez and most of her students were Spanish speakers. The students worked in groups as they shared ideas and resources on their projects. Some of their topics were: racism, the environment, and endangered species. While the whole class worked on their individual topics, Ms. Cortez sat beside a student to scaffold her English writing. She prompted the student to reread what she had just written, helping her to monitor flow and catch mistakes. In this writer's workshop, Ms. Cortez set high expectations while nurturing each student's language development.

In this scene, the students wrote about issues that are important to society. These issues interested the students and gave them a purpose for writing. They had opportunities to talk with each other as they worked on their projects, strengthening their oral language skills. Ms. Cortez helped students with the many tasks that are involved in writing including spelling, forming sentences, connecting ideas, and addressing an audience.

During writing, students' brains are very busy. Widespread regions of the brain are active due to the multiple components involved. Writers must attend to word meanings, grammar, and phonology. Other brain regions that are involved include emotion, memory, representing objects, and making meaning of the whole text. Brain areas are selectively activated as needed during writing (Sulpizio, 2020).

Bilingual Writing

As children progress through elementary school, they are capable of becoming biliterate in Spanish and English. Children receiving bilingual education reach equivalent English language outcomes to children who do not participate in bilingual education (Hopewell & Butvilofsky, 2016). As bilinguals move into middle and high school, first and second language writing proficiency continues to be strongly associated, as students mediate their writing with metacognitive knowledge and increasing linguistic fluency.

Research has shown that beginning at a young age and continuing through post-secondary school, students can strategically use multiple languages for writing. Emergent bilinguals will use what they know to represent letter sounds of English. They may even put together letter strings with non-Roman characters. They may copy from print in the classroom or other print they have seen to assist them in writing. This is part of the process of emergent bilingual literacy (Machado & Hartman, 2019).

Following are two examples of writing instruction. The first provides a way to support bilingual literacy in young learners (Rowe & Miller, 2016). The second example demonstrates how students can develop the use of their full linguistic repertoires by studying literature that was crafted to include more than one language (Flores & Machado, 2021).

eBook Composing

Preparation

Make a dual-language demonstration ebook.

Children will need access to computers or tablets, cameras or phones with cameras, and software for making an ebook.

Classroom LCD projector and speakers are needed if sharing the ebooks with a large class.

Goals

Use photos, drawing, writing, and speech in English and heritage languages to express experiences and ideas.

Use emergent writing, alphabet skills, and invented spelling.

Procedure

Explain the project and share your demonstration ebook. Talk about your process of developing the idea, designing, and organizing.

Children take photos in the classroom, bring photos from home, or draw pictures.

The teacher supports their photography or drawing and converses with children about their images.

Children write about their images. Converse with children about possible messages if needed and support their writing. Ask others to help you support heritage languages if needed.

Children record an oral narration in English and their heritage language.

The teacher supports the oral narrations.

Children read and listen to their finished compositions.

Share the ebooks in an independent reading center, with the whole class, and families.

Young children will use what is available to make meaning through print. Crayons, paper, pencils, pens, markers, envelopes, sticky notes, computers, smartphones, and tablets can all be used by children to send their messages out into the world.

Children in preschool, kindergarten, and first grade are connecting spoken language with the written alphabet and words. They need to make connections between what they know and what they are learning. Writing about themselves, their families, homes, and lives provides motivation to write and interest in what they are writing. Their classmates are a perfect audience for these young authors.

As children become more adept with writing, they can intentionally use their whole linguistic repertoire of English and their heritage languages. We know that both languages are controlled by the same language network in the brain. The language network is connected to other networks across the brain. During writing, students tap into these networks and may use other systems of signs and symbols such as numbers, photos, drawings, and emojis to help them express what they have to say. The next example provides a method for teaching the craft of writing using multiple languages.

In this example, students study how to craft language in their writing. They study how authors use semiotic resources including different languages. Semiotic resources are signs or symbols that convey meaning. Examples of semiotic resources include punctuation, drawings, photos, emojis, and words and phrases from various languages.

Crafting Stories

Preparation

Collect English books that use languages beyond English for literary effect. Select books that are authentic and affirming of students' cultures and languages.

Find a copy of a short story that uses languages other than English, such as "Chanclas" or "Eleven" by Sandra Cisneros.

Goals

Students study literature as models of how authors craft literature with languages and other semiotic resources.

Students use languages and various semiotic resources to support their goals for expression as they write.

Procedure

Explain the goals for the literature study and writing.

Demonstrate how to notice and note how authors craft literature using languages and other semiotic resources.

Begin by reading aloud and discussing a short story. Engage students in a discussion of the content as well as the language.

Briefly discuss each of the other books in the collection, then invite students to choose a book to read independently or in self-selected groups.

Students read their books, silently or quietly in their groups, stopping to notice and note the author's craft.

After some time reading, engage students in a discussion of the meanings in their books and the languages they discovered. Ask students why the author might have chosen to use the languages and other semiotic resources.

Students brainstorm ideas for their writing, drawing on their life experiences. Then they plan their writing including how they will use semiotic resources and languages to portray their ideas.

Provide regularly schedule time for students to write drafts, revise, and edit their writing.

Crafting writing using heritage languages shows students that their languages are valuable. When students see that multiple languages have been artfully used in published works of English writing, their own linguistic resources are truly seen as resources in the classroom and in society. By including multiple languages, students exercise important cognitive abilities. The brain's language networks and executive networks interact when students read and write in two or more languages. These assets can be developed in school and beyond for a lifetime of benefit.

Bilingualism beyond Childhood and Adolescence

Studies of bilingual adults are providing information on the potential benefits of bilingualism for brain development. Del Maschio et al. (2018) reported that bilingualism fostered neuroplasticity, which is the brain's ability to create new neural pathways. Bilinguals' neuroplasticity was enhanced in young adults and sustained into older age with the regular use of two languages. Plasticity seemed to promote cognitive reserves in healthy aging.

Bilingualism may be one environmental factor that helps to delay cognitive decline from aging (Bialystok et al., 2007). This may be due to the increased grey matter and white matter connections that are developed for monitoring the two languages. Studies suggest that bilingualism is a factor that can postpone the damaging effects of aging and poor brain health (Berkes et al., 2021).

Bilingualism and multilingualism are assets that can benefit you and your students. So don'thesitate to learn a language or use what you have learned in school or at home. Use what you know to translanguage when ordering Mexican, Italian, French, or Indian food at your favorite restaurant. Use greetings, like "hola," "ohayou," or "bonjour" and don't forget to say "gracias" to your language teachers.

Did You Know?

Informal assessment of multilingual learners' English oral language development can provide teachers with valuable information that can guide literacy instruction. Students need opportunities for oral production of English because oral language, reading, and writing progress together for language learners.

One method of informal assessment is to record a student as they talk. Then listen and note the language structures they are using, such as nouns, verbs, present tense, past tense, simple or more complex sentences, etc. Keep the notes in a cumulative portfolio to track progress over time.

Food for Thought

Is syntactic processing the major neural signature and the point of difference between a monolingual and a bilingual brain? A neuroimaging study with English-Spanish bilinguals and English only monolinguals showed increased activation in the left inferior frontal cortex of bilinguals when processing English compared to English monolinguals (Kovelman et al., 2008). This area of the brain is important to the reading network.

Bibliography

Abutalebi, J., & Green, D. (2007). Bilingual language production: The neurocognition of language representation and control. *Journal of Neurolinguistics*, *20*, 242–275.

Abutalebi, J., & Green, D. W. (2016). Neuroimaging of language control in bilinguals: Neural adaptation and reserve. *Bilingualism, Language and Cognition*, *19*(4), 689–698.

Alvear, S. A. (2019). The additive advantage and bilingual programs in a large urban school district. *American Educational Research Journal*, *56*(2), 477–513.

Berkes, M., Calvo, N., Anderson, J. A. E., & Bialystok, E. (2021). Poorer clinical outcomes for older adult monolinguals when matched to bilinguals on brain health. *Brain Structure & Function*, *226*(2), 415–424. 10.1007/s00429-020-02185-5

Bialystok, E., Craik, F. I., & Freedman, M. (2007). Bilingualism as a protection against the onset of symptoms of dementia. *Neuropsychologia*, *45*(2), 459–464.

Chang-Bacon, C. K. (2021). Monolingual language ideologies and the idealized speaker: The "new bilingualism" meets the "old" educational inequities. *Teachers College Record*, *123*(1), 1–28.

Chen, Y., Fu, S., Iversen, S. D., Smith, S. M., & Matthews, P. M. (2002). Testing for dual brain processing routes in reading: A direct contrast of Chinese character and Pinyin reading using fMRI. *Journal of Cognitive Neuroscience*, *14*(7), 1088–1098. 10.1162/089892902320474535

Crawford, J. (2004). *Educating English Learners: Language Diversity in the Classroom (5th ed.)*. Bilingual Educational Services.

Das, T., Padakannaya, P., Pugh, K. R., & Singh, N. C. (2011). Neuroimaging reveals dual routes to reading in simultaneous proficient readers of two orthographies. *NeuroImage*, *54*(2), 1476–1487.

Dehghani, M., Boghrati, R., Man, K., Hoover, J., Gimbel, S. I., Vaswani, A., Zevin, J. D., Immordino, Y. M. H., Gordon, A. S., Damasio, A., & Kaplan, J. T. (2017). Decoding the neural representation of story meanings across languages. *Human Brain Mapping*, *38*(12), 6096–6106.

Del Maschio, N., Sulpizio, S., Gallo, F., Fedeli, D., Weekes, B. S., & Abutalebi, J. (2018). Neuroplasticity across the lifespan and aging effects in bilinguals and monolinguals. *Brain and Cognition*, *125*, 118–126.

Di Pisa, G., Pereira Soares, S. M., & Rothman, J. (2021). Brain, mind and linguistic processing insights into the dynamic nature of bilingualism and its outcome effects. *Journal of Neurolinguistics*, *58*. 10.1016/j.jneuroling.2020.100965.

Flores, T. T., & Machado, E. (2021). The power of writing and telling our stories. *Language Arts*, *99*(1), 68–71.

Friedrich, N., Anderson, J., & Morrison, F. (2014). Culturally appropriate pedagogy in a bilingual family literacy programme. *Literacy*, *48*(2), 72–79.

García, O., & Kleifgen, J. A. (2020). Translanguaging and literacies. *Reading Research Quarterly*, *55*(4), 553–571.

Garcia, O., & Wei, L. (2014). *Translanguaging: Language, Bilingualism, and Education*. MacMillan.

Gort, M. (2012). Code-switching patterns in the writing-related talk of young emergent bilinguals. *Journal of Literacy Research*, *44*(1), 45–75.

Gunnerud, H. L., ten Braak, D., Reikeras, E. K. L., Donolato, E., & Melby-Lervag, M. (2020). Is bilingualism related to a cognitive advantage in children? A systematic review and meta-analysis. *Psychological Bulletin*, *146*(12), 1059–1083. DOI: 10.1037/bul0000301

Guo, T., Misra, M., Tam, J. W., & Kroll, J. F. (2012). On the time course of accessing meaning in a second language: An electrophysiological and behavioral investigation of translation recognition. *Journal of Experimental Psychology: Learning, Memory, and Cognition*, *38*, 1165–1186. 10.1037/a0028076

Hopewell, S., & Butvilofsky, S. (2016). Privileging bilingualism: Using biliterate writing outcomes to understand emerging bilingual learners' literacy achievement. *Bilingual Research Journal*, *39*(3/4), 324–338.

Kovelman, I., Baker, S. A., & Petitto, L. A. (2008). Bilingual and monolingual brains compared: A functional magnetic resonance imaging investigation of syntactic processing and a possible "neural signature" of bilingualism. *Journal of Cognitive Neuroscience*, *20*(1), 153–169. 10.1162/jocn.2008.20011

Krashen, S. (1985). *The Input Hypothesis: Issues and Implications*. Longman.

Kucer, S. B. (2015). Understanding readers' differing understandings. *Literacy*, *49*(3), 132–139.

Macbeth, A., Higby, E., Atagi, N., & Chiarello, C. (2021). Evidence for cognitive and brain reserve supporting executive control of memory in lifelong bilinguals. *Neuropsychologia*, *160*. 10.1016/j.neuropsychologia.2021.107958

Machado, E., & Hartman, P. (2019). Translingual writing in a linguistically diverse primary classroom. *Journal of Literacy Research*, *51*(4), 480–503.

Malik-Moraleda, S., Ayyash, D., Gallée, J., Affourtit, J., Hoffmann, M., Mineroff, Z., Jouravlev, O., & Fedorenko, E. (2022). An investigation across 45 languages and 12 language families reveals a universal language network. *Nature Neuroscience*, *25*(8), 1014–1019. 10.1038/s41593-022-01114-5

Padilla, A. M., Fan, L., Xu, X., & Silva, D. (2013). A Mandarin/English two-way immersion program: Language proficiency and academic achievement. *Foreign Language Annals*, *46*, 661–679.

Paris, D. (2012). Culturally sustaining pedagogy: A needed change in stance, terminology, and practice. *Educational Researcher*, *41*(3), 93–97.

Paris, D., & Alim, H. S. (2014). What are we seeking to sustain through culturally sustaining pedagogy? A loving critique forward. *Harvard Educational Review*, *84*(1), 85–100.

Paulesu, E., McCrory, E., Fazio, F., Menoncello, L., Brunswick, N., Cappa, S. F., Cotelli, M., Cossu, G., Corte, F., Lorusso, M., Pesenti, S., Gallagher, A., Perani, D., Price, C., Frith, C. D., & Frith, U. (2000). A cultural effect on brain function. *Nature Neuroscience*, *3*(1), 91.

Pliatsikas, C., Meteyard, L., Veríssimo, J., DeLuca, V., Shattuck, K., & Ullman, M. T. (2020). The effect of bilingualism on brain development from early childhood to young adulthood. *Brain Structure & Function*, *225*(7), 2131–2152. 10.1007/s00429-020-02115-5

Pugh, K. R., Mencl, W. E., Jenner, A. R., Katz, L., Frost, S. J., Lee, J. R., Shaywitz, S. E., & Shaywitz, B. A. (2001). Neurobiological studies of reading and reading disability. *Journal of Communication Disorders*, *34*, 479–492. 10.1016/s0021-9924(01)00060-0

Pugh, K. R., Shaywitz, B. A., Shaywitz, S. E., Shankweiler, D. P., Katz, L., Fletcher, J. M., Skudlarski, P., Fulbright, R. K., Constable, R. T., Bronen, R. A., Lacadie, C., & Gore, J. C. (1997). Predicting reading performance from neuroimaging profiles: The cerebral basis of phonological effects in printed word identification. *Journal of Experimental Psychology: Human Perception and Performance*, *23*, 299–318.

Rowe, D. W., & Miller, M. E. (2016). Designing for diverse classrooms: Using iPads and digital cameras to compose eBooks with emergent bilingual/biliterate four-year-olds. *Journal of Early Childhood Literacy*, *16*(4), 425–472.

Ryan, È. (2021). The impact of home literacy on bilingual vocabulary development. *Bilingual Research Journal*, *44*(1), 108–123.

Sandak, R., Mencl, W. E., Frost, S. J., & Pugh, K. R. (2004). The neurobiological basis of skilled and impaired reading: Recent findings and new directions. *Scientific Studies of Reading*, *8*, 273–292. 10.1207/s1532799xssr0803_6

Slavin, R. E., Madden, N., Calderón, M., Chamberlain, A., & Hennessy, M. (2011). Reading and language outcomes of a multiyear randomized evaluation of transitional bilingual education. *Educational Evaluation and Policy Analysis*, *33*, 47–58.

Steele, J. L., Slater, R. O., Zamarro, G., Miller, T., Li, J., Burkhauser, S., & Bacon, M. (2017). Effects of dual-language immersion programs on student achievement: Evidence from lottery data. *American Educational Research Journal*, *54*(1), 282S–306S.

Sulpizio, S., Del Maschio, N., Fedeli, D., & Abutalebi, J. (2020). Bilingual language processing: A meta-analysis of functional neuroimaging studies. *Neuroscience and Biobehavioral Reviews*, *108*, 834–853.

Teng, (Mark) Feng. (2020). The benefits of metacognitive reading strategy awareness instruction for young learners of English as a second language. *Literacy*, *54*(1), 29–39.

Thomas, W. P., Collier, V. P., & Abbott, M. (1993). Academic achievement through Japanese, Spanish, or French: The first two years of partial immersion. *The Modern Language Journal*, *77*(2), 170–179.

Williams, C., & Lowrance-Faulhaber, E. (2018). Writing in young bilingual children: Review of research. *Journal of Second Language Writing*, *42*, 58–69.

9

LITERACY NETWORKS

> Nate, a ninth grader, was building a computer game. He was learning computer coding in school, and he kept a spiral notebook where he drew and labeled game elements. He imagined how the game should be played based on his vast experience playing computer games. He excitedly discussed game building with his friends at school, his teacher, his brother, and his sister as he built his game over several weeks. He looked forward to interacting with other game builders in his class and talked to game builders through an internet group. Once the game was finished, he entered and won an online competition. Nate was thrilled to win and felt a sense of pride that he could excel at something he loved to do.

Nate's literacies for game building depended on his past experiences, social interactions, playing, watching, listening, and reading during gameplay. He tapped into his memories and skills as he wrote, drew, discussed, and coded. His emotions also played a big part in his perseverance through a difficult project. All the while, his receptive, developing brain was taking in information from his senses and body functions, the environment, and other people.

Nate's game-building literacies illustrate the ideas in this book. We have presented six areas of literacy that can be informed by neuroscience and literacy research. They are embodiment, social and emotional learning, multimodality, making meaning, phonology, and languaging. The connections between these areas of literacy and how our brain is shaped and developed can be thought of as literacy networks.

To elaborate on the ideas in the previous chapters, we use the metaphor of literacy networks. We view reading, writing, and other literacies as networks that connect with people socially (Street, 1984). Literacy networks involve emotion, one's body, languages, and one's brain. Reading and writing are interconnected processes. Literacy encompasses

DOI: 10.4324/9781003256199-10

visual, audio, and gestural representations. Literacy is a network of communicative practices.

The brain is also a network of interconnected processes and functions. Neuroscientists have moved from locating anatomical areas of the brain to describing the distributed networks connecting areas across the brain. The brain also receives information from the environment and the body. Embodiment is useful for thinking about networks that are being discovered by both neuroscientists and literacy researchers.

Embodiment

Embodiment describes how our minds and bodies interact with the environment and each other. Human development is an interconnected process in which brain development is influenced by social and cultural interactions (Immordino-Yang & Gotlieb, 2017). The human body develops in response to physical activity, the environment, and social interaction. The nervous and endocrine systems take in messages from the world around us and what is happening internally in our bodies. Emotional responses to our environment can lead to changes in our bodies and brains. And as the body develops through childhood into adolescence, hormonal changes affect both the brain and the body. Factors within our bodies and from the outside impact brain development.

Human development is impacted by the environment. When adverse situations occur, we react with stress and resilience. Stress or maltreatment affects how the body and brain function and lead to the release of stress hormones. When a person feels threatened, they must draw upon their resources to cope with the situation. Resources that help a person cope include optimism, self-esteem, and feeling like they are in control (Yao & Hsieh, 2019).

Cognitive flexibility is critical for coordinating overlapping brain networks that function during adverse experiences. Emotional regulation, physical pain perception, and cognitive control allow a person to adapt their behavior to cope with a bad situation. Educators have an important role to play in helping students develop cognitive flexibility and emotional control.

Resiliency is the ability to react flexibly and marshal the resources necessary when faced with an adverse event. We know that this ability varies depending on a person's situation and the event they are faced with. Schools, teachers, families, and friends can support students during stressful events. This support is necessary for helping children and adolescents develop resiliency (Lupien et al., 2009).

Embodied Literacy Learning

Social interactions, the environment, and the body influence the brain and literacy learning. When children and adolescents have not had enough sleep or are physically tired, it is difficult for them to concentrate on reading and writing. This is because adequate sleep is important for people to complete complex tasks. Sleep is needed for memory encoding, working memory, and long-term memory consolidation (Kopasz et al., 2010).

Children and adolescents must be cared for, adequately fed, and maintain good health; otherwise, their bodies and brains will be stressed, which affects their literacy learning. Nutrition plays a role in cognitive function and the potential for learning (Immordino-Yang, 2016). When children do not receive adequate nutrition, they may be unresponsive and less curious. That is why it is so important that children are provided with nutritious meals at home and in school. Nutritious food provides children and adolescents with the energy needed for learning.

A healthy body and intellectually engaging environment are necessary for literacy learning. High-quality instruction fosters intellectual engagement and curiosity (Jirout et al., 2019). An intellectually engaging classroom is filled with books and other interesting texts that students can choose from. Grade-level reading material is supported through discussion in whole group and small group settings. Writing instruction includes time to write about topics that interest students personally. A rich learning environment builds on students' cultural knowledge and expands students' view of the world.

For children and adolescents to respond to an enriched literacy environment, their physical needs must be taken care of while providing academic instruction. Literacy networks involve our bodies and the material conditions in which we live and learn. Students need healthy, motivating, and intellectually stimulating conditions to thrive.

Social and Emotional Learning

Social and emotional learning describes how our physical, mental, and emotional interactions with others promote learning. Joint attention is vital to learning from infancy onward (Gavrilov et al., 2012). In classrooms, teachers demonstrate skills as students follow along. Children and adolescents learn from each other and consider other perspectives when they engage in discussion.

Studies have shown that student interaction is associated with beneficial learning outcomes compared with other learning conditions (Tenenbaum et al., 2020). These benefits carried through regardless of the gender of group members, size of the group, or age of the students.

Interactions were more effective when the students had to reach a consensus. This means that the student must come to terms with their thoughts and the thoughts of others.

Instruction that includes collaboration and inquiry promotes opportunities for students to learn from each other, develop social and emotional skills, and think critically as they try to solve problems (Immordino-Yang et al., 2019). Inquiry learning allows students to pose their own questions about things that matter to them, their communities, or the world.

Reading and discussing literature that contains different, contrasting viewpoints develops critical thinking and the ability to understand how others might think differently. When students interact in peer groups, they consider the emotions of their peers in making decisions. Considering the perspectives and emotions of others is a part of literacy learning.

The emotions of children and adolescents are very important to their literacy learning. Emotions must be regulated to maintain focus, persist, and overcome frustration. Learning to read and write requires emotional self-regulation. For example, when children struggle with learning to read, they may feel frustrated (Liew et al., 2020). When adolescents struggle to express themselves in writing, they must overcome setbacks. Children and adolescents must self-regulate their emotions for successful literacy learning. Thus, literacy networks involve social interactions and emotions.

Multimodality

> High school student, Han chose the piano as his inquiry project. He was curious about this western instrument that seemed so different from the *erhu* he played back home in China. Using pen and paper, Han wrote notes about what he already knew about the piano and what he wanted to learn. He wanted to know who invented the piano and how it functions. Han used the internet to find informational text and photos. Then he visited the local university's music library that displayed an antique harpsichord, spinet, and pianos. He visited the practice rooms and listened to the music majors as they practiced. He even tried out one of the pianos and watched the hammers strike the strings as he depressed the keys. When Han returned to his classroom, he typed a text, then inserted photos and audio to create a multimodal presentation on the piano.

Multimodality is the way different modes such as sound, text, and images come together to communicate ideas. All these modes provide

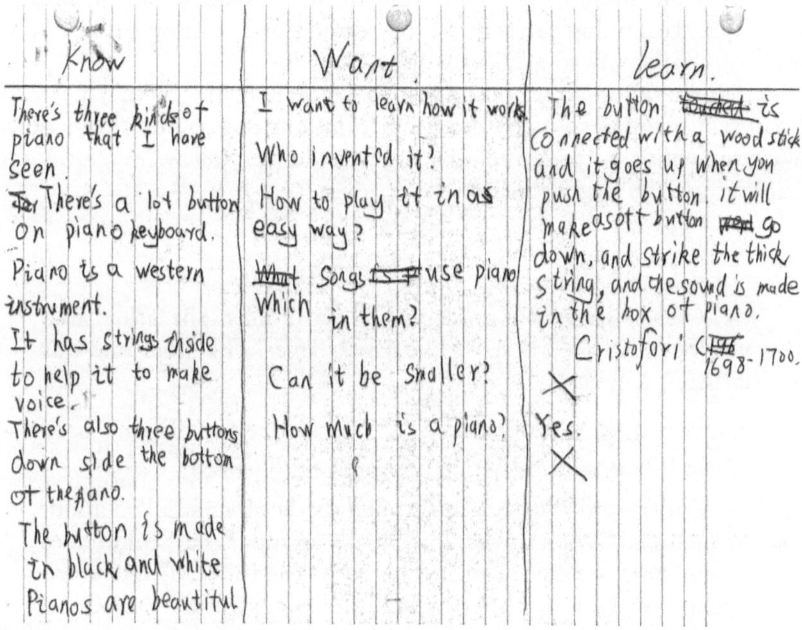

Figure 9.1 Han's KWL Organizer with Sections for Know, Want to Learn, and Learned.

great learning opportunities as shown by Han's inquiry project. He started by listing what he knew about the piano, and what he wanted to find out using a KWL organizer (Figure 9.1). He listened to piano music, used the keyboard, read about pianos, and watched videos about the piano. He presented his learning through multiple modes of communication.

Whether writing by hand or typing, we depend on interconnected brain areas to coordinate working memory, motor coordination, decision-making, and eye–hand coordination (Dinehart, 2015; Vinci-Booher, 2021). As we write, we use control strategies including generating ideas, drafting ideas, revising ideas, and choosing words to represent the ideas. We use monitoring strategies that include reading what has been written, reflecting, and reviewing (Hacker, 2018).

Human cultures determine what literacy entails in each place and era. In the current global information age, literacy includes modalities such as digital and visual texts. When students encounter these new literacies they must evaluate, make judgements, and engage in new ways (Turner et al., 2019). Reading and writing in our society have become richly multimodal. A text often contains visual and audio components. This creates more demand on the brain as we shift from one modality to another while monitoring the meaning of the message we are sending or receiving. Technological features of reading and writing add another layer of complexity to a literacy network.

Perhaps writing is the most obvious example of the literacy network because it involves so many brain functions and sociocultural functions. We write with a purpose and audience in mind then our written ideas add our voice to the larger culture.

Making Meaning

> Ms. Cotton gave first grader Alex two books. She asked him which one he liked best. "I like *Tiger, Tiger*. The other one was harder," Alex said.
>
> "Don't worry, Ms. Cotton said. I'll help you with the hard parts." She picked up the book, *Baby Lamb's First Drink*.
>
> Ms. Cotton and Alex paged through the book and talked about the pictures. "Look at the flowers, it's spring. What sound does spring start with?" This prepared Alex to read the word "spring" when it appeared within the context of the story.

Reading comprehension is the process of making meaning as we read. Ms. Cotton helped Alex to actively make meaning at the sound, word, and whole text levels. In the brain, this involves a distributed, large-scale cortical network that is active during reading comprehension (Aboud et al., 2016; Landi et al., 2013).

Because Alex did not have a lot of background knowledge about sheep and lambs, Ms. Cotton provided Alex with connections to things he was familiar with such as flowers blooming in spring. This helped Alex construct a mental model based on meaning cues, linguistic cues, and relevant background knowledge (van Moort et al., 2020). As new information is taken in, the brain's semantic system integrates it with previous information built over time. Combining information through the semantic system allows the reader to build meaningful representations of the text.

Context and background knowledge help the reader anticipate what a word will be (Kutas & Federmeier, 2000; Chow et al., 2014). Just as Ms. Cotton helped Alex predict upcoming words in the book, this process happens for all readers as they see the incoming word, recognize its meaning, and integrate the word into the unfolding sentence. Alex first did this with Ms. Cotton's help, then when he saw the word again, he recognized it. The process of retrieving the meaning of a known word involves multiple networks in the brain, yet it happens surprisingly quickly (Pu et al., 2020).

As students like Alex read books slightly above their ability level, they shape the reading networks in their brains and add to their long-term memory for words and text structures. The role of the teacher is to be a guide and model. Teachers demonstrate semantic, syntactic, and lexical reading strategies and then release the responsibility for these actions to the student.

Children become more fluent readers as they move into the upper grades and read increasingly complex texts. Teachers support their students' development as avid readers by providing a classroom environment that strongly encourages reading engagement. Relevance and student autonomy are especially important for engaging adolescent readers (Ivey & Johnston, 2013).

Texts are written to communicate ideas. Students' literacy networks expand through wide reading and critical discussions about the texts they read. Readers gain cultural knowledge and share ideas with others by discussing their texts. Readers gain insight into their own identities by experiencing actions and emotions through reading. Thus, the literacy network expands along with the readers' view of the world.

Phonology

> Jonah was seven years old when he read the book *The Thirsty Moose* by David Orme. Jonah read, "but the big mule would not listen" using the first two phonemes in "moose" he predicted the word "mule." Mr. Balan pointed to the "s" asking Jonah, "What does this letter say?" Then Mr. Balan asked him to read the sentence again, reading through the whole word, "moose."

Jonah knew all the sounds of the alphabet and was becoming more adept at figuring out unknown words using the alphabetic principle. He also knew that books conveyed meaning and were interesting to read. His teacher provided supportive opportunities for him to develop as a reader. They read together in a small guided reading group and he chose books during independent reading time. His parents took him to the public library and encouraged him to read at home. Based on these experiences, Jonah was gradually developing reading fluency.

Jonah and many other children's reading networks begin to develop at home when their parents teach them to recognize the letters of the alphabet. The reading network continues to build and become robust through associating words, letters, and meanings (Fischer-Baum et al., 2017). As the reading network develops, children move away from phonetically decoding word parts. They develop a rapid ability to extract word meaning from their memory. Continued reading builds a reading network of increasing strength.

Research-based instructional practices such as guided reading, interactive writing, learning centers, and wordplay can help children develop a strong reading network. Instruction that highlights meaning, demonstrates phonemes, and builds word memory develops connections between areas of the brain used for visual, phonological, and semantic processes.

Decoding processes involve the brain and body. Our eyes see the letters on the page or screen, and we hear the sounds the letters represent. We use a variety of voice organs including the lips and vocal cords. We also use our diaphragm, chest muscles, ribs, abdominal muscles, and lungs to produce sound.

Decoding also involves learning about our socio-cultural world including the books and other texts that are used in school. When children learn to decode, they may feel either stressed or confident, so emotion plays a role. The English language is culturally constructed and socially supported through parenting and schooling so that even decoding involves an extended literacy network.

Languaging

Languaging refers to using any of one's available linguistic resources to communicate with others and function in a social context (Garcia & Wei, 2014). In many classrooms, students and teachers speak multiple languages. Some of them grew up bilingually and others are in the process of learning a language. They are emergent bilinguals.

Many different factors influence brain functions in bilinguals. The age at which a language is acquired, the amount of exposure to a language, and knowledge of a language influence both brain structure and function. Yet neuroscience has not given us a complete picture of how the brain represents two languages (Sulpizio et al., 2020).

The bilingual brain engages in additional language tasks when communicating (Mohr et al., 2018). Because a bilingual child is learning two languages simultaneously, the child may have a smaller initial vocabulary and it may take them longer to retrieve a word from memory. Vocabulary is built over time and exposure to language. As children work at controlling their two languages, their brain's executive control functions show earlier development than monolingual children.

In the classroom, students who are not fluent speakers of a language may be hesitant to speak. Social interactions may produce stress or anxiety, impacting emergent bilinguals' classroom participation, reading, and writing. It is important to remember that languaging is a part of a complex literacy network that includes the brain, body, emotions, and social setting. When teachers reduce stress and increase motivation, they produce the conditions necessary for language use.

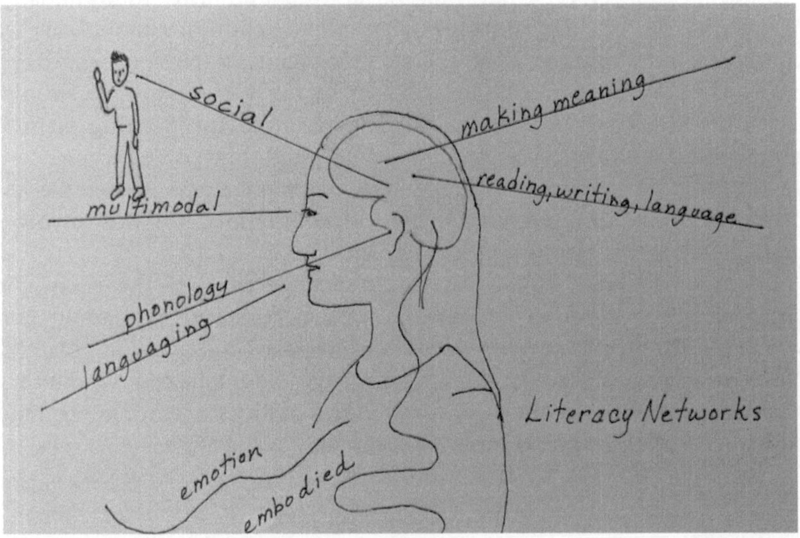

Figure 9.2 Literacy Networks.

Literacy Network

In this chapter, we have elaborated on six aspects of literacy: embodiment, social and emotional, multimodality, making meaning, phonology, and languaging. Putting them all together, we see a common theme, "literacy networks." Bringing together neuroscience and literacy research we understand literacy networks as connections throughout the brain, within the body, and connected to people and the environment. As literate human beings, we depend upon this literacy network (Figure 9.2).

Within the body, our central and peripheral nervous systems send information to the brain, strengthening and growing brain networks. Emotions, hormones, the gut, the heart, and other organs send information to the brain. Through our senses, we receive information from the environment around us and from the people we interact with. These experiences build and change the brain's networks.

In teaching and learning, students interact with materials, peers, and teachers, forming social connections and connecting information from the environment, source material, and dialog with others. Teachers can stimulate brain growth and emotional regulation by providing rich literacy environments. Frequent and sustained literacy experiences help to develop long-term memory, background knowledge, and schema.

Students today receive information and communicate multimodally. Visual images, text, digital formats, hyperlinks, and other modalities are commonly used and can even change our cognition (Firth et al., 2019). Students must navigate this network of literacies to communicate and learn in today's technology-saturated world. Making meaning of multimodal and complex texts requires using phonology, syntax, and connecting to background knowledge in an interactive and interconnected process. And in our interconnected world, communication often involves literacy networks with multiple languages.

Literacy networks involve the brain's connections to the body, the environment, and other people. From this perspective, reading and writing go beyond seeing words on a page and making sounds. Neuroscience and literacy research help us to understand the literacy networks involved in the uniquely human ability to read, write, and construct a society that is based on literacy.

Note to Readers

In writing this book, we have used our own experiences as literacy educators to highlight themes across literacy research that have impacted our own practices. We delved into neuroscience research to illuminate these themes through findings from brain imaging studies. With that said, we must stress the emerging nature of brain research. The technologies used to scan a brain and analyze the resulting data are rapidly improving. Some but not all the findings reported in this book have been replicated. If you are interested in neuroscience findings related to literacy and learning, you will want to stay current as future studies are published. New studies will surely shed additional light on emotion, reading, writing, and bilingualism.

Bibliography

Aboud, K. S., Bailey, S. K., Petrill, S. A., & Cutting, L. E. (2016). Comprehending text versus reading words in young readers with varying reading ability: Distinct patterns of functional connectivity from common processing hubs. *Developmental Science*, *19*(4), 632–656.

Chow, W.-Y., Lago, S., Barrios, S., Parker, D., Morini, G., & Lau, E. (2014). Additive effects of repetition and predictability during comprehension: Evidence from event-related potentials. PLoS ONE, 9, e99199. 10.1371/journal.pone.0099199

Dinehart, L. H. (2015). Handwriting in early childhood education: Current research and future implications. *Journal of Early Childhood Literacy*, *15*(1), 97–118.

Firth, J., Torous, J., Stubbs, B., Firth, J. A., Steiner, G. Z., Smith, L., Alvarez-Jimenez, M., Gleeson, J., Vancampfort, D., Armitage, C. J., & Sarris, J. (2019).

The "online brain": How the Internet may be changing our cognition. *World Psychiatry: Official Journal of the World Psychiatric Association, 18*(2), 119–129.

Fischer-Baum, S., Bruggemann, D., Gallego, I. F., Li, D. S. P., & Tamez, E. R. (2017). Decoding levels of representation in reading: A representational similarity approach. *Cortex: A Journal Devoted to the Study of the Nervous System and Behavior, 90*, 88–102.

Garcia, O., & Wei, L. (2014). *Translanguaging: Language, Bilingualism, and Education*. MacMillan.

Gavrilov, Y., Rotem, S., Ofek, R., & Geva, R. (2012). Socio-cultural effects on children's initiation of joint attention. *Frontiers in Human Neuroscience, 6*, 1-10.

Hacker, D. J. (2018). A metacognitive model of writing: An update from a developmental perspective. *Educational Psychologist, 53*(4), 220–237.

Immordingo-Yang, M. H. (2016). *Emotions, Learning, and the Brain: Exploring the Educational Implications of Affective Neuroscience*. W.W. Norton & Company.

Immordino-Yang, M. H., Darling-Hammond, L., & Krone, C. R. (2019). Nurturing nature: How brain development is inherently social and emotional, and what this means for education. *Educational Psychologist, 54*(3), 185–204.

Immordino-Yang, M. H. , & Gotlieb, R. (2017). Embodied brains, social minds, cultural meaning: Integrating neuroscientific and educational research on social-affective development. *American Educational Research Journal, 54*(1S), 344S–367S. 10.3102/0002831216669780

Ivey, G., & Johnston, P. H. (2013). Engagement with young adult literature: Outcomes and processes. *Reading Research Quarterly, 48*(3), 255–275.

Jirout, J., LoCasale-Crouch, J., Turnbull, K., Gu, Y., Cubides, M., Garzione, S., Evans, T. M., Weltman, A. L., & Kranz, S. (2019). How lifestyle factors affect cognitive and executive function and the ability to learn in children. *Nutrients, 11*(8). 10.3390/nu11081953

Kopasz, M., Loessl, B., Hornyak, M., Riemann, D., Nissen, C., Piosczyk, H., & Voderholzer, U. (2010). Sleep and memory in healthy children and adolescents – A critical review. *Sleep Medicine Reviews, 14*(3), 167–177. 10.1016/j.smrv.2009.10.006

Kutas, M., & Federmeier, K. D. (2000). Electrophysiology reveals semantic memory use in language comprehension. *Trends in Cognitive Sciences, 4*(12), 463–470

Landi, N., Frost, S. J., Mencl, W. E., Sandak, R., & Pugh, K. R. (2013). Neurobiological bases of reading comprehension: Insights from neuroimaging studies of word-level and text-level processing in skilled and impaired readers. *Reading and Writing Quarterly, 29*(2), 145–167.

Liew, J., Erbeli, F., Nyanamba, J. M., & Li, D. (2020). Pathways to reading competence: Emotional self-regulation, literacy contexts, and embodied learning processes. *Reading Psychology, 41*(7), 633–659. 10.1080/02702711.2020.1783145

Luke, A., Woods, A., & Dooley, K. (2011). Comprehension as social and intellectual practice: Rebuilding curriculum in low socioeconomic and cultural minority schools. *Theory Into Practice, 50*(2), 157–164. 10.1080/00405841.2011.558445

Lupien, S. J., McEwen, B. S., Gunnar, M. R., & Heim, C. (2009). Effects of stress throughout the lifespan on the brain, behaviour and cognition. *Nature Reviews Neuroscience*, *10*(6), 434–445. 10.1038/nrn2639

Mohr, K. A. J., Juth, S. M., Kohlmeier, T. L., & Schreiber, K. E. (2018). The developing bilingual brain: What parents and teachers should know and do. *Early Childhood Education Journal*, *46*(1), 11–20. 10.1007/s10643-016-0833-7

Pu, Y., Cheyne, D., Sun, Y., & Johnson, B. W. (2020). Theta oscillations support the interface between language and memory. *NeuroImage*, *215*. 10.1016/j.neuroimage.2020.116782

Street, B. (1984). *Literacy in Theory and Practice*. Cambridge University Press.

Sulpizio, S., Del Maschio, N., Fedeli, D., & Abutalebi, J. (2020). Bilingual language processing: A meta-analysis of functional neuroimaging studies. *Neuroscience and Biobehavioral Reviews*, *108*, 834–853.

Tenenbaum, H. R., Winstone, N. E., Leman, P. J., & Avery, R. E. (2020). How effective is peer interaction in facilitating learning? A meta-analysis. *Journal of Educational Psychology*, *112*(7), 1303–1319. 10.1037/edu0000436

Turner, K. H., Hicks, T., & Zucker, L. (2020). Connected reading: A framework for understanding how adolescents encounter, evaluate, and engage with texts in the digital age. *Reading Research Quarterly*, *55*(2), 291–309. 10.1002/rrq.271

van Moort, M. L., Jolles, D. D., Koornneef, A., & van den Broek, P. (2020). What you read versus what you know: Neural correlates of accessing context information and background knowledge in constructing a mental representation during reading. *Journal of Experimental Psychology. General*, *149*(11), 2084–2101.

Vinci-Booher, S., James, T. W., & James, K. H. (2021). Visual-motor contingency during symbol production contributes to short-term changes in the functional connectivity during symbol perception and long-term gains in symbol recognition. *NeuroImage*, *227*, 117554. 10.1016/j.neuroimage.2020.117554

Yao, Z., & Hsieh, S. (2019). Neurocognitive mechanism of human resilience: A conceptual framework and empirical review. *International Journal of Environmental Research and Public Health*, *16*, 5123.

INDEX